THEY
WENT
THAT-
A-WAY

THEY
WENT
THAT-
A-WAY

HOW THE FAMOUS,
THE INFAMOUS,
AND THE GREAT DIED

MALCOLM FORBES
WITH JEFF BLOCH

BARNES
&NOBLE
BOOKS
NEW YORK

1998 Barnes & Noble Books

ISBN 0-7607-0774-X

Printed and bound in the United States of America

98 99 00 01 02 M 9 8 7 6 5 4 3 2 1

QF

CONTENTS

8   CONTENTS

FOREWORD

WHEN I asked my editor, Michael Korda, if he'd be interested in publishing *They Went That-a-way* . . . he responded with positive enthusiasm. But with a "but": "People are going to want to know why Malcolm Forbes is writing about death. I do too. So right off the bat you must explain. And tell us about your own attitude toward death."

He took me back a bit, because I don't really think this is a book about death; I think rather it's about satisfying an oft-expressed curiosity on the part of Us, the Living. When some well-known name pops up in conversation, how many times have we said, "Whatever became of him/her?" In digging up final answers we've unearthed some pretty fascinating stuff about many a famous person's flame-out.

As for my own attitude toward death—which is quite extraneous to this work—I'm reminded of the way *Time* in its earliest convoluted-sentence days used to begin all "Milestones" obits: "As it must to all people, death came to . . . ." Since it's life's only certainty, and since being against it isn't apt to affect the result, dwelling on death strikes me as a woeful, wanton waste of time.

Time's all we really have in life. How much of it we have, we don't know till it's run out. To spend all this life solely preparing for the next with blissful dead certainty as to what it'll be is a form of optimism I'm not up to. It seems to me life is for living.

How we come into this world is routine—except perhaps for the Divine, which most of us are not. How we leave is very personal.

This book describes in some detail the extraordinary exits of 175 of our famous.

Some reaped what they'd sown, and for others the way they went was apropos or ironic.

There were those who went with epitaphic final words, while a few departed muttering epithets.

Not liking the music here, a number departed suicidally to take a chance that the next tune they'd hear might be better.

Some fought to their last breath to stay. A number were shoved out.

There are even those who achieved celebrity solely because of how they left their life, not because of how they lived it.

Each and every one is fascinating. As with eating peanuts, potato chips, or popcorn, once started you'll not be able to stop consuming these chapters. Though the book's about people passing, it's absorbing—not morbid or depressing.

After all, we all know that from the moment we enter this world we're on our way out, and while being dead may or may not mark another beginning, certainly for our here-on-earth phase it's an end. Whether the next round is better or worse or whether there is or isn't one or what form it takes, if any, is a matter of one's conjectural convictions. Countless millions have gone to their graves over violent differences as to what's next. Certainly none of us is personally acquainted with anyone in mortal form who's made the trip and returned with a first hand account.

But while we're here we are intrigued by how some of the mighty have met mortality. As you read along you will often say with a shake of your head—"So, they went that-a-way!"

Enjoy—before you experience!

M.F.

AESCHYLUS

525 or 524 B.C.–456 B.C.

AESCHYLUS, the founder of Greek tragedy who dominated Athenian theater for a generation (until he was succeeded by Sophocles), wrote plays packed with moral meaning. In his works, such as *Oresteia* and *Seven Against Thebes*, his characters act according to their own symbolic wills, but subject to the influence of the divine gods. Everything operates by grand design and, though it might sometimes require years and years of suffering and evil, ultimately events conclude for the better. His plays are loaded with freak violent acts. In *Prometheus Bound*, for example, a rock is struck by lightning and later some women are swallowed by an earthquake.

How, then, would Aeschylus have dramatized his own fate? A note of caution here: history books offer scant information on the playwright's death, and most scholarly biographers and literary critics have chosen to evade addressing the event entirely, one calling it "clouded in fable." Nevertheless, the legend so matches the man, it could well lurk in one of the dozens of his plays that didn't survive the ages. The story goes that Aeschylus, while staying in Gela on the island of Sicily, was killed when an eagle mistook his shiny bold head for a rock and dropped a tortoise on it to crack the shell. The tortoise shell, according to legend, remained intact.

ALEXANDER THE GREAT
356 B.C.–323 B.C.

ALEXANDER became the Great because his influence far outlasted his battle victories. It is said that Julius Caesar was very upset when he read that the early Greek conqueror had died at 33, an age at which Caesar had yet to accomplish anything. Napoleon kept a history of Alexander by his bed. And Michelangelo laid out the courtyard of the Vatican in the design of Alexander's shield.

Alexander was raised with such a sense of destiny. When at 20 he inherited the throne of Macedonia, after his father was assassinated, he promptly set out with 35,000 troops to conquer whatever he could. In the next eleven years, never returning to his kingdom, Alexander marched more than 11,000 miles and, despite enemies with hundreds of thousands of soldiers, never lost a battle. By his victories he sent Greek culture and commerce throughout Egypt and into much of Asia and India.

Through much of his career, Alexander was adored by his troops. He eagerly joined them on the front lines and set an example of avoiding rich foods and heavy drinking. But by 324

B.C., Alexander's own power became too intoxicating. He withdrew from his soldiers after he discovered plots against his life. He declared he was the son of Zeus. And for the first time in his life, be began drinking heavily.

Alexander and his army were in Babylon in 323, preparing to begin their next campaign. Three days before they were to depart, Alexander got involved in a drinking contest at a banquet. He is believed to have gulped down six quarts of wine. By the next day, not surprisingly, he was sick, not only from the wine but also from a chill he had caught in the cold weather. From his bed he continued to issue orders for the upcoming march, but he grew weaker each day. When it was clear he was dying, his troops filed past him in his tent. Alexander could only weakly try to raise his head and greet them. Within ten days of his drinkfest, the conqueror was dead.

Alexander had always believed he was descended from Achilles. If that's true, then Achilles' heel was Alexander's ego.

HORATIO ALGER, JR.
January 13, 1834–July 18, 1899

HORATIO ALGER wrote so many rags-to-riches novels that his name became synonymous with going from poverty to great pelf. But if he had written his own story, he definitely would have given it a different ending. Alger's characters always ended up triumphant, happy, and rich. He wrote more than 100 happy endings, to tales such as *Dan the newsboy, Ben the luggage boy, Phil the fiddler*, and *Paul the peddler*. There were *Andy Grant's pluck* and *Joe's luck*. Most famous of all was one of his earliest stories, *Ragged Dick*. At least an entire generation of boys learned that virtue and hard work always were rewarded by wealth and honor.

Alger stuck by his poor-boy-makes-good formula, often basing his stories on youths he met in post–Civil War New York City at the Newboys' Lodging House. He churned out some books in just a few weeks, earning him an estimated $20,000 a year, an incredibly successful sum a century ago. But even though he did better than many of his characters, Alger couldn't hold on to it. He was so taken with many of the boys in the lodging house that he freely gave them money whenever they asked. He bought magazine subscriptions for them, gave them money just to get by, and provided funds for those who wanted to start their own businesses. Not all of the boys, however, were as well-meaning as Alger, and some of his money wound up in poker games and saloons.

Nor was Alger happy with his success. He had gone to New York to be a serious writer, and his serial novels didn't qualify. As his books grew more popular—they often were awarded as Sunday-school prizes—Alger's interests, and then his mind, wandered. He tried to produce a play and run a curio shop. Both failed. He chased fire engines so he could watch the flames. For a time he was not infrequently seen parading down Broadway clad in a cape and wig and preaching loudly. After suffering a breakdown, he passed the time at the Newboys' House writing epitaphs for himself. Among them, "Here lies a good fellow who spent his life while he had it."

Broke, and suffering from one of his many respiratory illnesses, Alger moved to South Natick, Massachusetts, to live with his sister in 1896. There he stayed until, three years later, bedridden with a painful cough, he died one hot day in July. He left almost no estate, though his books had sold 800,000 copies during his life. Millions more continued to be sold as dime novels after he died, with the profits going to the publishers.

SAINT THOMAS AQUINAS
1225(?)–March 7, 1274

EVERYONE who went to Catholic school has Saint Thomas Aquinas to thank for it. The most important theologian and philosopher in the Catholic Church, Aquinas set down the fundamental doctrines that have been taught for centuries afterward. And for his efforts he is considered the patron of Catholic schools. So intent was Aquinas on devoting his life to the church that even after his family kidnapped him, he persisted and a year later took the vows of poverty of the Dominican Order. Studying in France and Italy in the 13th century, Aquinas became famous for his incisive lectures and scores of writings, most notably his *Summa Theologica*.

Aquinas literally devoted every waking moment to his religious studies, and would often appear lost in his deep concentration. Once, at a banquet with French King Louis IX, Aquinas came out of a long, detached stare by suddenly banging on the table and shouting, "That settles the Manichees!" Just as suddenly, after celebrating a Mass at the feast of Saint Nicholas on December 6, 1273, the prolific Aquinas stopped writing. The 48-year-old man told one of his assistants, "I cannot go on. All that I have written seems to me like so much straw compared to what I have seen and what has been revealed to me." Whether he had experienced a divine revelation or simply a stroke, Aquinas lived in a sort of permanent dazed state afterward. He said, "The only thing I want now is that as God has put an end to my writing, He may quickly end my life also."

Early the following year, Aquinas, living in Naples, was summoned to Lyons to attend a meeting with the Pope. Though not well, Aquinas set out with his assistants in early February. One day early in the trip, Aquinas was hit in the head by a low-hanging tree branch and was knocked off his donkey. The others rushed up and asked him if he was hurt. The scholar replied, "A little," but clearly it was more serious. They continued on their journey, but in a few hours Aquinas was so exhausted that he was taken to a nearby castle where his niece lived. There he grew weaker throughout the month.

Near the end of February, and feeling he was near death, Aquinas asked to be taken to a nearby abbey at Fossanuova. "If the Lord is coming for me," he said, "I had better be found in a religious house than in a castle." He was carried six miles on a donkey to the abbey, where he died about a week later.

JOHN JACOB ASTOR IV
July 13, 1864–April 15, 1912

JOHN JACOB ASTOR IV died on the *Titanic*. By the way, so did more than 1,500 other people. Such was the slant of some of the news reports after the famous unsinkable ocean liner sank in the icy Atlantic on April 15, 1912. Astor was no world leader or even a world-beater. But he was very rich. The post office would deliver to him letters addressed to "The Richest Man in the World." And Astor, the great-grandson of the founder of the family's 19th-century fur fortune, only had to sit back and watch New York City boom to get richer. "The Astors," testified the president of the Board of Assessments and Taxes, "are not looked upon as people who dispose of real estate after they once get possession of it." J.J. Number Four presided over some 700 parcels of Manhattan and owned more skyscrapers than anyone else in the early 1900s.

Astor also had the prestige of more than twenty corporate

directorships, but he usually voted by proxy, preferring to tinker with mechanical devices and write science fiction. Perhaps partly he tinkered to get away from his domineering wife Ava. Astor ended the unhappy eighteen-year marriage in 1909, a scandalous act made worse by his marriage two years later to an 18-year-old girl when he was 47. To escape the severe social criticism, Astor took his young bride abroad on a long trip to Egypt and England. There Madeleine learned she was pregnant, so Astor booked passage to New York on a most spectacular new ocean liner, the *Titanic*.

Such was Astor's prominence that after the ship's hull was fatally gouged by the iceberg, the captain informed him privately of the danger before sounding the general alarm. Survivors said Astor remained chivalrous to the end. After all the women and children had boarded lifeboats and there appeared still to be room in the final boat, Astor climbed in and sat beside his wife. But just as the boat was to be lowered into the water, a group of women ran on deck. Astor quickly gave up his place, saying, "The ladies have to go first." When his wife attempted to join him, he told her firmly, "Get in the lifeboat, to please me." He lit a cigarette and said, "Good-bye, dearie. I'll see you later."

Astor's body was recovered ten days later with $2,500 in his pockets. Madeleine gave birth to John Jacob Astor VI in August. Astor had left a $5 million trust for Madeleine, but she soon had to give it up in order to remarry. The bulk of his fortune he left to his oldest son from his first marriage, Vincent Astor, who gave much of the wealth away in a tradition carried on today by his widow, Brooke Astor.

ATTILA THE HUN
406–453

JORDANES, the 6th-century historian, described the barbaric Huns this way: "They made their foes flee in horror because their swarthy aspect was fearful, and they had . . . a shapeless lump instead of a head, with pinholes rather than eyes." He summed up Attila, King of the Huns, like this: "He was short of stature, with a broad chest and a large head; his eyes were small, his beard was thin and sprinkled with gray. He had a flat nose and a swarthy complexion, revealing his origin."

Attila, whose name meant "Little Father," and his tribe could neither read nor write, but by the middle of the 5th century they had conquered their way from the plains of Mongolia to the threshold of the fallen Roman Empire. Based in what is now Hungary, with an army of 500,000 men, Attila massacred entire towns, disrupting commerce routes for centuries to come. The leaders of Western empires paid him hundreds of pounds of gold annually in hopes of preventing his wrath. Finally in 452, Attila was slowed, but not defeated, in a battle that left 162,000 men slain on the bloody Catalaunian Plains.

Attila planned to invade Italy again in 453 in what well could have slaughtered the development of Western civilization. But that winter Attila got married. He added a beautiful young girl, Ildico, to his harem. During the wedding celebration Attila, who usually restrained himself during feasts, ate and drank heavily, then retired to the wedding tent with his bride. There he was found dead the next morning, his bride weeping over him. Attila had burst a blood vessel in his nose and, being dead drunk, had choked to death as the blood pooled in his throat.

Some have speculated that Attila's blood vessel broke due to the King's overexertion, shall we say, with his bride. Or possibly it was simply a bloody nose like others that had bothered him before. Either way, Western civilization was saved.

SIR FRANCIS BACON
January 22, 1561–April 9, 1626

WHEN HE WAS alive Sir Francis Bacon rarely got the attention he deserved. After he died the British statesman, philosopher, scientist, and writer got far more credit than he asked for. Bacon, a gifted writer himself, often is alleged to be the real Shakespeare, who was his contemporary, or at least the author of several of the plays. Some historians also speculate that Bacon was the son of the supposedly childless Queen Elizabeth. The irony is that the Queen often rejected the counsel of Bacon, and he was ousted as lord chancellor under King James for politically motivated charges of bribery. "I was born for the service of mankind," the none too humble Bacon once said. And what mankind wasn't yet ready to accept, Bacon wrote down for later generations in major works such as *The Advancement of Learning* and his famous essays.

Among his achievements, Bacon formalized the scientific method. At a time when scientists accepted preconceived ideas and then looked for evidence to support them, Bacon developed principles for systematic trial and error that would lead to the correct conclusion. "I have taken all knowledge to be my province," he declared. A man of nervous energy, he was always devising new experiments, especially after the bribery scandal in 1621 left him with little else to do.

In early April 1626, Bacon was traveling in his coach with a physician friend. As he saw the still-thick snow along the road, he got an idea for an experiment to find out if ice would preserve flesh as well as salt. He stopped at a cottage and bought a hen, which the lady of the house killed and gutted for him. He then stood out in the frigid air and stuffed the bird with snow. The procedure apparently took some time, and before he was through Bacon had developed a chill. He and his friend rode several more miles before seeking refuge at the home of an earl friend, who himself was a prisoner in the Tower of London for displeasing King Charles. Bacon was cared for by the earl's servants, but he did not recover. On April 9, Bacon died of bronchitis. But he had been right about the chicken.

FLORENCE BALLARD
June 30, 1944–February 22, 1976

FROM DETROIT's Brewster Housing Project to the top of the pop music charts, the three young black girls who made up the Supremes rode one of the most phenomenal star trips of the 1960s. Their number-one hits like "Come See About Me" and "Stop, in the Name of Love" often were the only songs preventing a complete British invasion by the Beatles and the Rolling Stones.

And in the beginning it had been Florence Ballard's idea. Ballard was planning to be a nurse when she got her friend Mary Wilson to help her form a singing group. Only after another girl dropped out did they enlist their final member, Diana Ross. The Supremes signed with Motown in 1961, fresh out of high school, and at first the three teenagers swapped the lead vocals. But with their first number-one hit in 1964, "Where Did Our Love Go?" Diana Ross became the star and Wilson and Ballard were left singing oohs and aahs and moving their arms in sync.

Ballard didn't like singing backup, but the Supremes were so successful that for a while she enjoyed the whole heady trip. They appeared on all the variety and talk shows on television, performed in London, wore stunning gowns, and were featured in fashion magazines. In 1965 it was estimated that each girl, barely 21, earned $250,000, though most of that was held and invested by Motown. Ballard bought a beautiful home and drove a plum-rose Cadillac Eldorado.

By 1967, however, all the glamorous tours just seemed to make Ballard tired. She began drinking, had trouble keeping her weight down, and would miss recording sessions and concerts with no explanation. That summer, during an engagement at the Flamingo Hotel in Las Vegas, Ballard either quit or was fired. After some time in a hospital for exhaustion, she signed with ABC Records as a solo singer. Motown wouldn't allow her to bill herself as a former Supreme, and after a couple of unsuccessful singles Ballard was dropped from the record label.

The next time Ballard got much attention was in 1975, when the headlines said she was on welfare, receiving $95 a week from the Aid to Dependent Children program for her three children after she had split up with her husband. Before that she had lost a suit against Motown for back royalties, had lost her home to foreclosure, and had moved in with her mother in a duplex apartment a half mile from the Brewster projects. She weighed almost 200 pounds and was taking medication for her diet and high blood pressure. "When I go to sleep at night," she said in an interview, "I have dreams of what it was like when Diana, Mary, and I worked great places like the Copa. Once I had it all. I was Supreme. Now? Now I have nothing."

Shortly afterward Ballard reconciled with her husband and the family moved into its own home in Detroit. Then on the evening of February 21, 1976, the 31-year-old Ballard noticed her arms and legs were becoming numb. She checked into a hospital that night, where she died the next morning of a heart attack.

P. T. BARNUM
July 5, 1810–April 7, 1891

"THERE's a sucker born every minute," declared Phineas Taylor Barnum, and the greatest born schemer spent his life proving it. As a child he ran his own lottery in Connecticut. He began making his real fortune in 1835, when he latched onto a slave whom he claimed was 161 years old and had been George Washington's nurse, drawing huge crowds and $1,500 a week. Many didn't believe the woman was that old once they saw her. But Barnum didn't care what they thought as they left his American Museum in New York City because by then he already had their money. And they paid again and again to see his mermaid, his bearded lady, and the midget he named General Tom Thumb.

The master promoter, who didn't create his legendary circus until he was 60 years old, remained active until he suffered a stroke at the age of 80 in November 1890. Only then did he write a will. But what nagged Barnum was not the fate of his own affairs, but the fate of his name. The man who professed he didn't care what the newspapers said about him as long as they spelled his name right, Barnum now had a strong hankering to know exactly what people would say about him after he died. The word got out, and the New York *Evening Sun* obliged. On March 24, 1891, with Barnum still alive, the newspaper published his obituary. Above four columns chronicling his life, the headline read, "Great and Only Barnum. He Wanted to Read His Obituary; Here It Is."

Several days later Barnum told his secretary, "I'm going to die this time." He went on to talk about plans to build houses on some property he owned on Long Island. "Why, Mr. Barnum," said Ben, his secretary, "you just said you were going to die!" "Yes, Ben, yes," replied the 80-year-old showman. "But I ain't dead yet, Ben, am I?"

Three days after that Barnum died. In an obituary he didn't get to see, *The Times* of London wrote, "He early realized that essential feature of a modern democracy, its readiness to be led to what will amuse and instruct it. He knew that 'the people' means crowds—paying crowds."

JEREMY BENTHAM
February 15, 1748–June 6, 1832

THERE IS a convenient, though not verifiable, tale about a conversation late in the life of Jeremy Bentham. The British philosopher and father of utilitarianism—the idea that man has a propensity toward pleasure and good and against pain and evil—was at the time over 80 and ill. From his bed he asked his doctor if there was any hope of recovery, to which the doctor said there wasn't. "Very well," replied Bentham. "Be it so. Then minimize pain."

Bentham was a man of exhaustive detail, writing some 10 million words that have been published and almost as many that have not. His essays on ethics, logic, jurisprudence, and political economy, as well as his harsh critiques of the British government, sparked major reforms, including bureaucratic reorganization, a national education system, and a modern police force.

When Bentham couldn't find the words to describe his thoughts, he invented new ones. His most successful new word was "international." Less timeless was the term "auto-icon," which had to do with preserving dead bodies as statues. Bentham spent his last months writing and revising an essay entitled "Auto-Icon, or the Uses of the Dead to the Living." He wrote, "If a country gentleman has rows of trees leading to his dwelling, the auto-icons of his family might alternate with the trees; copal varnish would protect the face from the effects of rain."

Bentham did his best to ensure his own postmortal future. As per his will, Bentham's friends gathered with doctors and medical students in the Webb Street School of Anatomy in London three days after his death. Bentham's body lay on the dissecting table in his nightshirt. As a thunderstorm flashed lightning on Bentham's face from a skylight, his doctor, also a well-known utilitarian, delivered a eulogy. Then, in best utilitarian fashion, the doctor dissected Bentham's body as friends and physicians looked on.

Besides being an odd funeral, the event also was an act of political protest, just as Bentham intended. At the time the only bodies dissected for the education of medical students were those of executed murderers. Dissection was intended as further punishment after the convict had been put to death.

Alas, Bentham did not get his final wish to be propped along a "country gentleman's" driveway. Instead, his skeleton sits in a box in a corridor of University College in London, clad in his own clothes and holding his favorite walking stick. The only change: officials decided Bentham's head looked too distasteful following the dissection, so that was replaced with a wax replica. Bentham's auto-icon to this day is wheeled out for utilitarian gatherings of Benthamites.

THOMAS HART BENTON
April 15, 1889–January 19, 1975

A GOVERNOR's beautiful wife once asked Thomas Hart Benton to paint her portrait. He said he wouldn't do it. "Your beauty is only skin deep," he told her. "You wouldn't like it if I painted you." His art was just as straightforward. While most of the art world was becoming more abstract in the 1920s and 1930s, Benton vividly painted realistic portraits of his youth in southern Missouri—Jesse James committing a holdup, black sharecroppers picking cotton, and gaunt Ozark hillbillies. Critics found Benton's work unsophisticated, but the public loved it.

His huge murals of American life adorn several public buildings, including the Truman Library, whose namesake called
Benton "the best damned painter in America."

As he grew older Benton continued to paint in his studio in
his stone mansion in Kansas City, Missouri. "You can't retire
from life," he said. "You can't retire like a man would retire
from business or a job. It is life to me. What the hell would
I do?"

In 1974, at the age of 84, Benton began yet another ambitious
mural, this one called "The Sources of Country Music," commissioned by the Country Music Foundation in Nashville. He
lately had become afraid he might die before he completed a
painting, so he tried to stay ahead of schedule. By the next
winter he had finished it, and after dinner on January 19, 1975,
he told his wife he was going to go sign the vast mural. Soon
after his wife found him collapsed on the floor of his studio, dead
of a massive heart attack. His last work remained unsigned.

BUSBY BERKELEY
November 29, 1895–March 14, 1976

IF EVER things start looking bad in a Busby Berkeley musical,
just wait for the final reel and rest assured, it will turn out
happily ever after. So it was with Berkeley himself. Hollywood's
star director of *Gold Diggers of 1935*, *Babes in Arms*, with Judy
Garland and Mickey Rooney, and the dance numbers in *42nd
Street* couldn't get a job in the 1940s. But wait for the final reel.

Berkeley began directing on Broadway in the 1920s, but it
was in Hollywood where he created an original art form. "A lot
of people used to say I was crazy," said the man with a face

suitable only for broad comedy. "But I can truthfully say one thing—I gave 'em a show." That he did. With scores of beautiful girls, innovative camera tricks and lavish sets—100 chorines playing neon-lighted violins, dozens of white baby-grand pianos—Berkeley made moviegoers forget about the Depression for a while.

But then the Depression ended and movie production costs soared. By the end of World War II, Berkeley was without a hit, had divorced his fifth wife, and even lost his studio contract. In 1946, a month after his mother died of cancer, the 50-year-old director slashed his throat and wrists, but not deeply enough to seriously injure himself. "I'm a has-been and know it," he said. "I can't seem to get myself straightened out for any length of time. Every time I get married it seems to turn out wrong. I'm broke. When my mother died, everything seemed to go with her."

Berkeley began drinking heavily. When he did land a picture, *Take Me Out to the Ball Game*, in 1949, he was arrested for drunk driving during the filming. Berkeley created the musical numbers for a few other movies, but finally gave up and, declaring himself "semiretired," bought a small home in Palm Desert, California.

There he lived long enough to get his happy ending. By the 1960s, Berkeley's movies began showing up on late-night television as Hollywood classics. Suddenly the man whose career had long since faded was invited to speak at film societies and conduct college lecture tours. In 1970 he was hired to supervise production of a Broadway revival of *No, No, Nanette*, starring his *42nd Street* leading lady, Ruby Keeler. On opening night in 1971 there were rave reviews and a standing ovation for the aging Berkeley. His financial condition, unsteady since the 1940s, improved enough for Berkeley to retire for good in a retirement home in Palm Springs. He died there at the age of 80, survived by his sixth wife. Now you can roll the credits.

AMBROSE BIERCE
June 24, 1842–1914?

"DEATH IS NOT the end; there remains the litigation over the estate." Such was the wit of Ambrose Bierce, once called "the wickedest man in San Francisco" and, less kindly, "Bitter Bierce." His "Prattler" column for William Randolph Hearst's *Examiner* was scathing. He attacked public officials, journalists, and ministers indiscriminately, calling them liars, scoundrels, or cowards, depending on the subject. The tenth of thirteen children of poor Ohio farmers, Bierce became part of a group of influential writers based in San Francisco in the late 19th century that included Mark Twain and Bret Harte.

Much to his dismay, Bierce never achieved as much success with his short stories, which often were compared to Poe's, as he did with his newspaper columns. By 1913, Bierce was tired of writing his column and had suffered the humiliating critical and financial failure of the publication of his collected works. Bierce, 71, decided it was time to move on. "Good-bye," he wrote. "If you hear of my being stood up against a Mexican stone wall and shot to rags please know that I think it a pretty good way to depart this life. It beats old age, disease, or falling down the cellar stairs. To be a Gringo in Mexico—ah, that is euthanasia!"

Bierce, then living in Washington, planned to go have a look at the revolution under way in Mexico. Then he would travel through Mexico to the Pacific, sail to South America and cross the Andes, then perhaps sail to England. "Naturally," he wrote, "it is possible—even probable—that I shall not return. These being 'strange countries,' in which things happen; that is why I am going. And I am 71."

After bundling his personal belongings and distributing them to his daughter and friends, Bierce left Washington on October 2, 1913. He stopped through Tennessee and Mississippi, visiting places where he had fought during the Civil War fifty years earlier. He crossed the Texas border into Mexico in early December. There he signed on as an observer in Pancho Villa's army. On December 26, 1913, he posted a letter in Chihuahua to a close woman friend. It was the last trace of the writer.

Speculation as to Bierce's fate was wide-ranging. "Authoritative" stories said Bierce was shot by a firing squad, shot during a battle, residing in a California state insane asylum, or living happily in Europe. Several inquiries by family and friends turned up no certain information. Historians believe Bierce's most likely demise occurred on the battlefield. He was, after all, 71 and suffered from asthma, and many stronger men were left unidentified and buried.

In his witty *The Devil's Dictionary*, published in 1906, Bierce defined "grave" as "a place in which the dead are laid to await the coming of the medical student." As the writer knew, that was no place for him.

SENATOR THEODORE GILMORE BILBO
October 13, 1877–August 21, 1947

THE U.S. SENATE has long attracted orators, some eloquent, some just long-winded. It made perfect sense, then, for Theodore Bilbo, Mississippi's leading politician in the first half of this century, to seek his place there. Bilbo's blend of Latin phrases, Shakespearian rhythms, and down-home Delta humor had carried him from a rural farm in Juniper Grove, Mississippi, where he had no formal education until he was 13, to the governor's mansion twice before he arrived in the Senate in 1934.

Bilbo was short, measuring five feet two inches. But admirers and critics agreed that "on the stump, he's seven feet ten inches tall." "It's my ancestors," Bilbo explained. "Half French, where I get my loquacity and my gestures. The other half Irish, where I get my audacity. With that combination, a man can talk forever."

What he had to say was a different matter. In the Senate, Bilbo loudly advocated the voluntary return of blacks to Africa. "I might entertain the proposition of crowning Eleanor [Roosevelt] queen of Greater Liberia," he said. A member of the Ku Klux Klan, Bilbo filibustered against an antilynching bill and one that would end poll taxes. In Bilbo's obituary *The New York Times* said of his speeches, "Little heed was paid to them except as crackpot utterances."

By 1946, after Bilbo's first two terms in the Senate, the times had changed enough so that Bilbo's fellow Democrats began to consider him less an annoyance than a real threat to the party's reputation. The Senate launched an investigation accusing Bilbo of accepting bribes from government contractors.

But this time Bilbo was uncharacteristically quiet. The summer before, doctors had found cancer in his jaw. He underwent two operations to remove part of his lower jaw, causing the loss of several front teeth as well. At the Senate hearings Bilbo sat sagging in his chair, his mouth twisted from the surgery, his vibrant cheeks now sunken. He had no more loquacious speeches to give. He sat calmly, still familiarly smoking a cigar. He acknowledged receiving gifts from government contractors, including a Cadillac, but called them "just an old Southern custom."

Senators wanted to block Bilbo's oath of office for his third term, denying him the right to be seated. Bilbo showed up anyway, and because senators are seated alphabetically, the confrontation left thirty-five other senators also barred from their seats. Finally, the next day, Bilbo and the senators agreed to delay his fate until after he had another operation, this one to remove more of his lower jaw and his throat glands.

Bilbo never recovered. Already weakened by a liquid diet, he became partially paralyzed and developed a persistent fever and a blood clot. He died August 21, 1947, "drugged and speechless," in a hospital in New Orleans. The man who ended one of his filibusters with the prayer "God forbid that the right of speech be taken from us" had no more to say.

HARRY BLACK
August 25, 1863–July 19, 1930

As AN EARLY megadeveloper in New York City, Harry Black had the kind of optimistic and opportunistic outlook that the real estate business seems to inspire. Never one to pull back, Black took advantage of real estate slumps to buy more land and push skyscrapers to new heights. His first major project, the triangular Flatiron Building at Madison Square in 1902, instantly was famous and controversial, as it was the slimmest building yet built for its height and many stood watching for it to topple over during strong winds. Black went on to build another triangular tower for *The New York Times*, creating the namesake of Times Square. He also built Macy's at Herald Square, the original Pennsylvania Station, and countless other landmarks.

Meanwhile, the self-made, Canadian-born, former wool salesman merged his Fuller Construction Company, which he had inherited from his father-in-law, with other real estate firms to make his United States Realty Company the dominant developer in New York and other major East Coast cities. By the mid-1920s, Black served on the boards of a dozen companies, was worth an estimated $15 million, and lived like it. Early in 1929 he devised even bigger plans to finance his new projects by selling shares instead of acquiring mortgages, which was unheard of at the time. Needless to say, the stock-market crash later that year ended Black's idea.

But by then Black was suffering more personal problems. Ten days before the market collapsed Black was found unconscious with his head underwater in the bathtub at his suite at the Plaza Hotel, which he owned. A rescue squad worked for nine hours and saved his life. Doctors said Black simply had passed out in the hot water.

Nine months later his death was no accident. Black was staying at his country home on Long Island, his wife was in Ireland visiting friends. About 8 A.M. on July 19, Black's butler heard him pacing in his bedroom. As usual, the butler turned on the radio in the next room. A couple of hours later the butler looked in on Black and found him collapsed in his pajamas with a bullet wound in his right temple and a pistol in his hand. Black died that evening. He left no note, but everyone thought that he, like so many others, had been killed by the market crash. In fact, largely due to Black's savvy and liquidity, United States Realty had survived the crash in good shape. His death, doctors said, was due to "melancholia."

BLACKBEARD THE PIRATE
About 1680–November 22, 1718

CAPTAIN EDWARD TEACH would have loved the fact that he became a legend. After all, he worked hard to build his reputation as the most notorious swashbuckling pirate during the golden era of seafaring thuggery in the Caribbean. Teach began, after taking command of a large ship he had captured, by calling himself "Blackbeard," for the thick scraggly growth that virtually carpeted his face below his eyes. He braided his beard with different colored ribbons and tied cannon fuses under the brim of his hat, which he would light during battle to surround his face in mystifying smoke. After a few heists his reputation so preceded him that merchant vessels would surrender at the sight of the black-flagged mast of his *Queen Anne's Revenge*, stocked with 40 cannons and 300 men.

Many believed Blackbeard, a towering man dressed in black and laden with knives and pistols, to be the Devil incarnate, and he liked it that way. He is said to have awed a tavern crowd one night by mixing gunpower and rum, which he then lit and drank as it burned. He rarely killed his robbery victims if they cooperated, but a man who hesitated to give up a ring could quickly find his finger chopped off. His romances during island layovers also were notorious, and he married at least thirteen prostitutes on his ship before setting sail, never to see most of them again.

Blackbeard got away with so much because in his day pirating was actually encouraged by some colonial governments—as long as it was another country's ships that were attacked. In April 1718 the British government offered a general pardon to all pirates if they would simply stop what they were doing. After blockading the harbor of Charleston, South Carolina, for a week and plundering eight ships, Blackbeard accepted the offer in June. He settled in Bath, North Carolina, where, not feared on land, he became a celebrity. He was married (for the fourteenth time) in a ceremony performed by the colonial governor.

It was just a few weeks, however, before Blackbeard got restless and returned to pirating. He operated off the craggy North Carolina coast, and from his land base at Bath began arranging to sell his loot in major cities like Philadelphia and New York. None of this much bothered North Carolinians, but the governor of Virginia was extremely alarmed. He commissioned two ships, led by Lieutenant Robert Maynard, to capture Blackbeard.

They found him in his usual hideaway in the Ocracoke Inlet, about 30 miles south of Cape Hatteras. Blackbeard, who was operating on a much smaller scale with only one ship, the *Adventure*, and about twenty-five men, was lax in his defenses because he had been left alone so long. Virginia's two ships weren't spotted until they were well into the inlet at dawn on November 22, 1718. Though outnumbered and still with room enough to escape, it was Blackbeard who fired the first shot. As the ships got closer he wheeled all his eight cannons to one side and fired them, killing half his attackers and nearly crippling both ships.

But, unlike most of Blackbeard's previous opponents, Maynard and his men didn't give up. Maynard sent most of his men below deck and then sailed up to the side of the *Adventure*. Blackbeard, seeing only a few men on the approaching ship, ordered his pirates to "board her and cut them to pieces!" Blackbeard was the first aboard, slipping on the deck, which was slick with the blood of the cannon victims. As ten of his men followed him, Maynard's hidden crew sprang from below and attacked in brutal hand-to-hand combat.

Blackbeard broadly swung his cutlass, a thick, curved sword, preventing anyone from approaching him. Maynard stood back and shot him, but Blackbeard didn't slow down. Then, as he raised his cutless to kill Maynard, another attacker slashed him deeply in the neck from behind. Now, with blood spurting from the wound, Blackbeard continued to swing his blade and fire his pistols, each of which he had to discard after one shot. Finally he weakened, and several attackers moved in to jab him with their swords. Blackbeard fell dead, ending a battle that had lasted less than ten minutes. Maynard examined the body and counted five bullet wounds and twenty deep cuts.

Maynard ordered Blackbeard's head severed and hung from a beam at the front of the officer's ship. The rest of the pirate's body was dumped overboard. The decaying head and its thick beard dangled from the ship for weeks, as Maynard paraded through ports in Virginia and North Carolina. Legend has it that the skull then hung from a high pole at the mouth of the Hampton River in Virginia as a warning to other pirates. Legend further has it that eventually Blackbeard's skull was fashioned into the base of a large punchbowl and placed into service at the Raleigh Tavern in Williamstown, Virginia.

As for the rest of his body, Blackbeard's ghost is said to be roaming the coast of North Carolina, afraid that the Devil won't recognize him without his head—and his beard.

ALFRED S. BLOOMINGDALE
April 15, 1916–August 20, 1982

CONSIDERING THAT he spent almost no time in the family's store, Alfred S. Bloomingdale didn't do too badly for himself. The grandson of the founder of the trendy department store ventured out on his own to become a successful Broadway producer in the 1940s and the founder of a credit-card company in 1950 that eventually made him chairman of Diners Club. Bloomingdale retired in 1970, but he and his longtime wife, Betsy, stayed very active on the Los Angeles social circuit. He was known as "King Alfred" and she was dubbed "Good Queen Betts." Along the way they became close friends of the Reagans, and Bloomingdale even was a member of the President's unofficial group of advisers called the "kitchen cabinet."

But what may stick in many minds about the life of Alfred Bloomingdale exploded a month and a half before he died. It was then, in July 1982, that 29-year-old Vicki Morgan, a former model, filed a $10 million lawsuit claiming she and Bloomingdale had carried on a twelve-year affair and that he had broken a promise to provide her with financial support and a suitable home for the rest of her life. She filed the suit after Bloomingdale began losing his long battle with cancer and was hospitalized in June, whereupon Betsy cut off Morgan's monthly $18,000 checks.

As Bloomingdale lay dying, Morgan's palimony attorney, Marvin Mitchelson, released photographs of the couple and made public details of the relationship. Depositions in the lawsuit said the business executive had met Morgan when she was an usher at Grauman's Chinese Theater in Hollywood. She was 17 years old, married at the time, and had an illegitimate son. The suit said they slept together the third time they met, in a tryst that included two other women. Morgan claimed Bloomingdale eventually promised her lifetime support if she would give up her job and devote all her "time, effort and energies" as his "confidante, companion and business partner." The suit said Bloomingdale had given Morgan $1.5 million over the course of their twelve-year affair.

Given the circles that Bloomingdale ran in, the lawsuit became the summer's most sensational story, especially when Morgan said in an interview that Bloomingdale's wife had known about the affair since 1974 after the illicit couple accidentally ran into Nancy Reagan. The First Lady denied that. There were more headlines when Mitchelson claimed he had spent two hours discussing the lawsuit with a special assistant to the President.

Before the scandal had faded the 66-year-old Bloomingdale died of cancer at a hospital in Santa Monica on August 20. He had written a new will, dated seventeen days after Morgan filed her suit, that left everything to his wife and a family trust. Three weeks after her husband's death Betsy Bloomingdale asked the court to dismiss Morgan's claim, saying it had been a strictly sexual affair. Later in September a Los Angeles judge agreed and threw out most of the suit, calling the relationship "no more than that of a wealthy, older, married paramour and a young, well-paid mistress."

The remnants of the suit never were resolved. On July 7, 1983, Morgan was beaten to death with a baseball bat in her Los Angeles condominium. Her live-in 33-year-old boyfriend confessed to the murder. But even that didn't end the late Bloomingdale's troubles. A few days after Morgan was murdered Los Angeles attorney Robert Steinberg announced publicly that Bloomingdale and Morgan were included on videotapes that he possessed showing high government officials having sex with mistresses. A day later, just before he was to be subpoenaed, Steinberg reported the tapes stolen. The tapes never did turn up and Steinberg later was charged with falsely reporting a theft. And there, finally, ends the sordid obituary of an accomplished man.

JOHN WILKES BOOTH
May 10, 1838–April 26, 1865

As HE LAY hiding in the pine thicket along the Potomac River, seven days after assassinating President Lincoln, John Wilkes Booth began to think his act had been in vain. "I am here in despair," he wrote. "And why? For doing what Brutus was honored for—what made Tell a hero. My action was purer than theirs. . . . I have too great a soul to die like a criminal. O, may He spare me that, and let me die bravely!"

Booth, a strikingly handsome, successful actor and strong supporter of the Confederacy, had planned for months to abduct Lincoln to force the release of Southern prisoners. But after Lee surrendered on April 9, 1865, Booth's plots were rendered useless. He spent the next few days glumly drinking much brandy at John Deery's billiard hall in Washington, D.C. When he shot the President on April 14 the act apparently was unplanned until that day, when Booth happened to hear that Lincoln was to see *Our American Cousin* at Ford's Theater that night.

It was during the second scene of the third act, after 10 P.M., that the 26-year-old Booth entered Lincoln's box and shot him in the back of the head. He stabbed an officer who tried to grab him, then leaped to the stage 12 feet below, yelling, *"Sic semper tyrannis! The South is avenged!"* As he jumped his boot spur got caught in the folds of an American flag draped along the President's box, causing him to fall and break his left leg as he hit the stage. Booth managed to limp quickly past the stunned actors and go backstage, where he stabbed the orchestra conductor, who tried to stop him, then struggled down the rear stairs to an awaiting horse that was being held by a stagehand.

As Booth fled the city—his fractured leg tearing deeper and deeper into his flesh—he was joined by 19-year-old David Herold, who as one of eight in Booth's gang had shot and wounded Secretary of State William Seward. Two men who were to kill Vice President Andrew Johnson backed out. Booth and Herold rode through the night southward into Maryland. They turned eight miles out of their way to arrive at the home of Dr. Samuel Mudd, who set Booth's leg at 4:30 A.M. From there the two men rode on to the Potomac, where they hid along the banks for a week, surrounded by Army troops but supplied food and newspapers by a Confederate sympathizer.

The troops finally caught up with the two men in the early morning hours of April 26, after they had crossed the river and reached the home of Richard Garrett in Virginia. After the soldiers surrounded the barn where Booth and Herold were sleeping, one of Garrett's sons was ordered to go in and convince them to surrender. Booth told the boy, "Damn you. You have betrayed me. Get out of here or I will shoot you."

Herold surrendered, but Booth stayed inside the barn, intent on a hero's final blaze of glory. He yelled, "Captain, this is a hard case, I swear. Give a lame man a chance. Draw up your men 20 yards from the door, and I will fight your whole command." When the troops refused Booth called out, "Well, my brave boys, you can prepare a stretcher for me."

Soldiers set the barn afire. Booth was seen briefly against the light of the blaze, leaning on a crutch, before a shot was heard. Booth was pulled from the barn with a bullet in the side of his neck that had broken his spinal column. A soldier, saying "Providence directed me," claimed he had shot Booth through a crack in the barn even though orders were to take the assassin alive. But some historians believe Booth had shot himself. The actor spent his final hours lying on the porch of Garrett's house. Before he died at 7 A.M. he mumbled, "Tell mother, tell mother, I died for my country." And then: "Useless, useless."

Although Booth's body was identified by several people before he was buried outside Washington, near the U.S. Arsenal, legend had it that the Army had gotten the wrong man and Booth remained alive. He was spotted, it was said, in Europe and India, and many believed the self-acclaimed hero wandered around Texas and Mexico for the rest of the 19th century before committing suicide in Enid, Oklahoma, in 1903.

MARGARET BOURKE-WHITE
June 14, 1904–August 27, 1971

MUCH OF THE history of the 1930s and 1940s we remember through the eyes of Margaret Bourke-White. Primarily as a founding photographer of *Life* magazine, but also through the compelling portraits in her books, Bourke-White created some of the most memorable images of the era, from World War II and Depression farmers to new mammoth dams and industrial plants. She photographed President Roosevelt, Winston Churchill (who gave her twelve minutes), and Stalin, and captured the classic portrait of Mahatma Gandhi simply spinning cotton for his own clothes. "Generals rushed to tote her cameras and even Stalin insisted on carrying her bags," a friend said of this tall, slender, handsome woman. She and her camera were everywhere, surviving torpedoes in North Africa and an ambush in Korea.

It was on her way home from the Korean War in 1952 that Bourke-White noticed a dull ache in her left leg and arm. When her doctor told her she had Parkinson's disease, she knew immediately what she faced. "A terrible disease," she said in her autobiography, *Portrait of Myself*. "You can't work because you can't hold things . . . you grow stiffer and stiffer each year until you are a walking prison . . . no known cure." Her craft required not only her clear vision of what made a photograph, but also demanded her steady hand to guide the camera and click the shutter at the precise instant.

She did not give up. She crumpled balls of newspaper and squeezed and twisted wet towels to try to preserve the flexibility and control of her hands. She demanded that *Life*'s editors send her on rugged assignments in Canada and elsewhere so she could get her daily rigorous walk. As her legs grew weaker and stiffer she got an aerial assignment covering the new St. Lawrence Seaway. Once she struggled into position in the airplane, she made photographs with her usual clarity.

Bourke-White completed her last assignment for *Life* in 1957, when she said she would stop working until she could perform as before. She underwent a complicated new surgery twice, in 1959 and 1961, that involved drilling into the skull to lessen the effects of Parkinson's. After the first operation she went in front of the camera as the subject of a *Life* story on her rehabilitation. With the starkness of her own work, the pictures showed this shaven-headed woman struggling to relearn words and recapture the use of her limbs.

The operations helped only temporarily. She had to dictate most of her autobiography, published in 1963, because her fingers couldn't press the typewriter keys. But in the final chapter of the book, she eagerly reported that *Life* had chosen her as its first representative to travel to the moon. Bourke-White suffered eight more years before she died in a Stamford, Connecticut, hospital after she had fallen and broken several ribs. Her clear eyes must have seen the Apollo landings, but her body was helpless to follow.

DIAMOND JIM BRADY
August 12, 1856–April 13, 1917

THE PHRASE "living high on the hog" could well have been created for Diamond Jim Brady. The greatest salesman of railroad equipment in the golden age of trains, Brady was quite literally the fattest cat in town. He'd travel around the country for nine months, then burst into New York City eager to lavish his enormous commissions and his unlimited expense account on parties, gambling houses, and first-night theater tickets, often with chanteuse Lillian Russell on his arm. The self-made son of an Irish saloon owner, Diamond Jim got his nickname from his jewel collection, which ultimately totaled some 20,000 diamonds and 6,000 other gems, including twenty-one complete sets of diamond-studded cuff links, scarf pins, rings, and shirt studs.

But Brady's real trademark was his appetite, which was the epitome of the voracious Gay Nineties. Here is an oft-documented sample of a Brady meal. Breakfast: steak, eggs, chops, pancakes, potatoes, grits, corn bread, muffins, and milk. Lunch: a tray of oysters and clams, another steak and maybe a lobster, a salad, several slices of fruit pie, and for dessert the better part of a box of chocolates. After a snack he would sit down for dinner, at which he was known to put away double orders of a fifteen-course meal.

The high life finally got to him in 1912, when he was admitted to Johns Hopkins Hospital in Baltimore suffering from gallstones. The hospital had to get a special bed and surgical table to support the fat man. In fact, doctors discovered his stomach was six times normal size and was covered with so many layers of fat that they could not operate. Brady recovered, even though he replaced his hospital diet with food he ordered from a top hotel.

He plunged back into New York during a dance craze and, after spending thousands to learn the fox trot and the turkey trot, would pay women $25 a night to dance with him. But his revelry was short-lived. Because of his diet Brady suffered from diabetes and persistent indigestion. His doctor told him he could live another five or ten years if he would just follow a special diet regimen. "Who wants to live ten years if he has to do all them things?" Brady replied. "I'm gonna go on eatin' what I please as long as I can keep my food down. Then when I cash in my chips it'll be because my number's up anyway."

His number started to make its appearance in November 1916, when Brady suffered severe ulcer attacks. His doctor told him he needed to get out of New York to rest, so Brady moved to Atlantic City. But his enjoyment of the Boardwalk mostly was limited to his view from the enclosed balcony he had built as part of his $1,000-a-week apartment. There he sat day after day with diabetes, bad kidneys, and chest pain. At 4:30 A.M. on April 13, 1917, Brady called for his valet to bring him a glass of water. After Brady went back to sleep the valet decided to let him sleep an extra hour that morning. But when he went to awaken Brady at 8:30 A.M. the 61-year-old man was dead of a heart attack. The doctor said he had died in his sleep only five minutes before. Brady left the bulk of his fortune to the Brady Urological Clinic at Johns Hopkins.

TYCHO BRAHE

December 14, 1546–October 24, 1601

TYCHO BRAHE, the Danish astronomer who provided vital links between the theories of Copernicus and the discoveries of Sir Isaac Newton, was an arrogant man. When he was in college he got into a duel with a fellow student over a mathematical question. Much of Brahe's nose was sliced off in the fight and for the rest of his life he sported a shiny nose cap made of silver and gold. As an esteemed astronomer, Brahe persuaded the King of Denmark to build him a huge observatory on Hveen, an island near Copenhagen, but he was less adept at playing the politics needed to support his studies. Everyone—royal officials, Brahe's students, other residents of the island—found the brilliant star-tracker temperamental and high-handed.

So it is perhaps surprising that Brahe allowed the situation to develop that led to his death. Brahe in 1601 was living near Prague, where he had moved after he fell out of favor with the Danish King's successor. On October 13 he was dining at the home of a baron. Brahe had had bladder trouble, but on this night he neglected to relieve himself before the meal began and then proceeded to drink copiously. In those days it would have been a supreme insult to leave the table before the meal was finished. So Brahe, raised a nobleman, remained at the table until his bladder burst. He suffered painfully for eleven days before he died.

LENNY BRUCE
October 19, 1925–August 3, 1966

"I'M NOT a comedian. I'm Lenny Bruce," he would say, and some people were only too quick to agree. Bruce made a career out of offending people, and his foul-mouthed humor got him arrested several times on obscenity charges as well as banned in Australia and England. But to others he was a profound social satirist, "in the tradition of Swift, Rabelais and Twain," according to a statement signed by 100 artists and scholars to protest one obscenity arrest in Greenwich Village in 1964.

Bruce also was arrested several times for possession of narcotics. Heroin had been part of his creative process since the Long Island–born World War II veteran began performing as the between-acts comic in cheap strip joints in the 1950s. "Look," Bruce explained when he was 28, in 1953, "you only have 65 years to live. Before you're 20, you can't enjoy anything because you don't know what's going on. After you're 50, you can't enjoy it either, because you don't have the physical energies. So you only have around 25 years to swing. In those 25 years, I'm going to *swing!*"

His swinging, which included wild sex orgies and occasional drug-induced incomprehensible performances and near-fatal illnesses, didn't slow his career. But the arrests did. By 1964 many club owners refused to book him, fearing their own arrests for obscenity. Bruce was followed constantly by law-enforcement officials waiting to slap another obscenity or drug charge on him. In 1965 the former headliner was declared bankrupt.

At a San Francisco hotel that same year, clearly aggravated by his many court battles, Bruce woke up in a frenzy in the middle of one night and fell—or jumped—out the window. He flipped in midair and hit the pavement 25 feet below on his feet. He broke both ankles and one leg and almost died from infection. After he insisted that the heavy plaster casts be removed early, he was left partly crippled. In the next year the always slender and short man grew fat and his heroin habit grew worse. He barely worked at all, preferring to stay fairly secluded in his home on Hollywood Boulevard in Los Angeles.

On August 3, 1966, he was found facedown on the floor of the bathroom next to his office in his home. A needle was sticking out of his arm, and apparently he had been sitting on the toilet when he fell forward, dead from an overdose of morphine. It wasn't clear whether he intended to kill himself or whether he just shot up a little too much, accidentally. Or maybe he had just calculated wrong, and twenty-five years of swinging was more than his 40-year-old body could take.

CHANG AND ENG BUNKER
May 11, 1811–January 17, 1874

CHANG AND ENG BUNKER were the original Siamese twins. They weren't, of course, the first pair of humans physically joined together at birth, but they were the first to make a highly successful career out of it. Chang and Eng were so famous in the 1800s that the term "Siamese twins" came to mean their condition, even though they were in fact sons of a Chinese fisherman and merely grew up near Bangkok. They were bound together at the base of their chests by a strong, thick ligament that was about five inches long and eight inches around. When they were children their "third arm" held them face-to-face, but as they grew up the ligament stretched, allowing them to stand almost side by side, as well as walk and even swim together.

When they were 17 in 1829 they were spotted by a British merchant who, after paying their mother a few hundred dollars, presented them first to the medical community and then to sellout audiences in the United States and Europe. The amazing pair would answer questions and then perform a little act that featured somersaults and back flips. Offstage, however, they were two very different individuals. Chang, who stood on the left and was an inch shorter than five-foot-three-inch Eng, was the more boisterous one. He drank heavily and got very drunk while Eng, despite their link, remained sober. Even their pulse rates were different, and when one got sick the other usually stayed well. Still, doctors were unsure of what internal organs or arteries they shared and could not guarantee that either one could survive an operation to separate them.

After ten years of being exhibited as freaks, Chang and Eng retired and bought a tobacco farm in North Carolina. Four years later, in 1843, they married Sarah and Adelaide Yates, local daughters of a poor Irish farmer. The union sparked much speculation among doctors and the popular press, which the two couples fueled by producing a total of twenty-one children—ten by Chang and Adelaide and eleven by Eng and Sarah. The four slept in one, specially made, oversized bed for fourteen years before they built a second house. Then the twins would alternate households every three days.

Over the years Chang and Eng, who took the last name Bunker when they became American citizens, returned to show business whenever they needed money to support their growing families. In 1870 they joined with master promoter P. T. Barnum for a sensational European tour. It was while on board a ship home that Chang suffered a stroke. Chang, who probably because of his drinking had always been the weaker twin, was paralyzed on his right side, nearest his brother. Eng, who remained healthy, was left to lie beside his brother during his long recovery.

In January 1874, Chang was suffering from bronchitis. They were sleeping by themselves at Eng's house on the night of

January 16 when Chang woke his brother. He complained of chest pains and insisted they get up and build a fire. Eng reluctantly agreed. A couple of hours later Eng convinced Chang to go back to bed, though Chang said his chest hurt when he lay down. About 4 A.M. Eng's 18-year-old son looked in on the pair. He found his father sleeping soundly. He found Chang dead.

Eng, who for years had been terrified of this possibility, woke up, and when he was told his twin was dead he wailed, "Then I am going!" He began shaking and complained of pain all over his body, and asked his wife and children to rub his arms and legs. Some minutes later Eng said he was choking. He started to sit up, then fell back and put his arm around his dead brother, saying, "May the Lord have mercy upon my soul." He fell into a coma and died an hour later, just before their doctor, who had promised to separate them if one died, arrived.

The autopsy showed that Chang and Eng were, indeed, deeply joined. Their livers were connected and a small amount of blood flowed between their abdominal cavities. Doctors concluded that separating them would have killed them. But they also determined that Chang's fatal illness did not kill Eng because the briefly surviving twin showed none of the effects of his brother's ravages. What had killed Eng, doctors believed, was the shock of Chang's death. Eng, literally, had been scared to death.

GEORGE GORDON, LORD BYRON
January 22, 1788–April 19, 1824

IT IS IRONIC that the creator of the Byronic hero was himself almost lame, born with a club foot. But then part of Lord Byron's appeal as one of the most widely read and shocking

poets of his day was the speculation about which of his characters' flamboyant adventures—especially those of his dashing
Don Juan—were fictional and which were autobiographical.
"People take for gospel all I say, and go away continually with
false impressions," the handsome poet once said gleefully. *"Mais
n'importe!* It will render the statements of my future biographers more amusing—as I flatter myself I shall have more than
one. Indeed, the more the merrier, say I."

Byron shocked staid England with more than his poems. The
son of a lord who had burned out and died when he was three,
Byron left his seat in the House of Lords and fled England alto-
gether in 1816 to escape his debts and a sex scandal involving
his wife's half sister. He traveled Europe, living openly for a
time as the kept man of a married woman in Italy and making
his famous acquaintance with another poet-in-exile, Percy Bysshe
Shelley, at Lake Geneva.

In 1823, Byron embraced a cause that his poetic heroes would
have relished. He decided to launch a ship to aid the Greek
war for independence from the Turks. He raised a substantial
amount of money and even sold some of his poems to pay for
a 120-ton vessel—less kindly described as a "tub"—that he
christened the *Hercules.* Byron hired some soldiers and sailed
to Greece in July, only to find his mission anything but glorious.
The Greek factions were stifled by infighting, so for months
Byron sat on the sidelines, unsure of with whom to join arms.

The poet settled in a small villa near the Ionian Sea where
he often was sick, largely because he fought his tendency to
be overweight by subsisting on a meager diet of rice. Byron
was so ill much of that winter that the zestful poet told his
doctor, "Do you suppose that I wish for life? I have grown
heartily sick of it and shall welcome the hour I depart from it.
Why should I regret it? Few men can live faster than I did.
I am, literally speaking, a young old man."

By February 1824, Byron had recovered enough to resume
his daily horseback rides. On April 9 he stubbornly insisted on
riding, even though the weather looked threatening, and three

miles out he was caught in a heavy downpour. He returned home soaked and chilled and soon developed a fever. His condition so worsened over the next week that his doctors finally persuaded him to be bled, which was accomplished by attaching twelve leeches to his temples. The doctors also gave him castor oil to induce diarrhea, which also was somehow supposed to purge the fever. Byron became delirious and spoke in fragments of English and Italian. On the night of April 18 the 36-year-old poet regained consciousness long enough to say "Now I shall go to sleep." He did until twenty-hour hours later when, drained and far from the battlefields, he died.

CALIGULA

August 31, A.D. 12–January 24, A.D. 41

"REMEMBER THAT I have the right to do anything to anybody," Caligula once told his grandmother, whom he later drove to suicide. What a charmer this 25-year-old Roman emperor was. At one banquet he cheerfully reminded his guests that he could have them all killed if he wanted to. Often he would put his arms around his wife or his mistresses and say "Off comes this beautiful head whenever I give the word." He slept with everyone, including his sisters, and made senators kiss his feet. He levied huge taxes so he could throw lavish parties and encouraged citizens to name him in their wills.

Some of that was not unusual in the violent decline of the Roman Empire. Caligula's predecessor had, after all, been smothered to death by a pillow. But Caligula, a tall, hairy man with a bald spot, who was given to seizures and practiced making scary expressions in the mirror, broke all bounds. He declared himself a god, equal to Jupiter, and replaced the heads of statues of the gods with his own likeness, though in his brief four years as ruler his likeness changed drastically as his excesses left him fat and hollow-eyed.

Not surprisingly there developed plots against his life. When he discovered one such conspiracy he ordered that his victims be killed "by numerous slight wounds, so that they may feel that they are dying." Another plot emanated from the emperor's own palace. Caligula was protected by a personal police force called the Praetorian Guard. One of the guards, Cassius Chaerea, was responsible for getting the daily password from the emperor. Caligula delighted in embarrassing and insulting Chaerea by giving him obscene words.

The guard struck back on the last day of the Palatine Games in the fourth year of the emperor's reign. The stage of the theater was covered with blood, as Caligula had performed a human sacrifice as part of the ceremony and two plays, a tragedy and a farce, both called for lots of blood. At the lunch recess Caligula left the theater and walked through a secret underground corridor toward the palace to bathe. In the passageway he was met by Chaerea, who with two other guards stabbed the emperor to death.

Romans at first hesitated to rejoice at the news of Caligula's death, fearing it was another of his ploys to smoke out his enemies. Only after his assassins and their supporters killed Caligula's wife and beat his daughter to death against a wall did the city celebrate.

AL CAPONE
January 17, 1899–January 25, 1947

ALPHONSE "SCARFACE" CAPONE was a gangster straight out of the movies. Actually it was the movies that took after him, as his iron-handed control over Chicago during Prohibition—punctuated by bombings and machine gunnings—inspired films such as *Scarface* and *Public Enemy* in the early 1930s. Capone operated out of a six-room suite at the Hotel Lexington on Michigan Avenue, complete with gold fixtures and a secret passageway behind a mirror. Wearing custom-made suits or Sulka silk pajamas, the heavyset but solid man with three scars on his left cheek ruled some 1,000 men and in his prime grossed more than $100 million a year from bootlegging, gambling, and prostitution. His gang wars killed more than 300.

Capone, however, didn't die by a bullet. He surrendered under indictment for income tax evasion. He was convicted in 1931 for not paying $215,000 in taxes and sent to a federal penitentiary in Atlanta. During his initial medical exam there Capone admitted that he had contracted syphilis three years before. He apparently got it from one of his mistresses who previously had been a prostitute in one of his brothels. But Capone somehow believed he had been cured and refused a painful spinal tap to determine if he was still infected.

The husky mob boss settled into prison life fairly well. He lived in an eight-man cell, worked eight hours a day making shoes, and got money smuggled to him so he could bribe privileges and protection. Two years later Capone was moved to a new federal prison, Alcatraz. At the island fortress, where everyone had their own cells, Capone worked in the laundry room and later the bathhouse. His powerful reputation gone, Capone once was stabbed in the back with a pair of scissors.

Then one day in 1938, Capone was found staring blankly in the mess hall. Doctors determined that his supposedly cured syphilis was in fact in its advanced stages. Capone spent his last eleven months of imprisonment in the hospital ward, where injections and shock treatments slowed his disease. In November 1939, Capone was released, but by then *The New York Times* said charitably, "He was a slack-jawed paretic and overcome by social disease, and paralytic to boot."

Capone retired to his Palm Island estate in the bay near Miami Beach. There, having held on to several million dollars that the IRS had been unable to seize, he continued to lose his mind. He was paranoid, especially of cars carrying men. Physically uncoordinated, his speech garbled and confused, he would fish off the dock for hours, dressed in his pajamas. In 1942 he received one of the first doses of the new drug penicillin, used to treat the disease. Like earlier treatments, it couldn't reverse his already severe brain damage.

Finally on January 19, 1947, Capone suffered a brain hemorrage at 4 A.M. while in bed. Last rites were administered and United Press International reported him dead. Instead, the 48-year-old man lingered almost a week, until he died at home on January 25. Long since deposed as a murderous gangster, Capone at his death only made page seven of the *Times*.

CATHERINE THE GREAT
May 2, 1729–November 17, 1796

WHAT YOU'VE probably heard about the death of Russian Empress Catherine the Great is wrong. The poor maligned woman, insatiable lover though she was, did not die in flagrante delicto with a horse that, according to the famous rumor, crushed her when the truss broke. No, the 67-year-old ruler was alone when she collapsed, having dismissed her lover—a 27-year-old man—earlier that morning.

It is not completely surprising that such a kinky tale would develop about Catherine. The daughter of a minor German prince, Catherine married Peter III, the incompetent heir to the Russian throne, and then overthrew him and had him killed seventeen years later when he became Emperor in 1762. Catherine was aided in her coup by her lover, who at the time was Gregory Orlov, one of the twelve or twenty-one lovers during her life. Unlike her late husband, with whom she consummated the marriage only after nine years and then just long enough to produce an heir, Catherine treated her lovers very well. She paid them big salaries and gave them large apartments near her chamber. She made one of them King of Poland. When she was ready to move on and dismissed them, usually it was with an estate or a title to support them.

Catherine was a vivacious, hardworking ruler who was not happy to grow old. In her youth a beautiful woman with blue eyes and lush black hair, Catherine in her later years took to wearing heavy cosmetics. By the age of 60 she had lost all of her teeth, which deeply embarrassed her, and in her last years her legs were so swollen with varicose veins that she could barely walk and mostly was wheeled about in a wheelchair.

On September 11, 1796, Catherine sat regally enthroned at

the wedding of her granddaughter, who was the daughter of her only legitimate son, Paul. But the groom, the son of the King of Sweden, never showed up, and later that night Catherine suffered a minor stroke. About two months later, on November 16, the empress seemed nearly recovered. She arose from bed early, had her usual cup of coffee, and discussed plans for a trip to Crimea in the spring. After she dismissed her lover and her secretaries, Catherine went into her dressing room. Normally she stayed there for ten minutes, so when her attendants didn't hear from her for half an hour, they summoned her private secretary. After he got no answer at the door he entered and found Catherine lying on the floor, gasping and unconscious.

The powerful Empress had suffered a severe stroke. Doctors bled her and raised blisters on her feet, but the next night she died, most unspectacularly, without regaining consciousness. For her funeral her son Paul, who never had been close to her and still was bitter about his deposed father's fate, had Peter III's tomb opened and his coffin placed next to Catherine's. Thus she was buried alongside the man in her life she had slept with the least.

CICERO

January 3, 106 B.C.–December 7, 43 B.C.

MARCUS TULLIUS CICERO, the most eloquent orator and writer of the Roman Empire, wasn't exactly savvy, especially for a politician. The middle classes may have adored his speeches in the courts or the Senate Forum—the way he called his opponents "swine" and "pests"—but his outspokenness regularly got him in trouble with his murderous, power-hungry colleagues. "My own applause has the greatest weight with me," admitted Cicero, who left a colorful and prolific legacy of 57 orations and 864 letters. But in his day, when Roman leaders were killing each other, Cicero's simple vice of vanity could be deadly.

Twice Cicero was forced to flee to Greece for his blunt opposition to Julius Caesar's drive to turn the Roman republic into a dictatorship. By the time Caesar was assassinated in the Senate in 44 B.C., the 62-year-old orator was living peacefully in political retirement in Rome. But he jumped back into the fray soon after, as he found plenty to say about the turmoil and rivalry sparked by the emperor's death.

He loudly attacked Mark Antony, at the time the leading contender to replace Caesar, who was murdering his rivals and surrounding himself with armed guards—an unprecedented act, even in bloody Rome. "Is it not better to perish a thousand times than to be unable to live in one's own city without a guard of armed men?" Cicero declared. "Believe me, there is no protection in that. A man must be defended by the affection and goodwill of his fellow citizens, not by arms."

It was a lovely thought, but hardly practical during the decline of the Roman Empire. A year after Caesar was killed lines were drawn that put Antony and Octavian in a temporary alliance on the winning side and Cicero and the entire Senate on the other. The forthright speaker now found himself squarely at the top of the list to be executed.

Cicero boarded a ship to flee Rome, but bad weather made him seasick in port and he was forced back ashore, where he spent the night in one of his villas. By the next day Cicero had decided to await his assassins calmly, but his slaves forced him to be carried back to the ship. On the way he was stopped by Antony's soldiers. Cicero, bedraggled and unshaven, willingly bent down and stretched out his neck so the soldiers could behead him. Antony also had ordered that Cicero's right hand be cut off.

Antony, who himself had only thirteen years left before the Roman Empire would turn against him, was so delighted with his soldier's accomplishments that he paid them 250,000 drachmas. Then the great Cicero drew the attention of Rome one final time. Again on the orders of Antony, his decapitated head and writing hand were hung in the Forum.

CLAUDIUS

10 B.C.—A.D. 54

IT WAS the Roman Emperor Claudius who received that most noble proclamation "Hail, Caesar, we who are about to die salute you!" How ironic that such a supreme gesture of honor should be bestowed on a crippled, stuttering old man who spent much of his life mocked for his supposed stupidity. But as it turned out a reputation for being stupid wasn't such a dumb thing during the most violent era of the Roman Empire. While everyone else was getting killed this great-nephew of Caesar Augustus wasn't considered worth the trouble. Then after the murderous Caligula was killed by one of his own guards in A.D. 41, 50-year-old Claudius was chosen Emperor precisely because he seemed to lack any capability for power, much less the ability to corrupt it.

Claudius proved to be a powerful and adept leader everywhere except in his own home. After his fourth wife was executed for plotting to overthrow him, the Emperor, then 57, married Agrippina, who was his 32-year-old niece. She was also the widowed mother of Nero, whom she was determined to see become Emperor (and who, after she got her wish, reportedly fiddled while Rome burned). Agrippina gradually stole power from the aging, increasingly feeble Claudius. When he finally caught on it was too late. Realizing that he was on to her, Agrippina fed the Emperor poisonous mushrooms. Claudius, who had waited fifty years to be taken seriously, gagged speechlessly for twelve hours before he died.

CLEOPATRA

69 B.C.–30 B.C.

LEGEND HAS IT that Cleopatra was beautiful, but there is no real record or even an authentic statue. Legend also has it that the original femme fatale killed herself with the bite of a poisonous asp, but that too was never proved. What is certain is that Egypt's last queen knew how to get her man. As Julius Caesar led his Roman troops into Egypt, the 20-year-old Queen captured the 54-year-old ruler with her charm and bore him a son. After Caesar was murdered in the Senate, Cleopatra took up with the virile Mark Antony, whom she was betting on to replace Caesar and make her Queen of the Roman Empire.

Of course it didn't work out that way. She bore him twins and four years later they were married, but in 31 B.C. Antony was defeated by Octavian and was forced to flee out of Rome with Cleopatra. Back in Alexandria, the Queen took care of herself. She had already built a huge marble mausoleum near the palace. And as Octavian approached to complete his empire, Cleopatra had her treasures—jewels, ivory furniture, and rare spices—moved into the secure vault. Her doctor prepared for her several poisons, which were tried out on prisoners in her presence. The Queen was not satisfied, as some potions seemed to cause too much pain and others severe convulsions.

Meanwhile, Octavian and Antony fought one last battle outside Alexandria. When Cleopatra's husband lost he returned to the palace, raging wildly at his defeat—and at reports that Cleopatra had secretly tried to make a separate peace with Octavian that would preserve her throne in Egypt. Cleopatra fled to her mausoleum and had word sent to Antony that she was dead. Distraught, Antony plunged his sword into his stomach. He died slowly and was taken to Cleopatra's mausoleum, where he passed away in her arms.

Just as Cleopatra was about to stab herself, Octavian's troops broke in and stopped her. She was held prisoner in her tomb. After several days Cleopatra visited Antony's tomb. When she returned her attendants bathed her, painted her with beautiful makeup, and dressed her in a white silken gown embroidered with pearls. The Queen then wrote a message to Octavian asking to be buried with Antony. When Octavian received the letter he rushed to the mausoleum, only to find Cleopatra lying regally on her bed, dead. Her two attendants also lay dead on the floor.

What killed the Queen was never determined. Some said she carried a dose of poison in a hair ornament. Others said a basketful of figs, delivered that morning, hid a poisonous asp that would have caused instant death. In fact, two small marks were discovered on Cleopatra's left arm, but no asp was ever found in the sealed mausoleum. When Octavian returned to Rome he paraded a statue of Cleopatra, dead on her bed with a gold asp wrapped around her left arm. And that's how legends get started.

MONTGOMERY CLIFT
October 17, 1920–July 23, 1966

IF YOU DIE at the height of your fame, you can achieve immortality. If you live long enough for your fame to fade, you are forgotten. Montgomery Clift belongs in the latter category. In the early 1950s his moody, sensitive performances in *A Place in the Sun* and *From Here to Eternity* made him a major heartthrob. More than that, he added an introspective, psychological dimension to those roles which made him the idol of two men who would become the most popular actors of the decade, Marlon Brando and James Dean. But by the time Clift died a little over a decade later, his obituary wasn't front-page news. And unlike other ill-fated stars of the decade, such as James Dean and Marilyn Monroe, the twenty years since Clift's death have produced only three or four biographies of his life.

Clift had been on Broadway since he was 14, but fame in Hollywood seemed to strike him differently. Three years after his first film, in 1948, he was treated for alcoholism. Some said it had to do with his insecurity concerning his many clandestine homosexual affairs. But whatever the cause, it turned a thoughtful, delicate actor into an inarticulate one. He soon began mixing pills, mostly depressants, with his drinks. He threw food at dinner parties, threw childish tantrums, and suffered blackouts. By the late 1950s movie studios were reluctant to cast Clift, especially since his last few films had not been hits. He showed up in supporting and cameo roles, but even then his long scenes would have to be chopped up because he couldn't remember all his lines for one take.

In 1966, after not working at all for four years, Clift was cast as the lead in *The Defector*. It was a B-movie spy thriller and he knew it, but he treated it as his comeback. To prove to the studios that he was a reliable star, he insisted on performing all his own stunts, including a grueling swim in the freezing Danube River, even as he was suffering from phlebitis and cataracts and was trembling.

Clift, still drinking, seemed happy with his performance. But then he saw a rough version of the movie. In it the 45-year-old actor looked like an old man. He returned to New York that summer deeply depressed and drinking even more. In mid-July he saw or spoke to several of his remaining friends. He was uncharacteristically emotional, and some later believed he was telling them goodbye. He spent Friday night, July 22, alone in his bedroom, which was not unusual. But his male nurse was concerned when he found the door locked at 6 A.M. Saturday. He discovered Clift lying faceup on his bed, dead, and wearing only his glasses.

An autopsy revealed that the faded film star had suffered a heart attack. But one friend, reflecting on Clift's last thirteen years, called it "the slowest suicide in show business."

CHRISTOPHER COLUMBUS
1451–May 1, 1506

UP TO HIS death, Christopher Columbus thought he had found a new route to China instead of discovering the Americas. But the Italian-born explorer who sailed for Spain at least had a good idea of what his find was worth. He dubbed himself "Vice-King and General Governor of the Islands and Terra Firma of Asia and India," and he got King Ferdinand and Queen Isabella to grant him one-tenth of all the revenues generated in the new lands. After his famous first voyage across the Atlantic in 1492, Columbus made three more trips to the Caribbean. But each was less successful than the one before.

The tall, ruddy former mapmaker was a better explorer than administrator. By his third voyage in 1498–1500, Columbus had alienated so many of his sailors that the King and Queen appointed a royal administrator to govern the new settlements. The commissioner promptly put Columbus in chains and shipped him back to Spain. It took Columbus—whose initial great discovery had faded since so many others had followed—six weeks to gain the attention of Ferdinand and Isabella and be released from prison.

The royal couple took away Columbus's power over the new lands, and only after he pleaded persistently and promised he would find rich gold mines did they grant him a fourth voyage. In 1502, as the aging explorer searched the coast of Nicaragua for a passage around the world, a terrible storm destroyed all eight of his ships. After being stranded on Jamaica for a year, Columbus returned to Spain in 1504, physically drained and carrying no gold. This time he was not welcome in the royal court. Columbus obsessively tried to press his claims of ownership and wealth, but his many letters went unanswered. Bitter and stubborn in his complaint, the 58-year-old white-haired man followed the King from palace to palace seeking what he believed was his.

Even after King Ferdinand saw him, Columbus remained unsatisfied. So when the royal court moved to the town of Valladolid in 1506, Columbus followed painfully on the back of a mule. A sailor gave him a room to stay in and cared for him as his condition worsened. Columbus suffered from heart disease and his legs and belly grew swollen. On May 1 the man who opened the modern world died dejected.

He had not, however, made his last trip to the New World. His body first was taken to Seville, but in 1536 his bones were shipped to a cathedral in Santo Domingo, in what is now the Dominican Republic, on the island he had named Hispaniola. When France took over the island in the late 1700s, Columbus was moved to Havana. And after the Spanish-American War the explorer crossed the ocean once again, where he remains in Seville.

SAM COOKE
January 2, 1931–December 11, 1964

SOME OF THE greatest soul singers of the last twenty years speak of their debt to Sam Cooke the way rock 'n' roll singers talk about Buddy Holly. Cooke, the good-looking son of a Chicago preacher, applied his gospel training to pop music and was one of the first black singers to score a major crossover hit with "You Send Me" in 1957. Unlike many music stars, Cooke was not careless about his career. As the hits continued he set a precedent by forming his own publishing company to get a bigger share of the profits. Often dressed in a white shirt and tie at the studio, Cooke looked like a businessman who happened to boogie down for a living.

By 1964, Cooke was living in a beautiful Hollywood home with his wife and two children. Their third child drowned that summer in their swimming pool. In October, Cooke had a Hollywood screen test and his career seemed poised for another big breakthrough. Then on the night of December 10, while dining at a restaurant with some friends, Cooke picked up a young Eurasian model named Elisa Boyer. He drove her to a cheap motel called the Hacienda. Boyer later told police that Cooke dragged her into the motel room and started ripping off her clothes. When he went into the bathroom for a moment, Boyer grabbed Cooke's pants and ran outside.

Cooke ran after her, wearing only a topcoat. When he couldn't find her he banged on the door of Bertha Lee Franklin, the motel manager, accusing Franklin of hiding Boyer. Franklin wouldn't open the door, and Cooke went to his Ferrari and started the engine. But then he changed his mind and went back to Franklin's door. This time he kicked in the door and, Franklin said later, began hitting her. The 55-year-old woman pointed her pistol and fired three shots, one of which hit the 33-year-old singer in the chest. Police ruled the death a justifiable homicide.

HART CRANE
July 21, 1899–April 27, 1932

HART CRANE, who was on his way to becoming a great American poet when he died, traveled constantly during his life to get away from those who knew him too well. He moved to New York City when he was 17 to get away from his parents and become a writer, and he spent the next dozen years jumping from New York to Cleveland to Cuba to Los Angeles and to Paris, among other places. Even in Paris his reputation for drunken and homosexual binges caused him to flee to Marseille.

Despite his growing reputation as a major literary figure, especially after his epic poem *The Bridge*, Crane was racked with self-doubt. He feared none of his work was good and felt guilty for not producing more poems. In 1931, ashamed of his personal life in New York, where he had been arrested for drunkenness and solicitation, Crane got a Guggenheim Fellowship to spend a year in Mexico researching and writing an epic poem about the Spanish conquests.

That it was a huge bite for someone who severely doubted his talent became clear immediately, as he began drinking heavily as soon as he sailed from New York. He spent the year depressed, adrift, and often drunk, and soon began talking of suicide almost daily. At the end of his year Crane had almost nothing to show for his fellowship, including not a word of his epic poem. This time, seeing no prospect of escape, he faced returning to New York and the people from whom he had fled.

In March 1932, a few weeks before he was to sail back to New York, Crane invited two women friends over, then greeted them at the door drunk and announced he had swallowed a bottle of iodine and would be dead in three hours. After the women determined the dose wasn't fatal, Crane made them spend the afternoon helping him write and repeatedly revise his will. He left most of his estate, recently inherited from his father, to a sailor. "Won't be living at all any more if this ever reaches you," he wrote in an accompanying note. "I remember so many things, and I have loved you always, and this is my only end."

By the time he sailed on the *Orizaba* on April 24, however, Crane seemed in good spirits. He was traveling with Peggy Baird, a writer who had lived next door to him in Mexico and had become a close friend. The ocean liner stopped in Havana, where Crane had caroused years before. He returned to the ship drunk that night, and after the ship was back at sea, he rambled the decks. Apparently during his wandering, he was beaten and robbed, probably in an escapade with some sailors. Shortly after, Crane stood near the edge of the deck and looked as if he were about to jump overboard, but the night watchman grabbed him and returned him to his cabin.

The next morning the handsome poet with prematurely gray hair and a youthful face had breakfast with Baird in his room, wearing a topcoat over his pajamas. Later he stopped by her room. "I'm not going to make it, dear. I'm utterly disgraced," Crane told her, but apparently she thought he meant he wouldn't be joining her for lunch. Then, as other passengers gawked at his strange dress, he walked along the deck to the stern. He quickly took off his coat and jumped over the rail.

Life preservers were thrown to him, but the poet bobbed only once above the water and made no effort to reach the white rings. The ship halted in the water, about 10 miles off the Florida coast, and circled the area for an hour before finally proceeding to New York. Ship Captain J. E. Blackadder sent this message to Crane's relatives: "Hart Crane went overboard at noon today. Body not recovered."

CRASSUS

115 B.C.–53 B.C.

You CAN sum up the character of Crassus with the root of his name—crass. The richest Roman in the time of Julius Caesar, Marcus Licinius Crassus was legendary for his money-grubbing. Crassus organized one of the first fire brigades in Rome and would have his men show up at a fire and sell their services. Meanwhile, Crassus would quickly negotiate to buy nearby endangered buildings—at fire-sale prices—then put out the flames before his new properties were damaged. He amassed several hundred houses in Rome and charged high rents, giving him a fortune nearly equal to the annual revenue of the state treasury. Crassus used his money to finance Julius Caesar's campaign for the crown, and for his deep pockets he became one third of the First Triumvirate and governed the empire with Caesar and Pompey.

Crassus had his own standard by which to measure his wealth. "No man is rich," he said, "who cannot support an army." Crassus got his chance to put his money where his mouth was in 54 B.C. when, as governor of Syria, he raised an army against the Roman Empire's constant enemy, the Parthians. But unfortunately for Crassus, financing an army wasn't the same thing as managing one. He led his troops across the Euphrates River only to be routed in a battle at Carrhae that killed his son.

With his troops ready to mutiny, Crassus accepted an invitation by the Parthian general to meet for a peace parley. Upon arriving, he was summarily beheaded. His head was sent to the court of the Parthian king, Orodes II, where according to legend it was tossed into a performance of Euripides's *Bacchae* as one character mourned the death of another. Orodes, who had heard of the self-bought general's unscrupulous business reputation, had molten gold poured down Crassus's throat, saying, according to one translation, "Sate thyself now with that metal of which in life thou wert so greedy." For the record, Crassus had invested in silver.

MARIE CURIE
November 7, 1867–July 4, 1934

WHEN SHE WAS 60 years old and had already won two Nobel Prizes for discovering radium and radioactivity, Marie Curie wrote to her sister, "Sometimes my courage fails me and I think I ought to stop working, live in the country and devote myself to gardening. But I am held by a thousand bonds, and I don't know whether, even by writing scientific books, I could live without the laboratory."

Marie Curie was extraordinarily devoted to science. And it killed her. But not until after the physicist had accomplished decades of painstaking research that led to the X ray, early treatments for cancer, and, ultimately, the nuclear bomb. In 1898 she and her husband, Pierre, began their tedious experiments, which required them to process two tons of pitchblende, a raw ore, to obtain a few centigrams of radium chloride. In primitive conditions—an abandoned Paris warehouse with an asphalt floor and a patched glass roof—Marie Curie would stir a caldron of molten mass to isolate the new radioactive substance they had discovered.

After Pierre was killed suddenly in 1906 when he was run over by a horse-drawn wagon in a crowded Paris street, Marie worked even harder. At scientific conferences the small woman with ash-gray eyes would read her scientific papers with a timid, monotone voice. But in World War I, Curie staunchly worked in the battlefields with portable X-ray equipment that quickly located bullets and shrapnel.

Besides exposing herself to the dangers of war, Curie also received high levels of radiation from the primitive X-ray equipment. She had been exposed to radiation since she began her research, and as she grew older its mounting total took its toll. She was often ill from exhaustion and the radiation made each malady worse and the recoveries longer. She occasionally developed painful, burning lesions on her hands from handling the radioactive material. But even after periodic blood tests showed increasing deterioration, Curie insisted on working in her lab. From 1923 to 1930 she underwent four cataract operations. As her vision worsened she simply used giant lenses and taped large colored signs on the dials of her instruments.

In the winter of 1934, at the age of 66, Curie was healthy enough to go skating at Versailles and skiing. On an Easter trip to southern France she caught a cold. Back in Paris, her condition worsened as she continued to work at her lab. If she was too weak to go in, she would write at home. By early summer her doctors recommended that she be moved to a sanitorium in the French Alps where the air was better.

But air wasn't the problem. She died a few weeks later from anemia, a nonfatal condition that her contaminated body could not fight. In a biography of her mother Curie's daughter wrote, "On the morning of July 3, for the last time Madame Curie could read the thermometer held in her shaking hands and distinguish the fall in fever which always precedes the end. She smiled with joy."

ADELLE DAVIS
February 25, 1904–May 31, 1974

"YOU ARE what you eat," insisted Adelle Davis, and the renowned dietitian meant it absolutely. "A woman who wants to murder her husband can do it thoroughly in the kitchen," Davis said. "There won't even be an inquest." It was that kind of direct talk that made the five-foot-four-inch, deep-voiced woman one of the most listened to authorities of the health-food movement. Her four books, including *Let's Eat Right to Keep Fit* and *Let's Cook It Right*, sold over 10 million copies by extolling whole-grain bread, fresh fruits, milk, and fish. She herself swallowed dozens of vitamin supplement pills every day.

So Davis was understandably shocked when she learned in 1973 that she had bone cancer. "I have been a failure," was her first thought, she said later. "I thought this was for people who drink soft drinks, who eat white bread, who eat refined sugar and so on." She had often said that cancer was related to your diet and was worried that her illness would discourage many who had followed her advice toward a healthier diet. Later she said she believed her cancer was caused by her years in college and a few thereafter when she admitted she had eaten junk food before she began following her own training as a nutritionist. Davis underwent chemotherapy to treat her cancer. But a year after it was diagnosed she left the hospital and returned to her Los Angeles home, where she died.

JAMES DEAN
February 8, 1931–September 30, 1955

ACTOR MARTIN SHEEN said of James Dean, "There were only two people in the fifties: Elvis Presley, who changed the music, and James Dean, who changed our lives." It's an amazing assessment, considering that Dean died midway through the decade. In fact, he was in Hollywood less than two years and made only three movies, two of which—*Rebel Without a Cause* and *Giant*—had yet to be released when he died.

The car crash that killed him rated only four short paragraphs on an inside page of *The New York Times*. But the West Coast newspapers knew better. Their front-page banner headlines above a picture of his crumpled Porsche was more attention than Dean had ever gotten when he was alive. But it was merely a hint of the legend that would follow, unfettered by the bounds of a living human subject. "You haven't Heard the Half About James Dean, by Natalie Wood" and "Here Is the Real Story of My Life—by James Dean As I Might Have Told It to Joe

Archer" were two of the early postmortems in the movie magazines.

The 24-year-old achieved immortality a few days after he completed filming *Giant*, a sweeping epic that, rising star that he was, matched him with Elizabeth Taylor and Rock Hudson. Dean had taken an interest in race-car driving, but Warner Brothers had forbidden him to race during the filming. On a Friday, the day after a party celebrating completion of the movie, Dean and one of the film's stunt men headed for a weekend racing event. Dean was driving his new gray Porsche that he had bought for $7,000 a few days before. The car was capable of doing 150 miles per hour, and Dean named it "The Little Bastard."

About 3:30 that afternoon Dean got a speeding ticket outside of Bakersfield, California. A little over two hours later, as he was driving west on a rural two-lane highway, Dean saw an eastbound car slowing at an intersection, apparently to turn left across the highway. "That guy's got to stop," Dean told his companion. "He'll see us." But Dean's gray Porsche blended into the late afternoon twilight. The impact tore open the hood and trunk on the little sports car and crushed the driver's side of the car. Dean died almost immediately; his passenger was thrown from the convertible and seriously injured. The driver of the other car, a 23-year-old college student, received minor injuries.

In one of those classic ironies, Dean had filmed a commercial for safe driving while on the set of *Giant*. "People say that racing is dangerous, but I'll take my chances on the track any day than on the highway," Dean, slouched in a chair and toying with a small lariat, had mumbled in his style. "Take it easy drivin', uh, the life you might save might be mine, you know?"

JOHN DILLINGER
June 22, 1903–July 22, 1934

GANGSTERS, like movie stars, can rise to the top very quickly. John Dillinger, who got caught robbing his first grocery store when he was 21, used his nine years in prison to polish his skills so that less than a year after he was released in 1933 he was named "Public Enemy Number 1" by the FBI. That was no small distinction, considering that some of the other gangs roaming the Midwest at the same time included Bonnie and Clyde and Ma Barker. Dillinger robbed with galling confidence. When the police got close he would step up his activity. When he was low on weapons he raided a police station. He shot his way out of jail twice, and once fooled prison guards with a gun he carved from a piece of wood and covered with black shoe polish. In less than a year Dillinger robbed over $500,000, which is impressive considering he got it a few thousand dollars at a time.

But Dillinger was not unaware of the odds. "A guy in this racket is living on borrowed time. Mine, something tells me, is short," he said during one brief prison stay. "When I go, I hope it's quick, in the midst of a thrill. Naturally, I'll prefer to shoot it out. I might win some of the time, but the time will come when some cop will hit me and—Poof!—that'll be all for John."

In May 1934, Dillinger got a face-lift that straightened his nose and slimmed his eyebrows. He dyed his reddish-brown hair black and grew a mustache. He also had his fingertips treated with acid to blur his fingerprints. Dillinger felt confident enough of the disguise that that summer, although he was the subject of a nationwide manhunt, he lived openly on the North Side of Chicago and took up with Polly Hamilton, a 26-year-old waitress who was divorced from a Gary, Indiana, policeman. She thought

Dillinger's name was Jimmie Lawrence, but her landlady, a 42-year-old Romanian woman named Anna Sage, soon caught on. Sage faced deportation for running a whorehouse, so she tipped off police about Dillinger to try to gain favor and stay in the United States.

On Sage's information, sixteen federal agents staked out the Biograph movie theater on North Lincoln Avenue on July 22, 1934. Dillinger apparently was planning to leave for Mexico the next day. At 8:30 P.M. on what had been a sweltering day over 100 degrees, the agents saw Dillinger, wearing a white silk shirt, gray tie, gray flannel pants, and a white straw hat, enter the theater with Hamilton and Sage. Two hours later, after the three had watched *Manhattan Melodrama*—a gangster movie with William Powell in which Clark Gable is sentenced to the electric chair—they walked out the front door. As agents approached, planning to arrest him, Dillinger ran toward an alley and pulled a .38-caliber pistol from his belt. Before he could fire a shot he was hit by three bullets, two in his chest and one in the back of his neck that exited below his right eye. He died within minutes.

Two women passing by were shot in the leg. But Dillinger's two female companions ran back to their apartment. Later there were rumors that a mysterious "woman in red" had fingered Dillinger by pulling out a handkerchief as they left the theater. The tale referred to Hamilton, whose dress had been orange and who hadn't been the snitch anyway.

Meanwhile, as Dillinger was taken to the hospital, some souvenir hunters who gathered outside the Biograph dipped newspapers and handkerchiefs in the pools of blood he left on the sidewalk. The hospital refused to accept the gangster because he was already dead, so agents laid his body on the grass in front of the hospital to await the arrival of the coroner's van.

As with most legendary gangsters, there are those who insist that it wasn't Dillinger who lay dead on that grass or who had been shot coming out of the Biograph that hot evening. They say Dillinger's cosmetic surgery had fooled the feds, but agents were too embarrassed to admit their mistake after they had already gunned somebody down. That would have been salt in the wound to Anna Sage, who was deported anyway in 1938.

BOBBY DRISCOLL
March 3, 1937–March, 1968

How's THIS for a Disney script? Once upon a time there was a little boy in Cedar Rapids, Iowa, whose parents took him to Hollywood for a screen test. The blue-eyed blond got his first role when he was six and went on to become Disney's first real-life child star, the first live actor the studio signed to a long-term contract. He starred in *Song of the South* and *Treasure Island* and also was the voice of Peter Pan. Bright and cute and spontaneous, he worked with such major stars as Myrna Loy, Lillian Gish, Don Ameche, and Joan Fontaine. One of his directors called him "the greatest child find since Jackie Cooper played 'Skippy.'" In 1949 he won a special Academy Award for outstanding juvenile performance of the year in the thriller *The Window*.

But there the Disney part of the script ends. Bobby Driscoll got married when he was 19 and the same year was arrested on felony narcotics charges. He was later arrested on assault, robbery, forgery, and more drug charges. "I had everything," he once said in court. "I was earning more than fifty thousand dollars a year, working steadily with good parts. Then I started putting all my spare time in my arm. I was seventeen when I first experimented with the stuff . . . mostly heroin, because I had the money to pay for it. Now, because of my arrests, no one will hire me."

Cut to March 30, 1968. Two children playing in an abandoned tenement on New York City's Lower East Side found a corpse. His arms were dotted with needle marks, but he had no identification. The actual cause of death was recorded as hardening of the arteries and a heart attack. The body was buried in a pauper's grave.

A year and a half later, Bobby Driscoll's father was dying and wanted to find his son. Authorities ran a check on Bobby's fingerprints and found they matched the corpse buried in New York. Not the way a Disney story is supposed to end.

THE DUKE OF WINDSOR
June 23, 1894–May 28, 1972

EDWARD VIII didn't give up only the British throne to marry Wallace Warfield Simpson. He also gave up his country. The eleven-month King refused to live in England as long as the royal family refused to publicly accept his Baltimore-born, twice-divorced bride. After he abdicated on December 11, 1936, for "the woman I love," Edward, demoted to Duke, spent the rest of his life in self-imposed exile, primarily living in France, though he and the Duchess never made many close friends there.

That is not to say they were lonely. They were perhaps the social center of the international jet set in the 1940s and 1950s. "Wherever the Duke and Duchess go, the world goes," party-giver Elsa Maxwell said in 1950. As they hopped to Paris, New York, or the Riviera, society and the press hopped too. The Duke declined to comment on political issues, so instead was quoted on other matters. "Miniskirts are too mini," proclaimed the Duke.

"I think the maxi is just dreadful." All in all it was a fairly vapid life for a man who would be king, filled with golf, gardening, and an endless string of parties that the Duchess reveled in but the Duke seemed simply to tolerate.

They went out less as they aged into their seventies. In 1971, after the Duke, a longtime heavy smoker, grew hoarse, doctors discovered a tumor in his throat. It was malignant and inoperable. In Paris that November he began six weeks of daily cobalt treatments, which weakened him but didn't slow his cancer. After the treatments the Duke refused to remain in the hospital, saying, "I want to die in my own bed."

On May 18, 1972, the Duke received a visit from his niece, Queen Elizabeth II. He had demanded that his intravenous tubes be removed for the visit, and he greeted her dressed and seated in an armchair in his Paris home in the Bois de Boulogne. He was unable to speak, but the Queen chatted for half an hour while he just smiled. Nine days later the 77-year-old Duke fell into a coma. He awoke after midnight on May 28 and called for the Duchess. When she arrived he said nothing, then died in her arms at 1:30 A.M.

Finally in death he returned to England, as he had wished after Queen Elizabeth agreed to allow his wife also to be buried there when she died. Some 57,000 people filed past his coffin at St. George's Chapel at Windsor Castle, and he was buried nearby at Frogmore Mausoleum, near his great-grandmother, Queen Victoria. The Duchess was even invited to stay in Buckingham Palace while in England for the ceremonies. She died in 1986 at the age of 89 and was buried next to her husband.

ISADORA DUNCAN
May 26, 1877–September 14, 1927

ISADORA DUNCAN's death was a telling denouement to her life. Always flamboyant and controversial, the early modern dancer also suffered serious tragedies. Denouncing the institution of marriage, Duncan had two illegitimate children, one by a stage designer, the other by a millionaire. In 1913 both children were killed in Paris when the driverless car they were sitting in rolled down a hill into the Seine. Later she did marry a Soviet poet, who committed suicide after she divorced him. Duncan herself had attempted to drown in the Mediterranean and had been in two serious car accidents.

But her public persona remained dramatically dazzling. She often walked around Paris in a Roman toga, with bare legs and sandals. Onstage, she performed her breakthrough interpretive dances often clothed only in thin, translucent material, causing her to be banned in Boston in 1922. Her career was sporadic in the United States, so the native San Franciscan lived in Europe, where she was more popular.

Facing heavy debts because of her extravagance, Duncan was writing her memoirs in Nice when she was killed. The day before she died she had told a reporter from the Associated Press, "Now I am frightened that some quick accident might happen." It did. Despite her lack of money, Duncan had taken an interest in a small racing car, a Bugatti, and had asked the owner if she could ride in it. She was, it seems, also interested in the driver.

On the night of September 14, after an evening walk along the Promenade des Anglais in Nice, Duncan, as usual wearing an immense red silk scarf draped around her neck and streaming behind her in long folds, got into the sports car. Neither she nor the driver noticed that one end of the scarf had fallen outside the car and under a rear wheel. As the car pulled away the scarf wound around the wheel, yanking Duncan over the side of the car and dragging her behind it for several yards before the driver turned to see what had happened and stopped. The dancer's scarf had broken her neck, killing her almost instantly.

WILLIAM CRAPO DURANT
December 8, 1861–March 18, 1947

"FORGET MISTAKES. Forget failures. Forget everything except what you're going to do now and do it. Today is your lucky day." If that sounds like something a compulsive gambler would say, it is not incongruous that the words actually came from William Durant, the founder of General Motors. When the self-made carriage-maker bought out Cadillac, Oldsmobile, and others to instantly become the biggest carmaker in 1908, Wall Street financiers called it "Durant's Folly." Durant, on the other hand, wasn't finished with his dream, but he couldn't raise the $2 million down payment to buy Henry Ford's company.

After an economic downturn caused the bankers to force Durant to give up control of GM in 1910, he turned around and started Chevrolet. He took back control of GM in 1916, then lost it for good after a severe stock plunge four years later. It was upon launching Durant Motors a few months after that that he remarked, "Today is your lucky day." And for a while it was. Durant Motors had a few good years, and even when it sagged Durant kept busy playing the stock market. At its height his fortune was estimated at $120 million. His busy brokers earned $6 million in commissions one year and it is believed he traded at an average rate of 5,000 shares per hour. Durant might have lost his dream company, but he went home to a lavishly over-decorated Fifth Avenue apartment stuffed with Flemish tapestries, Louis XV furniture, and high-priced collectibles.

It was no surprise that Durant, heavily margined, was one of the major victims of the stock market crash in 1929. As he was forced to sell off his surviving holdings to pay his debts, he also resigned his corporate directorships that at least had given him the semblance of an active business life. In 1936, Durant declared bankruptcy, listing debts of $914,000 and assets of $250 in clothing. Two years later he and his wife auctioned her jewelry and the furnishings of their Fifth Avenue apartment. Durant was shunned by most of his former business partners back in Flint, Michigan, but a few, including his successor at GM, Alfred Sloan, and Charles Stewart Mott helped him get by with loans that he would never repay.

In 1939 the GM founder opened an eighteen-lane bowling alley in Flint near a GM factory. True to form, he told reporters it wasn't just a bowling alley, it was "the first of a chain of recreational centers . . . for clean sports in cities throughout the United States." Durant, whose short height and acquisitiveness had once led him to be compared to Napoleon, cheerfully continued, "I haven't a dollar, but I'm happy and I'm carrying on because I find I can't stop. Many people value money too highly. I'm trying now to do good for as many people as possible. After all, money is only loaned to a man. He comes into the world with nothing and he goes out with nothing."

How true that would be. On October 1, 1942, the former car magnate awoke during the night at the Durant Hotel in Flint suffering from a stroke. For the next four years a series of smaller strokes gradually reduced his mental and physical abilities until he required full-time care, which left him almost penniless and finally had to be paid for by Sloan and others. Durant grew sentimental as he reflected on the dramatic swings in his fortunes. Sometime before the 85-year-old man died in his smaller New York apartment in 1947, he said to his wife, "Well, they took it away from me, but they cannot take away the credit for having done it."

AMELIA EARHART
July 24, 1898–July 2, 1937

WHEN AMELIA EARHART was hailed as the first woman to fly the Atlantic in 1928, one British newspaper sniffed, "Her presence added no more to the achievement than if the passenger had been a sheep." Technically that was correct, since she sat in back while a male pilot and navigator guided the airplane a year after Charles Lindbergh flew to Paris by himself. Despite the parades that welcomed her back to the United States, Earhart acknowledged, "I'm a false heroine, and that makes me feel guilty. Someday I will redeem my self-respect."

That she did. The tomboyish, tousled-hair pilot became the first woman to fly solo across the Atlantic in 1932. She went on to set flying records for both men and women, making the first flight from Hawaii to California and setting a speed record from Mexico City to Newark, New Jersey, by taking a shortcut across the Gulf of Mexico.

By 1937 about the only record left was to fly around the world. Earhart took off May 20 from Oakland, California, with her navigator, Fred Noonan. The plan was to fly east roughly along the equator. In Miami the 38-year-old Earhart told a reporter, "I have a feeling there is just about one more good flight left in my system and I hope this is it." It was spoken to the reporter in secrecy. Only after her twin-engine Lockheed Electra was 100 miles off the coast and headed for Puerto Rico did the world learn that Earhart had set out to do what no one had done before.

Through the month of June, Americans followed her across Africa and Asia. She survived buckled landing gear in Chad, sandstorms in the Middle East, and monsoons near Calcutta. Trouble with the plane's navigational instruments was repaired in Bandung, Java. In Australia, facing their longest flights across the Pacific, Earhart and Noonan dumped some baggage to lighten the load, including their parachutes. "A parachute would not help over the Pacific," Earhart said.

When they arrived in Lae, New Guinea, on June 30, the female pilot and her navigator had traveled about 22,000 miles in forty days. She hoped to be home for the Fourth of July. But again the navigational equipment was malfunctioning. Its performance was crucial, as the small plane would be aiming for Howland Island, a speck in the central Pacific 2,556 miles away. Already, back in Miami, Earhart had removed a 250-foot wire trailing antenna because it was too cumbersome. Over the empty seas the antenna might have picked up radio waves to guide the plane to the tiny island.

Earhart and Noonan took off July 2 (July 1 in the United States) at 10:30 A.M. with 1,150 gallons of fuel, more than enough for the journey. Two American ships were stationed on either side of Howland Island to offer assistance. Tracking radios heard regularly from Earhart through the day and the following night. At 6:45 A.M. the next day Earhart radioed with some urgency, "Please take a bearing on us, and report in half hour. I will make a noise in microphone. About 100 miles out." At

7:42 A.M., three minutes before her scheduled broadcast, Earhart pressed, "We must be on you. But cannot see you. But gas is running low. Been unable to reach you by radio. We are flying at altitude 1,000 feet." At 7:58: "We are circling but cannot hear you." Apparently the plane's radio was unable to receive messages.

At 8:45 A.M. Earhart gave their position—at least as recorded by the plane's troublesome navigational equipment—then said, "We are running north and south." That meant Earhart was zigzagging over the ocean hoping to spot land. It was the last the ground crews heard from the pilot. At 10 A.M. it was presumed that the plane would have run out of fuel.

Still there was the desperate hope that Earhart had been able to land the plane in the choppy sea, where it was designed to float. It was also possible that she could have landed on the beach of another island and was awaiting rescue. As Americans, stunned by Earhart's disappearance, followed intently, a massive naval and air search swept 250,000 square miles for sixteen days before giving up. Based on her last radio transmissions, naval officials believed she most likely ran out of fuel and crashed within 100 miles of Howland Island.

But another theory was asserted for more than twenty-five years. There had been rumors that during her final flight Earhart had conducted reconnaissance for the American military to mark Japan's encroachment into the Pacific. The pilot's final fate, according to some, was that she survived a crash landing only to be captured and later killed by the Japanese.

GEORGE EASTMAN
July 12, 1854–March 14, 1932

GEORGE EASTMAN may have done more than anyone else to change the way we look at ourselves. After first inventing the hand-held camera and the paper film roll, Eastman in 1900 came out with the Brownie, a small, cheap camera that was to photography what the Model T was to automobiles. The camera sold millions and the family photo album was born. It also sent Eastman well on his way to building one of the largest companies—Eastman Kodak—and fortunes in the first half of this century. He quickly gave much of it away, always showing great concern for his hometown and his employees.

So it came as a terrible shock when the man who always asked his friends "Are you happy?" committed suicide, leaving only this note as explanation: "To my friends: My work is done. Why wait? G.E."

Eastman had made his first $1 million by 1900 and promptly gave away more than half of it. "If a man has wealth he has to make a choice," Eastman said. "He can keep it together in a bunch and then leave it for others to administer after he is dead. Or he can get into action and have fun while he is still alive." Eastman had a lot of fun. During his life he gave away an estimated $75 million to $100 million, the bulk of his fortune.

Eastman shied away from the attention that came with his success and good works and, ironically, always tried to keep himself out of photographs. As he wrote in 1919 to my father, B. C. Forbes, founder of *Forbes* magazine, "I never made any talk on thrift [the subject of the letter], or for that matter on anything else, and as you know, like to keep out of the lime-light."

Characteristically level-headed and organized, Eastman in

1925 passed on control of his company to senior executives because he wanted to prevent instability when he died. A lifelong
bachelor, he continued to live fairly quietly in Rochester in a
huge home that displayed masterpieces by Rembrandt and Van
Dyck as well as several pictures of his mother. In his skylit con-
servatory, adorned with hanging ferns and a mounted elephant
head, he would host Sunday evening musicales and dinners for
100 guests.

By March of 1932, Eastman had grown weak from age and
illness. A lifelong friend had died a few weeks before. On Monday, March 14, Eastman called some close colleagues to his
home to witness a codicil to his will. Later he chatted with his
personal physician and his nurses, then asked them to leave,
saying, "I have a note to write." The following day the lead
story in *The New York Times* described what then occurred.
"As methodically as he had lived his seventy-one years [*sic*] he
penned a brief note, carefully put out his cigarette, placed the
cap back on his fountain pen and removed his glasses before firing a shot through his heart."

KING EDWARD II
April 25, 1284–September 21 (?), 1327

THE HISTORY of the British throne is fraught with sovereigns
who were forced to an early death, but none match the savage
end of Edward II. The unremarkable son of the very popular
Edward I, he had a lot to live up to and he simply wasn't up to
it. When he inherited the throne in 1307 at the age of 23, Edward II angered his already skeptical lords by openly carrying
on a homosexual affair with a palace squire, Piers Gaveston. Ed-

ward bestowed on Gaveston the lucrative title of Earl of Cornwall, a position never before doled outside the royal family. Within a year the noblemen's threat of revolt sent Gaveston into exile, and a few years later he was captured and beheaded.

That pretty much set the tone for Edward's twenty-year rule. He was forever putting down rebellions while he further appalled the noble classes by taking an interest in peasant skills such as shoeing horses and thatching houses. Finally it was Isabella, his long-ignored Queen, who rallied the troops and deposed Edward in 1326 on the ground of incompetence. His son, Edward III, was crowned in early 1327, but was largely controlled by Isabella's boyfriend.

Edward II, meanwhile, was held prisoner, kept out of sight, and shuttled among various lords' castles. For several months, according to legend, Edward was treated most unregally. He was forced to wear a crown of hay, and once, while being transferred from one castle dungeon to another, he was shaved by the roadside with ditch water. After some loyalists attempted to free him his captors realized it was dangerous for Edward II to remain alive. As they were reluctant to murder him outright, they placed him in a dark cell where the floor was covered with several inches of filthy water and hoped he would succumb to some disease.

That didn't work, but on September 21, 1327, it was announced in Parliament that Edward II had died at Berkeley Castle. The cause of death was not given, but many historians place credence in an account recorded some years later by a writer who knew someone who lived at the castle at the time. The former King, the account said, "was ignominiously slain with a red-hot spit thrust into his anus." The brutal act may have been committed, in part, so that when the deposed ruler finally was laid out for his funeral near Christmas, the body showed no signs of injury. Edward's heart was placed in a silver box and sent to Isabella, who mourned properly at the funeral.

KING EDWARD V
November 2, 1470–1483?

MANY A MONARCH has gone to an early grave after losing a war or riling the nobility. Edward V was killed simply because he was King of England, and not even a teenaged one at that. His exact fate, however, remains a mystery.

Edward was always an outsider to the throne. When he was born his father, Edward IV, was hiding across the English Channel in Flanders amassing troops to regain his title. Even after the father was successful the younger Edward grew up outside of London, raised by his mother's relatives. So when Edward IV died suddenly at the age of 42 in April 1483, Edward V and his entourage had a four-day journey ahead before the 12-year-old heir could claim his crown.

Meanwhile, a power struggle between the widowed Queen, Elizabeth Woodville, and the late King's brother, Richard, made that journey very long and treacherous. Along the route Edward's escorts were arrested by Richard, his uncle, who then escorted his nephew into London and placed him in the Tower. Young Edward wasn't officially under arrest—he had his servants and was seen playing in the Tower yard—but neither could he leave the fortress. His mother, Elizabeth, who had sought refuge at Westminster Abbey, sent her second son, a 9-year-old also named Richard, to keep his brother company. Edward's coronation, originally scheduled for May 4, kept getting pushed back.

As the young boy stood by helplessly his mother lost the fight. Richard III was crowned King on July 6. Edward V was dubbed "the Lord Bastard." But even after Richard III's coronation the young princes remained held in the Tower. No longer were they seen playing in the yard and they were restricted to the inner apartments. Even at 12, Edward knew what lay ahead. "Alas," he was said to have said. "I would my uncle would let me have my life yet, though I lose my kingdom." Nothing more was heard or seen of the young princes until some royal subjects demanded their release. Then it was learned that the boys were dead. It remains unclear when that was discovered or when they were killed.

The most widely believed version was recorded some years later by Sir Thomas More, who said Richard III sent his men to kill the boys a few weeks after his coronation, in late July or early August. According to More, the men smothered Edward and young Richard with the billowy bedclothes in which they were sleeping. But some documents seem to indicate the boys were alive in 1484 and even 1485. If that's true, they may have been put to death by the next king, Henry VII, after he killed Richard III in battle in 1485 and then may have conveniently passed on the blame to his dead predecessor.

Whatever the case the mystery stood unresolved until 1674, when workers rebuilding some stairs in the Tower found a buried wooden chest that contained the bones of two young boys. The workers threw the bones onto a pile of debris before others recognized the possible significance of the remains. The bones were declared to be those of the young princes and were entombed in a marble coffin designed by Christopher Wren in Westminster Abbey.

The story didn't end there either. In 1933 that tomb was opened. Scientists were unable to determine the age of the bones or the cause of death. They did discover, however, that one of the boys, believed to be Edward, had suffered from a serious jaw disease.

"MAMA" CASS ELLIOT
February 19, 1941–July 30, 1974

IT WAS WIDELY reported that Mama Cass died choking on a sandwich, a rather macabre end to one of the 1960s' best—and most overweight—folk singers.

Born Ellen Naomi Cohen, Cassandra Elliot and the rest of The Mamas and the Papas caught the lyrical side of the sixties with hits like *California Dreamin'* and *Monday, Monday*. At 250 pounds, Mama Cass was twice as heavy as the five-foot-five-inch woman should have been. But she cheerfully laughed at herself, allowing the joke to become part of the singing group's charm onstage. Still she pursued crash diets, once claiming to lose 120 pounds.

After the group split up in 1968, Cass Elliot had a fairly successful solo career, singing in nightclubs and small concerts. She was in a London apartment preparing for a concert when she died. The news that she had choked while eating certainly spread word of her death faster and farther than it otherwise might have.

But five days later a London coroner reported that Mama Cass hadn't died from choking. Found dead in her bed, she had died of a heart attack, apparently brought on by her overweight condition.

WILLIAM FAULKNER
September 25, 1897–July 6, 1962

"It is my ambition," wrote writer William Faulkner, "to be, as a private individual, abolished and voided from history, leaving it markless, no refuse save the books. . . . It is my aim, and every effort bent, that the sum and history of my life, which in the same sentence is my obit and epitaph too, shall be them both: He made the books and he died."

Of course it didn't turn out that way. Despite the "Keep Out" sign Faulkner painted and posted at the end of his driveway, there has been undying interest in the life of the Southern writer who won the Nobel Prize and two Pulitzers for his semiautobiographical novels, including *The Sound and the Fury* and *Absalom, Absalom!*, set in the fictional Yoknapatawpha County in northern Mississippi.

Yet for all his success as a writer, Faulkner insisted it was not his first love. Even more, he loved riding horses. "There is something about jumping a horse over a fence, something that makes you feel good," he said. "Perhaps it's the risk, the gamble. In any event, it's something I need." Over the years Faulkner's risks led to many bad falls. In 1952, then aged 55, he cracked two vertebrae, causing constant pain that also exacerbated his serious drinking problem. In 1959 he broke his collarbone in another fall, but half an hour later he was drinking bourbon with his arm in a sling. "It didn't hurt no worse than a hangnail," he drawled.

In 1962, after finishing his twenty-first novel, *The Reivers,* which would win him his second Pulitzer posthumously, Faulkner was spending his time riding on his farm near Oxford, Mississippi, and drinking to relieve the pains of his battered 64-year-old body. On June 17 he was riding alone along a road when his horse apparently spooked, throwing Faulkner onto the side of the road and injuring his back. After the riderless horse walked back to the stable, Faulkner's wife, Estelle, went searching for her husband. She found him limping angrily toward home. Faulkner proceeded to get the same horse out of the stable, mount him, and direct him through a series of jumps before the writer retired into the house in pain. "You don't think I'd let that damned horse conquer me, do you?" Faulkner told his appalled doctor soon after. "I had to conquer him." He also said to the doctor, "I don't want to die."

Faulkner's victory over the horse was brief. Because of the back injury, it was excruciating for Faulkner to sit or lie down. He walked with crutches, and even limped into the town's post office, but he grew weaker and more pale. And as had happened before, he began drinking heavily. Feeling particularly bad, Faulkner was taken to the hospital on the evening of July 5. At 1:30 A.M. the next morning he sat up on the edge of his bed, then slumped over from a heart attack. Doctors tried unsuccessfully to revive him for forty-five minutes before pronouncing him dead.

ARCHDUKE FRANZ FERDINAND
December 18, 1863–June 28, 1914

SOMETIMES it's the slightest fluke that changes the course of history. True, there were at least six assassins lurking in the crowds that lined the streets of Sarajevo as Archduke Franz Ferdinand, heir to the Austro-Hungarian throne, paraded by on June 28, 1914. But four of them chickened out, one threw a bomb but missed, and the last missed his chance to fire his revolver. Had it not been for a fluke, the last assassin might not have gotten a second chance an hour later, and World War I, while it may well still have occurred, at least would have been ignited differently.

Ferdinand might have known better than to venture into Sarajevo, which now is in Yugoslavia but then was a part of Bosnia that recently had been annexed from neighboring Serbia. Sarajevo was hot with rebels who wanted out of the Astro-Hungarian Empire, but the Archduke had the idea that an appearance by a member of the royal family would help ease tensions. And, indeed, the townsfolk showed warm support for Ferdinand and his wife during tours of the town and shopping trips.

On the fourth day of their visit, with Austro-Hungarian flags lining the streets and the Archduke's picture in many windows, the royal couple sat in an open limousine in a procession of four cars that drove down the main street, Appel Quay, toward a ceremony at the town hall. Ferdinand was in full uniform, bedecked with military decorations. His wife, Sophie, wore a white gown and a large hat. Suddenly a bomb flew from the crowd and landed on the Archduke's car. By some reports Ferdinand himself shoved the missile off the hood as his chauffeur sped away. The bomb exploded in the road, damaging the following car and injuring several bystanders. The Archduke ordered his driver to stop; then, after examining the damage, he said, "Come on. The fellow is insane. Gentlemen, let us proceed with our program." He even told his chauffeur to drive more slowly so people could get a better look at him.

The Archduke clearly was bothered by the attack. As the town's mayor began his speech at the town hall ceremony, Ferdinand blurted out, "It is perfectly outrageous! We have come to Sarajevo on a visit and have had a bomb thrown at us!" Then after an awkward pause he added, "Now you may go on." After the ceremony the Archduke's wife didn't want to drive back through the open streets, but a Sarajevo official assured her, "It's all over now. We have not more than one murderer in Sarajevo."

For at least some precaution they canceled a trip to a museum, which would have taken them along the narrow Franz Josef Street in a crowded part of the city. Instead they were to be driven straight back along the wide Appel Quay, which bordered the Miljacka River. An official stood on the running board next to the Archduke as further protection. But the new route wasn't passed on to all the drivers, so after the lead car made a right turn on to Franz Josef Street, Ferdinand's driver started to follow before he was told to turn back.

The driver put on the brakes and began to back up. At the same time Gavrilo Princip, the only willing assassin who had missed his chance during the first procession, happened to be standing on the corner of that intersection. Princip stepped into the street and fired his revolver twice. The first bullet struck Sophie in the stomach; the second pierced the Archduke's neck. As the car sped to a hospital Ferdinand said to his wife, "Sophie, Sophie, do not die. Live for our children." Both died within minutes, at 11:30 that Sunday morning.

After they were arrested Princip and his co-conspirators admitted they supported the separatist movement. But even though the evidence indicated that the assassins had not been aided by Serbia, troops were mobilized within a few days and in a month World War I had begun. If only the Archduke's driver had driven straight ahead.

W. C. FIELDS

January 29, 1880–December 25, 1946

W. C. FIELDS made drinking look like one long joke. In one of his best-loved movies, *Never Give a Sucker an Even Break*, Fields jumps out of an airplane window to retrieve his bottle. A publicity still from the 1930s shows him posed on the tennis court next to a liquor cabinet on wheels. "I'm an advocate of moderation," Fields would assert in his unique, raspy voice. "For example, I never drink before breakfast." The bulbous-nosed comedian, who ran away from home at the age of 11 after a beating and went on to become a star in the Ziegfeld Follies and then in Hollywood, made a career out of such cynical humor.

But it was more than a joke. Fields reputedly drank two quarts of martinis a day, even on the set. He never acted drunk and his red nose just added to his image. But his health was less laughable. In 1936 he spent a year in a sanitarium recovering from pneumonia and tuberculosis. He was told to stop drinking but he didn't. By the early 1940s, after turning out his classics *My Little Chickadee* with Mae West and *The Bank Dick*, Fields didn't have the stamina to complete the shooting schedule of an entire film. He appeared in cameo roles, wearing heavy makeup to mask the swollen red veins that blotched not just his nose but his entire face.

He gave his last, albeit uninspired, performance in 1944 in *Sensations of 1945*, though his joints were painfully stiff. In the next couple of years, as he continued drinking heavily, he suffered from cirrhosis and kidney trouble. When his abdomen became distended and bloated, his doctor told him his stomach was waterlogged. "God forbid!" Fields cracked. "I always knew that abominable, tasteless liquid would someday poison me."

The poison was the gin. By the fall of 1946, Fields had moved into a sanitarium in Pasadena. Doctors forbade him from drinking, but friends continued to smuggle bottles for him. On Christmas day, in severe pain, Fields died of a stomach hemorrhage. His longtime mistress Carlotta Monti later wrote that his last words were no joke. He said, "Goddamn the whole friggin' world and everyone in it but you, Carlotta."

JIM FISK

April 1, 1834–January 7, 1872

"BETTER TO HAVE lost and won than never to have played at all" was the bastardized philosophy of Jim Fisk, one of the most scorned and scurrilous Wall Street rogues of the late 19th century. The self-made, unschooled little fat man started out a peddler and eventually developed such finesse and outright gall that he and partner Jay Gould pulled a stock scam that wrested the Erie Railroad away from none other than Cornelius Vanderbilt. A year later, in 1869, Fisk and Gould tried to corner the gold market and caused half of Wall Street to collapse. In the near riots that followed, after a lynch mob banged on his office door, Fisk said, "A fellow can't have a little innocent fun without everybody raising a halloo and going wild."

Fisk, a flamboyant dresser with a flashy smile, relished his notoriety. He bought himself a lavish, marble opera house, from which he ran his railroad and where he often was seen in his well-placed box during performances. Directly above him in the next balcony sat his mistress, an out-of-work but beautiful actress named Josie Mansfield. That they did not sit together was one of Fisk's few attempts to be discreet about his scandalous relationship while his wife lived in Boston.

Fisk gave Mansfield a house and showered her with gifts, but the young lady, whom the press called the "Twenty-third Street Cleopatra," was not satisfied. Tired of the secrecy and Fisk's inattention when he was busy with business, Mansfield started her own secret affair with Edward Stokes, an extremely handsome business partner of Fisk. Fisk found out, and soon so did the press, as Fisk cut off payments to Mansfield and backed out of his business partnership with Stokes, and the three proceeded to fling lawsuits at each other.

On January 6, 1872, Mansfield's lawsuit, seeking more money from Fisk, went to trial. Stokes, already financially ruined by the jealous Fisk, took the stand and was humiliated as he tried to claim his relationship with Mansfield was innocent and that he spent the night at her home only during storms. Later that afternoon Stokes rode in Mansfield's carriage—which had been a gift from Fisk—to Delmonico's for lunch. There he was told that a grand jury had just indicted him on Fisk's charges of blackmail.

Stokes left the restaurant and parked outside of Fisk's home. He waited for Fisk to leave, then followed him to the Grand Central Hotel on Broadway, where Fisk was meeting some friends. Stokes darted inside the hotel before Fisk did, and as Fisk climbed the main stairs to the second floor, Stokes stepped out and pointed a revolver at him. "I've got you now," Stokes said from six steps away, then fired twice at his large target. "For God sake," Fisk yelled, "will anybody save me?" Stokes ran upstairs as Fisk, shot in his right arm and belly, staggered down into the lobby.

Fisk was taken to a hotel room, where a doctor was unable to retrieve the bullet from a four-inch-deep wound in his abdomen. "Doctor," Fisk said, "if I am going to die, I want to know about it." The doctor told him he wasn't going to die, at least not that night. Still, Fisk, who seemed to be in little pain except for what he called a "green-apple bellyache," made out his will as his wife, Lucy, from Boston and his good friend Boss Tweed, who was out on bail for corruption charges, sat at his bedside.

By the next morning Fisk was in a coma. He died at 10:45 A.M. Stokes was convicted of murder at his second trial and was sentenced to hang, but on appeal his term was reduced to six years in prison. Mansfield, who didn't see Fisk before he died, sued Fisk's widow, to whom Fisk had left the bulk of his $1 million estate. The newspapers, of course, had a field day with the whole thing. "What a scamp he was," said one. "But what a curious and scientifically interesting scamp!"

F. SCOTT FITZGERALD
and ZELDA
September 24, 1896–December 21, 1940
July 24, 1900–March 11, 1948

IT IS OFTEN SAID that F. Scott Fitzgerald and his wife, Zelda, were the original flappers. Living high on the profits from his successful first novel, *This Side of Paradise*, in 1920, the couple reveled in the Jazz Age. There they were, splashing in the fountain in front of the Plaza Hotel on Fifth Avenue. And there was Zelda, dancing on the table at dinner parties. When they weren't hopping about Europe they threw lavish weekend-long galas at their Long Island estate, which Fitzgerald used in *The Great Gatsby* in 1925.

Fitzgerald always wrote about what he knew, and as long as the Twenties roared his tales of the rich and famous were popular. But when the Twenties ended so did the Fitzgeralds' party. Zelda, who felt ignored by her husband and was desperate for a successful career of her own, suffered a nervous breakdown in April 1930. Diagnosed as schizophrenic, she spent most of the rest of her life in mental hospitals, and Fitzgerald spent much of his life worrying about her care. "I left my capacity for hoping on the little roads that led to Zelda's sanitarium," he wrote.

Fitzgerald's stories turned darker and became much less popular. His only completed novel of the decade, *Tender Is the Night*, was about a psychiatrist who falls in love with his schizophrenic patient. Already a heavy drinker since his party days, Fitzgerald became an alcoholic. He tried twice to commit suicide. Deep in debt, he went to Hollywood in 1937, but his screenwriting contract was not renewed after eighteen months.

Fitzgerald visited Zelda only occasionally, because usually they both seemed worse afterward. In the fall of 1940, Fitzgerald was working on a new novel, *The Last Tycoon*, the story of an ambitious movie producer who failed. Zelda had been released from the Highland Hospital in Asheville, North Carolina, after four years and was living with her mother in Montgomery, Alabama. Fitzgerald, who hadn't seen his wife for a year and a half and was living in Hollywood with another woman, wrote to Zelda promising he would visit her for Christmas.

But late in November the 44-year-old author had a heart attack. He continued to work on his novel in bed and promised his publisher a first draft by January 15. He felt well enough to go to a movie on the night of December 20, but he felt chest pains at the theater. The next day, sitting in an overstuffed chair writing notes for an article and waiting for the doctor to pay a visit, Fitzgerald suddenly stood up, reached for the mantel, then fell over dead of another heart attack. At the time all of his novels were out of print.

Zelda continued her shaky life. In 1948 she was staying again in Highland Hospital, in a room on the top floor. Just after midnight on March 11 a fire broke out in the kitchen downstairs, sending flames up a dumbwaiter shaft. With most patients trapped behind locked doors of the mental institution, nine women were killed. Six of them were on the top floor, including Zelda. She was buried next to her husband in Rockville, Maryland.

JIM FIXX

April 23, 1932–July 20, 1984

A FORMER 220-pound, two-packs-a-day smoker, Jim Fixx was hardly the likely candidate to lead Americans out of their easy chairs and into a long-distance-running craze. Having never exercised regularly in his life, Fixx didn't even begin running until he was 35. Then he quit smoking cold turkey and, by running, eventually shed 61 pounds. Ten years later, in 1977, Fixx wrote *The Complete Book of Running*, which stayed on the bestseller lists for more than a year and made the good-humored former magazine editor the guru of the sport.

In his book Fixx wrote, "Although the evidence is inconclusive, most of it clearly suggests that running is more likely to increase than to decrease longevity." Fixx himself became part of that debate when he died of a heart attack—after seventeen years of running—during one of his daily 10-mile runs. He was found by a motorcyclist late on a Friday afternoon, collapsed by the side of a road outside Hardwick, Vermont, wearing only running shorts and carrying no identification. Several passersby tried unsuccessfully to revive him.

How could a man who had run thousands of miles and lived the picture of a healthy life-style suddenly succumb to the rigors of his sport? It turned out he was not as healthy as perhaps even he thought he was. An autopsy revealed that one of his coronary arteries was 99 percent obstructed, another was 80 percent blocked, and the third, 70 percent. Doctors also found scars on his heart muscle that indicated Fixx had suffered three prior, undetected heart attacks in recent weeks. During that same time, even as he complained of chest pains and a tight throat—clear symptoms of heart disease—Fixx ran a 12-mile race and a 5-mile race.

But perhaps most telling of all was that Fixx's father had died of a heart attack at the age of 43. It was his second; he had survived one at 35. Given Fixx's family history, and his sedentary life-style until 35, some experts said running hadn't cut short the life of the 52-year-old. It probably kept him from dying a decade before.

HENRY MORRISON FLAGLER
January 2, 1830–May 20, 1913

WHEN THE ALMIGHTY John D. Rockefeller was asked once about the origins of the almightier Standard Oil Company, he said, "I wish I'd had the brains to think of it. It was Henry M. Flagler." Flagler was an original partner with the original Rockefeller in the oil business. But he probably is better known as the "Father of Florida," resulting from a later but equally monumental endeavor.

Flagler, who was already 55 when he first visited the state, sent thousands of people southward by building the Florida East Coast Railroad in the 1890s from Daytona to Miami, which at the time was little more than a swamp with a few shacks. He built fabulous resort hotels along the way, including the original Breakers on Palm Beach. He later sent tracks more than 100 miles over a loose string of islands to Key West and another line into central Florida that opened the state's richest agricultural region.

Flagler relished his role as the guiding and civilizing force over these former backwoods. He called those who followed his railroad into Florida "colonists." He wrote, "I feel that these people are wards of mine and have a special claim upon me."

In return his influence was so great that when his second wife suffered severe mental problems, Flagler bribed legislators to pass a law making insanity grounds for divorce. A week later he married his third wife. And for her he built a $2.5 million white marble palace on the shore of Lake Worth in West Palm Beach. Whitehall, with its Louis XIV furniture, Spanish tapestries, and full-time organist, was like a museum—and as cold and uncomfortable. It was a spectacular setting for parties during the winter season. But as Flagler grew older Whitehall saw fewer guests. He would tour the grounds of the estate in a wheelchair attached to the front of a bicycle. It was tiring for him even to walk through the house, and he once said, "I wish I could swap it for a little shack."

Near the end of the winter season in 1913, at the age of 83, Flagler slowly made his way on foot toward a first-floor bathroom off the grand hall. There was a narrow marble threshold above a short, steep flight of marble steps that led down to the bathroom. The doors featured the latest device: a pneumatic pump that automatically closed them behind you. Several hours later Flagler was discovered collapsed at the bottom of the short flight of stairs. He apparently had been shoved down the steps by the force of the pneumatic doors.

He suffered a broken hip and was badly bruised, but lingered for more than two months. As he lay bedridden in the stifling early summer heat, he asked his doctor, "Do you think that was just fair of God? I was old and blind and deaf, was it fair to make me lame?" And later: "Was it part of a plan to make me see my helplessness?"

JAMES FORRESTAL
February 15, 1892–May 22, 1949

JAMES FORRESTAL, Secretary of the Navy during World War II and charged with unifying the armed forces after the war, once was asked if he had any hobbies. "Obscurity," the tight-lipped, grim-looking man replied. It was a hobby he was not allowed to pursue. The president of the Wall Street firm Dillon, Read and Co., Forrestal volunteered his services in Washington as World War II approached. He played a major role in preparing the Navy for war, overseeing the construction of 65,000 ships and 110,000 naval aircraft.

For Forrestal the end of the war meant an even more difficult assignment. As the first Secretary of Defense, Forrestal faced uncooperative generals, especially in the Air Force, and a drastically reduced postwar military budget. Praise for his wartime achievements quickly turned into criticism on every decision. Forrestal became the scapegoat of the moment, attacked both professionally and personally. Finally, in March 1949, Forrestal resigned at the request of President Truman, who had just started his first elected term.

For Forrestal, who had had a lifetime of success and reward, leaving office was a devastating personal defeat. After his final day at the Pentagon he returned home deeply depressed. He told a close friend that he saw himself as a complete failure. He also believed he was the victim of a conspiracy and was considering suicide. As his friend watched in shock Forrestal searched his house, including the closets, for those out to get him. He was sent to relax in Hobe Sound, Florida, where his wife and friends were vacationing. There Forrestal tried to kill himself once. His friends quietly hid all razors, knives, and belts and accompanied him closely on the beach. But Forrestal's constant paranoia of being chased and watched by his enemies did not go away.

On April 2, Forrestal was admitted to the Naval Medical Center in Bethesda, Maryland. His illness, characterized as severe exhaustion, was followed closely in the press, evoking much sympathy but also some suggestion that his policies should be reviewed in light of his mental state. Forrestal seemed to be recovering, however, to the point that by May a guard was stationed outside his door instead of inside his sixteenth-floor room. Also because of his progress he was allowed to shave himself and wear belts with his hospital gown, even though he had told his psychiatrist that if he were to commit suicide, he would hang himself rather than jump out a window.

Saturday night, May 21, Forrestal declined his usual sleeping pill, saying he wanted to stay up and read. When the guard looked in at 1:45 A.M. Forrestal was copying a poem out of a book. Later the poem was found to be Sophocles' *Chorus from Ajax*. In part, it says:

> *Frenzy hath seized thy dearest son,*
> *Who from thy shores in glory came*
> *The first in valor and in fame;*
> *Thy deeds that he hath done*
> *Seem hostile all to hostile eyes. . . .*
> *Better to die, and sleep*
> *The never waking sleep, than linger on,*
> *And dare to live, when the soul's life is gone.*

Before he finished copying the poem Forrestal walked across the hall to a small kitchen. He tied one end of his robe sash around his neck, the other around a radiator by the window. He pushed open a screen, then jumped out the sixteenth-floor window. After a moment the sash broke and Forrestal fell, hitting a fourth-floor ledge before finally coming to rest on the roof of a third-floor passageway. He was found almost immediately after a nurse on the seventh floor reported hearing a crash outside.

Truman said Forrestal was "as truly a casualty of the war as if he had died on the firing line." On May 26 a letter to the editor was published in the Washington *Post*, signed by the "Wife of a Public Servant." It said, "What kind of country is ours that a foremost public official should choose death rather than a life in retirement? What kind of public office is it whose duties are so strenuous that they bring nervous exhaustion?"

STEPHEN FOSTER
July 4, 1826–January 13, 1864

HE WAS NO great composer, but Stephen Foster had a way with sentimental words and catchy melodies that has kept his songs popular for more than a century. There's something pleasantly wholesome and irresistibly old-fashioned about songs like "Jeannie with the Light Brown Hair" and "Oh! Susanna." Two have been adopted by states, "My Old Kentucky Home" and Florida's "Old Folks at Home" ("Swanee River").

What is ironic is that the composer of such unabashed sentimentality—born on the fiftieth birthday of the nation—ended up so miserably. Foster, who grew up singing but had very little musical training near Pittsburgh, was successful almost from his first published songs in 1848. He earned more than $1,000 a year in royalties and married in 1850. But he always spent more than he made and the marriage was unhappy.

He wrote fewer songs each year until he left his wife and daughter in 1860 and moved to New York City. There, desperate for cash, he churned out 105 songs—more than half of his entire work—in the last three and a half years of his life. Most were soon forgotten, and his previously lucrative publishing arrangement deteriorated to the point that Foster was selling songs out-right for a quick $25. The composer, who drank heavily and suffered symptoms of tuberculosis, grew bitter and lonely as he lived in a series of rooming houses.

On January 10, 1864, bedridden with fever, Foster got up to wash himself. Apparently as he stood over the washbasin he fell, shattering the porcelain bowl, which cut his neck deeply. He was found by a chambermaid delivering towels later that day. George Cooper, one of his few friends, was summoned to hear Foster whisper, "I'm done for," and plead for a drink.

Foster was taken to the city-run Bellevue Hospital, where he died, alone and unrecognized, three days later. The hospital, which had registered the 37-year-old composer as Stephen Forster, put his body in the morgue for unknown corpses until Cooper retrieved it.

Unlike nearly all that he wrote in his final years, Foster's last song, which he penned just a few days before he died, joined his earlier classics:

> *Beautiful dreamer, wake unto me.*
> *Starlight and dew-drops are waiting for thee.*
> *Sounds of the rude world heard in the day,*
> *Lull'd by the moonlight have all pass'd away.*

BENJAMIN FRANKLIN
January 17, 1706–April 17, 1790

BENJAMIN FRANKLIN said it: "In this world, nothing can be said to be certain except death and taxes." The wise and wise-cracking self-made statesman helped lead a revolution over taxes, but when his death was near he welcomed it with characteristic good humor. Franklin celebrated life and ascribed much of his happiness to two simple health tips: hot baths and cold fresh air. He slept with an open window and he said, "I rise almost every morning and sit in my chamber without any clothes whatever, half an hour or an hour, according to the season, either reading or writing. This practice is not in the least painful, but, on the contrary, agreeable."

It might have made him happy, but it didn't keep him well. Franklin had severe lung ailments as a young adult and suffered gout for decades. While minister to France in 1782 he developed a painful bladder stone that restricted his activity for the rest of his life. After he returned to Philadelphia in 1785, ending twenty-five years of almost continuous diplomacy abroad, his pain grew worse so that by 1789 he was almost confined to his bed. His characteristic chubby form was diminished by the opiates he took to relieve the pain of the stone. "For my own personal ease, I should have died two years ago," he wrote to George Washington after his inauguration in 1789. "But, though those years have been spent in excruciating pain, I am pleased that I have lived them, since they have brought me to see our present situation"—namely, the new nation.

In early April 1790, Franklin developed an abscess in his left lung that left him barely able to breathe. He continued to write and entertain visitors between fits of pain. During one bad spell he told a visitor, "Oh, no, don't go away. These pains will soon be over. They are for my good, and besides, what are the pains of a moment in comparison with the pleasures of eternity?" On April 12 the pain suddenly subsided. Franklin got up from his bed and asked that it be made up fresh so he could "die in a decent manner." His daughter told him she hoped he would recover. "I hope not," he replied.

On April 17 the abscess in his lung burst. Someone suggested he shift his position in bed so he could breathe more easily. "A dying man can do nothing easy," Franklin said, then fell into a coma. The final certainty overtook the 84-year-old man at 11

P.M. that night with his two grandsons watching. His doctor believed that Franklin himself had caused the fatal lung ailment by sitting for several hours in front of an open window. Franklin might have gotten a kick out of that. After all, his Poor Richard said, "Nine men in ten are suicides."

SIGMUND FREUD
May 6, 1856–September 23, 1939

"THE MIND is an iceberg—it floats with only one-seventh of its bulk above water," Sigmund Freud once said. As the founder of psychoanalysis, the Austrian doctor dove deep into those submerged waters and created a whole new way of thinking about thinking. He developed many of his theories from the scores of patients he treated in private sessions, during which he often puffed on one of the fifteen to twenty cigars he smoked every day.

He continued to smoke heavily even after he was diagnosed in 1923 as having cancer of the jaw. It was the tobacco, Freud said, that gave him his creativity and great capacity for work. It also probably exacerbated the last sixteen years of his life, during which he had thirty-one operations to remove tumors and fit and refit an extensive prosthesis that replaced half his mouth. In 1938 the "unwelcome intruder," as Freud called his cancer, temporarily prevented the expressive man from speaking. And this time doctors determined the tumor was malignant and inoperable. "It is tragic," Freud said, "when a man outlives his body."

That same year Hitler invaded Austria. Freud at first was reluctant to leave the country, and then when he tried the Nazis wouldn't let him go until they were paid 250,000 Austrian schillings as ransom. Leaving behind most of his rich library and other possessions, the dying Freud took up residence in exile at his son's home in London. There he continued to work, though his sessions were conducted by his daughter, Anna. Freud's face was hollow and drawn, but his mind remained clear, and despite the intense pain of his growing cancer he refused all medication for relief. Said the master of the mind, "I prefer to think in torment than not to be able to think clearly."

He relented only in his final, agonizing days in September 1939. Doctors had cut through his cheek to gain access to the fatal tumor, and the smell from the open wound was so bad that even Freud's favorite dog wouldn't go near him. The 83-year-old man couldn't eat, and he was surrounded by a mosquito net to keep the flies away. Two days before he died Freud told his doctor, "My dear Schur, you remember our first talk. You promised me then you would help me when I could no longer carry on. It is only torture now and it has no longer any sense." The doctor gave Freud a shot of morphine, and after another dose twelve hours later, Freud fell into a coma. He died early the next morning.

CLARK GABLE
February 1, 1901–November 16, 1960

IT IS SAID that Clark Gable never got over the sudden, tragic death of his wife, Carole Lombard, who was killed in a plane crash in 1942. Gable blamed himself for her death, believing that she wouldn't have been on the plane had he accompanied her on the trip to sell war bonds. Soon after the top box-office movie star left Hollywood and joined the Army, where he manned a camera to compile war documentary footage during hazardous bombing missions in Europe. When Gable returned to Hollywood his roles never matched his classic performances in films like *It Happened One Night* and *Gone with the Wind*, where he trademarked his dark, handsome features and wry grin. He began drinking heavily and married and soon divorced a fourth wife, who said she couldn't live in Lombard's shadow.

In 1960, then married happily for a fifth time, Gable finally got a role that interested him. He was cast opposite Marilyn Monroe in *The Misfits*, a Western directed by John Huston and written by Monroe's husband, Pulitzer-winning playwright Arthur Miller. Gable's salary was $750,000 plus a percentage of the film's profits—the biggest deal ever in Hollywood. At the time he was cast Gable weighed a bloated 230 pounds, but the 59-year-old actor eagerly jumped into a crash diet and exercise program that had him down to 195 when filming began.

In short the production was a nightmare. Monroe, who had less than two years to live, was late, unprepared, and threw tantrums, partly because her marriage with Miller was breaking up. For days Gable was left sitting in the 110-degree Nevada desert sun while filming dragged on from July to October. Gable was so bored and yet so tense from all the delays that he volunteered to do most of his own stunts, including being dragged in the dust behind a wild horse. The scene required several takes. Kicked, rope-burned, and bloodied, Gable finally left the desert on October 18 for two final weeks of shooting on the Paramount lot. Near the end of the production Gable complained to his agent about working with Monroe. "What the hell is that girl's problem? Goddamn it, I like her, but she's so damn unprofessional. Christ, I'm glad this picture's finished. She damn near gave me a heart attack."

On November 6, two days after filming ended, Gable complained of stomach pains. An electrocardiogram confirmed that he had indeed had a mild heart attack. He seemed to be recovering quickly. But just before 11 P.M. on November 16, after his wife had retired down the hall of the hospital to lie down, Gable flipped the page of a magazine; then his head fell back and he died.

He was entombed next to Lombard at Forest Lawn. Four months later his widow, who was fifteen years his junior, gave birth to a boy, Gable's only child.

YURI GAGARIN
March 9, 1934–March 27, 1968

FOR ONE brief moment the Soviet Union outshined the Kennedy administration when it launched into space Yuri Gagarin, the first man ever to make that trip. Gagarin's 89-minute orbit of the earth on April 12, 1961, embarrassed the United States space program and made him an unabashed hero in a nation that decried the "cult of personality." The 27-year-old cosmonaut parachuted safely to earth to find his name given to streets, a glacier, and hundreds of newborn babies. Hundreds of thousands of Soviets jammed Red Square to cheer him and Khrushchev even smothered him in kisses.

Gagarin, who had been born on a farm collective north of Moscow, now charmed the entire world. He toured Finland, Cuba, Brazil, and India and lunched with Queen Elizabeth II. At home, Gagarin's future was assured. He and his wife and two children were given a new four-room apartment in Moscow. He was promoted to colonel in the Soviet Air Force and became a deputy in the Communist Party's Supreme Soviet.

After the initial furor died down, Gagarin continued flying in the air force. It was during a training flight on March 27, 1968, that he crashed in a forest 50 miles northeast of Moscow. Unlike the wide publicity following his space triumph, very little information about his death was released by the government.

It was only after twenty years, in 1988, that Soviet officials released details of their hero's death. Gagarin and his copilot had been flying at an altitude of some 16,000 feet, above a thick layer of clouds, and were beginning their descent toward an airstrip. Suddenly a large military jet flew within 2,000 feet of Gagarin, causing a violent airstream that sent his plane plummeting into the clouds. Earlier, an air traffic controller had told

Gagarin that the cloud layer was at an altitude of 3,500 feet, so Gagarin apparently believed he had easily enough time to level his plane. In fact, the clouds were less than 2,000 feet high. By the time Gagarin saw the ground, Soviet officials said, he was two seconds too late to prevent the crash.

Gagarin's ashes were buried in the Kremlin wall and a town near where he grew up now is called Gagarin.

JAMES GARFIELD
November 19, 1831–September 19, 1881

As THE REPUBLICANS' compromise candidate for President in 1880, James Garfield was tied to nobody but ended up trying to please everybody. He waffled his way through the campaign and arrived in the White House with everyone believing he had promised them something. That was especially true when it came to civil service appointments. Virtually all federal jobs were politically assigned, and even though Garfield had wanted to reform the system, he privately had promised to give each faction of the Republican Party a share of the spoils. So immediately after his inauguration on March 4, 1881, Garfield was faced with hundreds of office seekers who lined the halls of the White House. "These people would take my very brain, flesh and blood if they could," Garfield sighed.

Among those Garfield met with in March was Charles Guiteau, who asked to be named consul general in Paris. Garfield didn't know the man, so he sent him over to the State Department as a polite way of getting rid of him. The State Department politely shuttled him back to the White House. This went on for a month and Guiteau could not figure out what was causing the delay. Guiteau, a self-anointed evangelist and former member of the Oneida "free love" experimental colony, believed he was responsible for Garfield's victory. He had written a ranting speech supporting the candidate—actually he had written the speech for Horace Greeley's campaign in 1872, then updated it for Ulysses S. Grant's failed bid in 1880, then revised it for Garfield. The speech was never spoken, but Guiteau had hung around Republican campaign headquarters passing out copies to anyone who would take them.

It was after he was barred from the White House, Guiteau said later, that he had a vision from God, who told him that Garfield needed to be "removed." He bought an ivory-handled .44-caliber revolver and tracked the President through the month of June. Garfield had no bodyguards. "Assassination can be no more guarded against than death by lightning," he said, "and it is best not to worry about either."

On Saturday morning, July 2, 1881, Garfield left the White House to travel to join his wife at their summer home in Long Branch, New Jersey. As he walked with his Secretary of State through the ladies' waiting room in the Baltimore & Potomac Railroad Station, Guiteau walked up behind the two men and fired two shots from less than a yard away. One bullet—it isn't clear which hit first—grazed the President's arm, the other entering his back four inches to the right of his spine. Garfield, a tall, husky, bearded man, threw his arms in the air and yelled, "My God! What is this?" then collapsed on the floor. Guiteau was arrested as he walked toward a carriage he had ordered to take him directly to jail to protect him from angry mobs. "I am a Stalwart," the assassin said, referring to Grant's faction of the Republicans. "[Chester] Arthur is now President of the United States."

Garfield, meanwhile, was taken upstairs in the train depot and laid on a mattress. Doctors tried to sound optimistic, but Garfield said, "I thank you, Doctor, but I am a dead man." He was given brandy to relieve the shock, then was carried back to the White House. He never got out of bed, but neither did he die quickly. For more than two months doctors probed the wound daily searching for the bullet and frequently performed surgery—without anesthetic—to relieve infection. Garfield wavered with fever and chills. He could keep down no food and was given milk from a cow that grazed on the White House lawn. Only once was he strong enough to sit up. He wrote *"Strangulatus pro Republica"*—tortured for the Republic.

To escape Washington's stifling summer heat, Garfield was moved in September to Elberon, New Jersey, near his beach home. His day of travel was declared a national holiday for prayer. Shortly after his arrival, on September 19, Garfield's temperature rose to almost 109 degrees. He died of blood poisoning at 10:35 P.M.

In 1883, President Arthur signed the Pendleton Act, which was the first step toward taking politics out of the civil service.

JUDY GARLAND
June 10, 1922–June 22, 1969

STANDING IN LINE outside the funeral home, a 23-year-old Queens housewife explained why she had joined thousands to pass by the coffin of Judy Garland. "Everyone's got sadness and problems, everyone gets lonely," she said. "Judy Garland made all of us feel something tied her and us together." It is not to say that Judy Garland would not have been a legendary entertainer had she led a happy life, but certainly part of what captivated her audiences was the awareness of what she brought onstage with her. She was a child star, a superstar at 17 in *The Wizard of Oz*, and the leading movie musical actress by 1948. She also was seeing a psychiatrist when she was 18, attempted suicide at 28, had four failed marriages, and had been addicted to uppers to perform and downers to sleep since her early years at the movie studio.

For almost the last twenty years of her life—more than half her career—Garland followed failures with smashing comebacks almost with regularity, most notably in *A Star Is Born* in 1954 and at London's Palladium in 1960. Even after her voice failed Garland pushed her frail legs and bony face through exhausting performances, so that, in 1967, Vincent Canby wrote in a review, "that the voice is now a memory seems almost beside the point."

In 1969, Garland was living in London with her fifth husband, Mickey Deans, a 35-year-old New York discotheque manager. She had performed unevenly at a London supper club earlier that year, but in June seemed happy in her new marriage. At 10 A.M. on Sunday, June 22, Deans was awakened by a telephone call from one of Garland's friends in the United States. His wife wasn't in bed, so he called to her in the bathroom. He got no answer, but found the door locked, which was usual for Garland since her early days on crowded movie sets. He climbed out onto the roof of their house to look in the bathroom window. He saw her sitting with her head slumped over in her lap.

Doctors said Garland had died of "an incautious self-overdosage of sleeping pills." They said it was not a suicide, that probably she had taken her usual dose of Seconal to get to sleep, then awakened and, confused, swallowed more pills. Liza Minnelli saw her mother's death in less clinical terms. "It wasn't suicide," she said in a statement soon after. "It wasn't sleeping pills, it wasn't cirrhosis. I think she was just tired, like a flower that blooms and gives joy and beauty to the world and then wilts away."

ELBERT HENRY GARY
October 8, 1846–August 15, 1927

AT AN AGE when many think about retiring, Elbert Henry Gary was just beginning the career that made him famous. The Illinois lawyer was 55 when he melded several steel companies, including Andrew Carnegie's, to create the United States Steel Company in a $1-billion merger unheard of in 1901. Folks who lived near U.S. Steel's main factories were so appreciative of the company's growth and jobs that when they incorporated in 1906 they named the town Gary, Indiana.

For twenty-six years "Judge" Gary (nicknamed from earlier days as a county judge) guided U.S. Steel, through a major antitrust suit and bitter strikes. He was one of the first business-men to try to cultivate public opinion and instituted the novel idea of issuing annual reports to stockholders. Even at the age of 80, Gary showed no signs of stepping down. On April 25, 1927, the chairman of the board told reporters at the company's annual meeting, "I would not blame the members of the corpo-ration if they should decide to say, 'It is time for that old gentle-man to lay himself on the shelf.' I might be justified in saying, standing on my feet here, that I have at least justified the con-clusion that I am still alive."

A few days later Gary suffered a freak injury. By May 20 he had recovered enough to attend a meeting of the American Iron and Steel Institute, where he explained why he hadn't prepared a speech. "I have been what seemed to me pretty busy, and although not of very much consequence, I might say that a few weeks ago, practicing a very foolish thing that I have been accustomed to, I put my feet up on my desk—at a directors' meeting, too, while I was thinking—my chair tipped over too far, and, of course, I struck the arm of my chair in the very worst place, in the small of my back. Since that time I have not been quite up to par, and my nerves were to some extent shocked, I think. This morning I am feeling first-rate, strong and vigorous and as happy as any man ought to be."

Gary had always looked on the bright side, but this time too much so. He had suffered from heart disease, an inflammation of the lining of his heart, for seven years. The fall out of his chair aggravated his condition so that by late June he could not go into his office in New York. He declined through the month of July, though rumors of his serious condition were firmly denied by the company. He last received visitors two weeks before he died, when he congratulated some U.S. Steel executives who recently had been promoted, but the strain was so great that his condition worsened.

A week later he and his wife moved into their newly remodeled four-story brick mansion at Ninety-fourth Street and Fifth Avenue. A week after that Gary died there on August 15. He was conscious almost until the end and had continued to work from his bed. One of the last things he worked on was a statement to be published that extolled the progress U.S. Steel had made in improving on-the-job safety for its workers.

KING GEORGE V
June 3, 1865–January 20, 1936

KING GEORGE V, grandson of Queen Victoria and grandfather of Queen Elizabeth II, was hardly one of Great Britain's greatest rulers. He maintained his reign through World War I and the demise of several other European empires, but the power of the British throne had long since passed to the Parliament. Still, the occasion of his death, though it meant little to the direction of England, was major news around the world.

Think how many more stories there would have been if what was revealed in 1986 had been known then, fifty years before. The King's life didn't just "move peacefully toward its close," as his doctor reported at the time. It seems the King was killed.

The notes of his physician, Lord Dawson, finally published in 1986, state that as the King lay comatose and near death, Dawson injected him with a fatal dose of morphine and cocaine. "At about 11 P.M.," the doctor wrote, "it was evident that the last stage might endure for many hours, unknown to the patient but little comporting with the dignity and serenity which he most richly merited and which demanded a brief final scene. I therefore decided to determine the end." Dawson's notes say that the King's wife, Queen Mary, and his heir, the Prince of Wales (who became Edward VIII and within a year abdicated the throne to marry Wallis Warfield Simpson), both agreed that the King's life shouldn't be prolonged if he was to die soon. Euthanasia was then, and still is, illegal in England.

That evening at 5:30 a bulletin stated that the King's strength was diminishing. He had been suffering for several months with chronic bronchial problems. Four hours later, as the Queen and their children dined, Dawson wrote on his menu card, "The King's life is moving peacefully toward its close." Reports at the time said that later the family gathered around the King's bed as the Archbishop of Canterbury read the 23rd Psalm and then "Death came peacefully to the King at 11:55 P.M." The King's last words were reported to be "How is the Empire?"

Dawson's notes say that after the Archbishop left he gave the unconscious King the fatal overdose. How would King George V, a straightforward, "ordinary" man in his own words, often annoyed with the pomp of his job, have reacted to knowledge of such an act? Dawson recorded that the King actually spoke later in the evening than had been reported. Dawson says he injected the King with a small dose of morphine—before the fatal shots—to help the monarch get to sleep. "Goddamn you," said the King.

GEORGE GERSHWIN
September 26, 1898–July 11, 1937

GEORGE GERSHWIN used to say he had more tunes in his head than he could put down on paper in a hundred years. How truly sad, then, that his career was cut short after only twenty years. His unbroken string of syncopated hits, many written with his lyricist brother, Ira, began when he was 18, with songs like "Lady Be Good," "Strike Up the Band," and "Funny Face." More serious works such as *Rhapsody in Blue* and *Porgy and Bess* placed his music in the great concert halls of Europe as well as on vaudeville stages in America.

Gershwin and his brother went to Hollywood in 1936 to write songs for Fred Astaire and Ginger Rogers. Despite their success, the normally athletic and cheerful Gershwin seemed less enchanted with the parties and womanizing he used to enjoy. After one affair ended, he wrote, "I am 38, famous, and rich, but profoundly unhappy. Why?" He perked up for two concerts in February 1937 at the Philharmonic Auditorium in Los Angeles. But during one selection, his mind went blank. He missed a few bars, then continued without interruption for the rest of the performance. Two months later, he had a similar blackout in a Beverly Hills barbershop. Each time, Gershwin said, the lapse was accompanied by the smell of burning rubber.

By June, Gershwin was experiencing growing confusion, loss of balance, and grogginess. He also suffered painful headaches and fits of irritability. But doctors could find nothing wrong and concluded that the problem was stress and Gershwin should stop working so hard. In late June, the composer collapsed at the Samuel Goldwyn studios. He had written five of nine songs for a new musical, *The Goldwyn Follies*. The last was "Our Love Is Here to Stay." After a week in the hospital doctors still found nothing, and Gershwin was sent to rest in the Beverly Hills home of a friend.

A week later, on Friday, July 9, Gershwin awoke so weak that he couldn't get out of bed without help. Once on his feet, he collapsed and fell into a coma. Finally, doctors diagnosed a brain tumor. Gershwin's condition deteriorated rapidly, and when doctors operated at 3 A.M. on July 11, they found they could not remove the tumor. Even if he lived, they said, he would probably be blind and disabled. Gershwin died at 10:35 A.M., before most of his friends even knew he was ill. He left no will, and his estate went to his mother.

Although Gershwin's prolific career ended after twenty years, his music quickly took on a life of its own. He wrote music for five movies, but after he died it was heard in at least eighteen more, including *An American in Paris* in 1951 and Woody Allen's *Manhattan* as late as 1979.

EUELL GIBBONS
1912–December 29, 1975

"EVER EAT a pine tree? Many parts are edible." With that odd statement and a Grape Nuts cereal commercial, Euell Gibbons got more fame and attention in the 1970s than he had in his entire career as a health-food writer. The rugged-faced, rough-voiced connoisseur of wild foods became a media sensation, as well as the butt of many jokes.

But strange berries and plant stems were no passing fancy for Gibbons. During one particularly lean stretch as a youth in Dust Bowl–era central New Mexico, he fed his family for a month with puffball mushrooms, piñon nuts, and other wild foods he found in the mountains. Gibbons later was a cowboy, a hobo, and a cotton picker among other things before he moved to Pennsylvania and, at the age of 50, began to write about his diet. His first book in 1962, *Stalking the Wild Asparagus*, was a best-seller, as were later volumes in which he stalked *The Blue-Eyed Scallop*, *Healthful Herbs*, and *The Good Life*.

In 1974, Gibbons developed an ulcer. He told readers of his monthly health-food column that the ulcer could have been caused by taking too many aspirin to relieve his arthritis. He doubted it had anything to do with his diet, which included dandelion greens, wild onions, and sassafras tea. The next year, however, the 64-year-old healthy eater died of an undisclosed stomach ailment.

HERMANN GOERING
January 12, 1893–October 15, 1946

WHEN NAZI Reich Marshal Hermann Goering was visited in prison by his wife for the last time, he told her, "You may be sure of one thing. They won't hang me. No, they won't hang me." Hitler's chosen successor spoke with a characteristic confidence that belied the recent verdict by the judges at Nuremberg, who had sentenced Goering and eleven others to death by hanging. Goering had promptly requested a firing squad instead—"At least I should be spared the ignominy of the noose," he said—but he was denied.

Of all the captured Nazi leaders at the end of World War II, Goering seemed the least shaken. The man who as chief of the Luftwaffe had devised the blitzkrieg attacks and firebombings of London, who had built a $200 million art collection mostly confiscated from Jews, and who had surrendered by driving into an Allied camp with his wife, valet, and forty-nine suitcases maintained a tight-lipped smile throughout the ten-month war crimes trial that ended in the summer of 1946. Enthusiastically ruthless during the war, Goering said before his trial, "This is like going into battle and I will show that I cannot only dish it out, but can take it as well. . . . In fifty or sixty years there will be statues of Hermann Goering all over Germany—little statues, maybe, but one in every German home."

Goering and the others had been sentenced on October 2, 1946, to be hanged within fifteen days. The men became aware that they would go to the gallows being erected in the prison gymnasium on October 16, but they weren't told the hour of their death. They were kept in solitary cells with guards outside each door to maintain a constant watch. Specifically to prevent suicide attempts, the prisoners' bodies, clothes, and spartan cells had been searched at least 100 times during their confinement. All the Nazi leaders were known to have carried cyanide capsules near the end of the war. After Gestapo Chief Heinrich Himmler bit into his vial soon after he was captured and died in less than a minute, Allied officials were acutely cautious to block any attempt to beat their judicial process. The prisoners at Nuremberg were never allowed unguarded contact with outsiders, even with their attorneys. Prison Commandant Colonel B. C. Andrus insisted that "suicide was impossible" at the Nuremberg jail.

On the night of October 15 the eleven men who were to hang the next day ate a final meal together of cold cuts and potato salad. Goering had spent the day reading a novel and writing a letter. After dinner he seemed to be sleeping quietly in his black silk pajama pants and pale blue silk jacket. The guard said later he thought he had seen Goering's hands outside his blanket at all times, as required by prison regulations. But suddenly the guard saw Goering twitching on his cot at 10:45 P.M. By the time officials entered the cell he was dead, three hours before he was to have been hanged. Goering had bitten a vial of cyanide. Glass from the capsule was found in his mouth.

Under his blanket guards found three penciled letters and a brass cartridge that had contained the glass vial. One of the letters was dated four days before and was addressed to Colonel Andrus. Goering wrote that he had carried three vials of cyanide when he had surrendered in May 1945. He purposely allowed one to be discovered—in a can of coffee extract—to make the guards think their search had been successful. One of the other two vials, Goering wrote, he hid on a clothes rack each time he had to change clothes and was searched. The third vial he pushed into a box of skin cream.

After Goering was found dead the remaining prisoners were manacled. Between 2 A.M. and 3:15 A.M. the ten Nazi leaders were hanged as scheduled, though Goering was to have gone first. All of their bodies, including Goering's, were taken to Munich, where they were cremated. Their ashes were dumped in a muddy gulch outside the city. The location was kept secret to prevent the future establishment of a Nazi shrine. And so far, anyway, the little statues that Goering hoped for have yet to find a home.

MAJOR GENERAL
CHARLES "CHINESE" GORDON
January 28, 1833–January 26, 1885

CHINESE GORDON embodied the British Empire. He fought in
the Crimean War, quashed rebel forces in China in the 1860s
(hence his nickname), served in South Africa and India, and
stabilized British and Egyptian positions in the Sudan against
bands of slave traders. Also—perhaps like the empire—Gordon
was brave to a fault. In Crimea and in China, he fought care-
lessly, brazenly swinging his sword on the front lines in hand-
to-hand combat. In the Sudan, he would ride ahead of his troops
to arrive alone at the enemy camp. Gordon talked often of his
desire to be a martyr, and he pursued his dream.

His victories on every frontier of the empire made him im-
mensely popular in England, but Gordon felt more at home
abroad. In 1884 he was sent back to the Sudan, this time to
evacuate Egyptian occupying forces against a rising tide of
Moslem fanaticism. But instead, the obstinate hero of so many
previous sieges directed the Egyptian soldiers under him to
begin fortifying their positions around Khartoum. He wrote to
his superiors, "I shall hold out here as long as I can, and if I can
suppress the rebellion I shall do so. If I cannot, I shall retire to
the equator and leave you the indelible disgrace of abandoning
the garrisons."

His noble plan was in trouble from the start. Moslem forces
cut off Khartoum by March of 1884, and it was not until August that Gordon's popularity finally forced the British government to agree to send relief forces. By December they still
hadn't arrived, and the unfortunate deaths of his aides left
Gordon the last British official in Khartoum. On December 14,
with little food left and dispirited troops deserting by the day,

he wrote solemnly, "I think the game is up. We may expect a catastrophe." That wasn't quite true. As the Moslem rebels closed in, their leader sent word to Gordon that he would be spared and sent back to England if he would give up. Gordon refused. On January 26 at 3:30 A.M., the rebels swarmed into Khartoum. The ragged troops under Gordon's command lasted half an hour.

Gordon himself stood outside his quarters in the palace, dressed in his white uniform, with his left hand on his sheathed sword and his right hand holding a revolver. He used neither as a Moslem fighter shoved a spear through Gordon's breast. Gordon fell forward on the palace floor as other rebels jabbed their spears into his body. He was decapitated and his head delivered to the Moslem leader.

Meanwhile, the British relief forces, who were having to fight their way toward Khartoum, were taking three days' rest before their final approach to the capital city. They arrived two days late, on what would have been Gordon's fifty-second birthday. From their steamships the British saw the smoking ruins of the city, and they turned back down the Nile without firing a shot.

Back in England, the general got his wish to be a martyr. His death provoked an onslaught of grief and anger. Gordon was hailed as a hero who had been cruelly neglected by the ruling Liberal Government. By the summer of 1885, that government fell, in no small part because of Gordon's death. Gordon got a statue in Trafalgar Square. Gordon windows were installed in cathedrals, and Gordon Clubs were created for boys. And fourteen years later, Gordon returned to Khartoum, in bronze and seated on a camel, after the British again conquered the Sudan.

ARSHILE GORKY
April 15, 1904–July 21, 1948

ARSHILE GORKY was one of the first painters to embrace the Abstract Expressionist movement of the 1940s. Because he died before the style reached its prime, it was only later that his work was recognized as a vital influence on more famous artists like Jackson Pollock and Mark Rothko. Gorky saw abstractionism as a way to make images on the canvas move. "Try to allow your mind the freedom to think in terms of constant motion or flux instead of paralysis," he wrote to his students. "I am destroying confinement of the inert wall to achieve fluidity, motion, warmth in expressing feelingness, the pulsation of nature as it throbs."

Gorky hardly was born to arrive at the forefront of the art world. He was named Vosdanig Manuk Adoian by his fairly prominent family in Kharkom, Armenia. As a teenager he fled the Turkish massacres only to watch his mother die of starvation in his arms. When he came to the United States in 1920, he fabricated a different history. He moved to New York City in 1924 and made up the name Arshile Gorky because he thought a Russian name would sound more familiar to Americans. He was no relation to the famous Russian writer Maxim Gorky, but Arshile was happy to allow people to believe they were cousins.

After World War II, Gorky was beginning to receive wide acclaim for his work. His paintings were shown in the top exhibitions, though the earnings had not quite followed yet. Then in January 1946 the artist's barn studio in Sherman, Connecticut, caught fire, destroying thirty of his recent paintings and his entire library. The next month Gorky underwent surgery for cancer. Despite these setbacks he continued to work prolifically, albeit with darker, more somber colors.

On June 26, 1948, Gorky was riding in a car driven by New York art gallery owner Julien Levy when they were in a serious accident near New Milford, Connecticut. Gorky's neck was broken and his painting arm was paralyzed. For the handsome, vibrant, six-foot-tall painter who cherished the motion of his canvases, the paralysis was insufferable. He soon regained some movement of the arm, but it was painful and the always temperamental painter grew deeply depressed. By mid-July his antagonism had sent his wife and their two children to her parents' home in Virginia.

On July 21, Gorky telephoned a neighbor and one of his art students to tell them he was going to kill himself. The 44-year-old painter was found later that day hanged in his barn studio. On a wooden picture crate he had scrawled in white chalk, "Goodbye My Loveds." Five months later his wife collected $11,000 in a lawsuit settlement from gallery owner Levy, who had driven the car in the accident that Gorky's wife claimed had led to his suicide.

ULYSSES S. GRANT
April 27, 1822–July 23, 1885

ULYSSES S. GRANT's mistake was in not quitting while he was ahead. From an impoverished former Army captain working in his younger brother's leather-goods store at the start of the Civil War, Grant rose to become the commanding general of the Union forces in three years and was hailed as the savior of the nation, next to Lincoln. Ten years later, after presiding over one of the most scandal-ridden presidencies ever, Grant left office in 1877 without even the $25,000 lifetime annual salary that had been awarded him as general. "The crisis came," wrote *The Nation* at the end of his second term, "when an ignorant soldier, coarse in his taste and blunt in his perceptions, fond of money and material enjoyment and of low company, was put in the Presidential Chair."

After an extensive tour of Europe and a failed, halfhearted attempt to win the 1880 presidential nomination, Grant settled in New York, where he planned to live off a trust fund of $250,000 that had been raised by some friends. But bad investments caused that fund to dwindle, and worse, Grant put all his own money, about $100,000, into his son's Wall Street firm. His son's partner turned out to be an embezzler, and Grant was wiped out. He even had to put up his swords and other memorabilia as collateral for a loan. Desperate for cash, Grant began writing personal accounts of major Civil War battles for *Century Magazine*, earning him $500 a story. They were so successful that he also began writing his memoirs under far more lucrative terms arranged by his publisher, Mark Twain.

Grant wrote rapidly under intense deadline pressure, though it wasn't one imposed by the publisher. In December 1884, a few months before he began the project, doctors diagnosed the pain in his throat and mouth as throat cancer. Facing the prospect of leaving behind a poor wife and four children, Grant raced to complete his memoirs, though by April 1885 he was in such pain that brandy was injected into his veins to relieve it. He dictated much of his work, but had to write the final chapters after it became too painful for him to talk.

The general turned in the final pages of the two-volume work on May 23. By July he was near death. During one lapse of consciousness his doctor again injected brandy into his veins. At the same time a Methodist minister took a bowl of water and baptized him. Grant awoke. "It is Providence! It is Providence!" exclaimed the minister. "No," replied the doctor. "It was the brandy." Grant suffered a relapse on July 21. An injection of morphine caused him to lose consciousness and he died at 8 A.M., July 23.

A few months later his memoirs became an instant best-seller. The financially strapped general never knew he had earned $450,000 for his wife and four children.

D. W. GRIFFITH
January 22, 1875–July 23, 1948

To GAUGE the impact of producer and director D. W. Griffith on the movies, consider that when he first used a close-up audiences jeered, "Where are their feet?" Easily the "Father of Film," Griffith pioneered techniques such as fade-outs and flashbacks and thereby transformed the movies from nickelodeon diversions to cinematic art. Starting in 1908, he produced and/or directed some 500 films, including *Birth of a Nation*, the first movie masterpiece, and *Intolerance*, the first spectacular financial flop. He co-founded United Artists and launched a Who's Who of early stars, including Lillian Gish, Mary Pickford, and Donald Crisp.

Griffith created many spectacles on film—he marshaled 16,000 extras for one scene in *Intolerance*—but he was just as ambitious off the screen. Besides United Artists, Griffith had his own production company, granting him a free rein to make exactly the movies he wanted to make. At the height of his career, in 1920, he spent a fortune to buy a Long Island mansion built by Henry Flagler and convert it into a film studio.

But soon after the picture changed. Making movies became more expensive, so Griffith's occasional flops were more costly. By 1925 he had lost his Long Island mansion and his production company. Griffith was forced to work for others, and since by then many directors had learned his techniques and improved on them, the old master himself was called on less and less. *The Struggle,* a 1931 movie about alcoholism, turned out to be his last film, a flop that left him so deeply in debt that he had to sell out of United Artists just as the company started making a profit and Hollywood entered its Golden Age.

Seemingly undaunted, Griffith moved into a less expensive hotel in New York. He worked on several plays and an autobiography, but he completed none of them. Many in the movie industry lamented his decline, but none offered him work. By the 1940s the former premier movie-maker was drinking heavily and could be found in Hollywood bars and restaurants telling tales of his former glory over and over to anyone who would listen. He got in bar fights, vulgarly propositioned young women, and at least once wound up in jail.

Those incidents helped break up his second marriage in 1947, when he was 72. The next summer, on the morning of July 23, Griffith suffered a cerebral hemorrhage in his modest rooms at the Knickerbocker Hotel on Hollywood Boulevard. He struggled down to the lobby and asked for help before he collapsed. He didn't regain consciousness before he died later that day.

At his funeral 300 of Hollywood's finest showed up to, according to *The New York Times,* "ruefully acknowledge years of ingratitude to his genius." Actor Donald Crisp eulogized, "It was the fate of David Wark Griffith to have a success unknown in the entertainment world until his day, and to suffer the agonies which only a success of that magnitude can engender when it is past. There was no solution for Griffith but a kind of frenzied beating on the barred doors."

M. ROBERT GUGGENHEIM
May 17, 1885–November 16, 1959

GRANDSON OF Meyer Guggenheim—the founder of the great mining fortune—and eldest son of successor Daniel, M. Robert Guggenheim was the clear heir apparent to everyone except himself. "Every wealthy family supports at least one gentleman in leisure," he declared early on. "I have elected to assume that position in mine." He followed through by being a poor student and showing such little interest in the family business that his father quickly scuttled him out of the office and set him up with a trust fund.

Thus established, M. Robert pursued his leisure earnestly. During his life he collected five yachts, four wives, and a variety of prize dogs, horses, and race cars. He sailed the world and maintained a 36-room mansion in Washington, D.C., where, with his fourth wife, he threw wonderful parties and so befriended many politicians.

In particular he was buddies with President Eisenhower, who reciprocated M. Robert's fund-raising activities by naming him ambassador to Portugal in 1953. There M. Robert continued to show great skill in party-giving, at least for a year. Then in 1954, at the palace of the Portuguese President, M. Robert was demonstrating a childish trick by flipping a teaspoon in the air when it landed in the cleavage of an esteemed female guest. M. Robert resigned soon after, ostensibly for health reasons.

Devoid of a diplomatic career or even the hope of a similar position, M. Robert reverted to his leisurely pursuits, primarily by womanizing quite openly. In 1959, at the age of 74, M. Robert collapsed, dead of a heart attack, after he had just left one of his mistresses and was hailing a cab on a Georgetown street. This may be one time when it actually fits to say he died as he had lived.

ALEXANDER HAMILTON
January 11, 1757–July 12, 1804

THERE IS IRONY in noting that Alexander Hamilton, an elitist who called the general public a "great beast," today gets his visage palmed by millions each day on the face of the $10 bill. An illegitimate orphan from St. Croix, Hamilton made his name as a powerful pamphlet writer against the British and went on to become the Founding Father who, as the first Secretary of the Treasury, laid the economic foundation of the new nation. But the views and manner of the arrogant Federalist rubbed many the wrong way, and he finally resigned from his controversial term in 1795. Still, Hamilton maintained great influence, loudly voicing his opinions both in person and in his pointed, sometimes vicious, writings.

In the end it might have paid for Hamilton to be a little less direct. He was at a dinner party in 1804 when—hardly for the first time—he began disparaging his longtime political enemy Aaron Burr, who was then the Vice President and also a candidate for governor of New York. What Hamilton didn't foresee was that his remarks, among which he called Burr "dangerous," would be overheard by someone who passed them on for publication just before the election. Burr lost the election and he blamed Hamilton's words for it.

Given a chance at a career's worth of revenge, Burr challenged Hamilton to a duel. Hamilton had gotten himself in this predicament before, but on every previous occasion he had been able to avoid actually going through with the gunfight. For even as ruthless as he was in words, Hamilton abhorred the idea of a duel, particularly after his son was killed in one in 1801. Hamilton offered Burr a carefully worded apology—never really denying that he thought Burr was dangerous—but Burr would not accept. So, adhering to his 18th-century view of honor, Hamilton quietly made out a new will and arranged to transfer his pending law cases. Even his wife was unaware of the impending duel, as Hamilton wrote her a letter the night before saying, "The scruples of a Christian have determined me to expose my own life to any extent, rather than subject myself to the guilt of taking the life of another. . . . But had rather I should die innocently than live guilty."

At 5 A.M. on July 11, Hamilton, with his law clerk and a surgeon, sailed from Manhattan across the Hudson River to the bluffs of Weehawken, New Jersey. Hamilton told his clerk he would let Burr shoot first, then would fire his gun into the air. The two men met at 7 A.M. on a narrow ledge, six feet wide and 20 paces long, about 20 feet above the water. Unlike cowboys, they didn't pace off, spin, and shoot. They simply stood 10 paces apart with their pistols at their sides. At the command the duelists were to raise their guns, aim, and fire. Burr did just that, and his bullet hit Hamilton in his right side, causing him to fall forward on his face. The surgeon rushed up and Hamilton said, "This is a mortal wound, Doctor." The autopsy later showed the bullet had cracked a rib, pierced his liver, and then lodged in a vertebra.

Burr approached his victim, then left the scene without speaking. Hamilton, barely alive, was carried back across the river to a friend's home on Jane Street. In severe pain, he summoned two ministers to give communion, but both refused because they disapproved of the duel. Before the 47-year-old man died the next afternoon, his last words to his wife were "Remember, my Eliza, you are a Christian."

Burr, who immediately fled the city for the South, never recovered his political career. On his deathbed in 1836, the 80-year-old man was asked if he wanted to repent his sins. He replied, "On that subject, I am coy."

DAG HAMMARSKJÖLD
July 29, 1905–September 18, 1961

THAT THE United Nations was taken seriously in its early years was due largely to Dag Hammarskjöld, who became its Secretary General in 1953. The Swedish diplomat ventured into the world's hot spots and frequently helped defuse them—for example, getting China to release some American prisoners during the Korean War and sending the first U.N. peacekeeping force to the Middle East. A bachelor and a loner, Hammarskjöld gained the respect of most in a thankless job.

One of the worst crises of 1961 flared up in the Congo (now Zaire), which recently had been granted its independence from Belgium and was promptly plunged into near civil war because of tribal disputes. Hammarskjöld's efforts to calm the fighting caused Soviet Premier Khrushchev to demand his resignation because the U.N. troops were hindering Soviet influence. Nevertheless, Hammarskjöld stood firm and in September he flew to the country to try to arrange a cease-fire. The violence was centered in the Katanga Province on the southeastern border of the Congo near Rhodesia. The president of that province, Moise

Tshombe, wanted to secede from the rest of the Congo and wouldn't even agree to meet with Hammarskjöld.

In a bold and dangerous move, considering the level of fighting, Hammarskjöld decided to go see Tshombe anyway. To fly into the Katanga Province would have been suicidal, since U.N. forces there had come under heavy attack, mostly from Belgian mercenary fighter planes. So Hammarskjöld and a few other U.N. officials took off from the Congo capital, Léopoldville, late Sunday afternoon, September 17, planning to land in Ndola, which is just across the Katanga border in Rhodesia. The DC-6 in which they were flying had already been pierced by a bullet in its left engine earlier that day. To protect the twelve passengers and crew, the pilot filed false flight plans and to avoid detection didn't use the radio. Also, instead of flying a straight path to Ndola the pilot flew due east and then south, skirting Katanga entirely.

Airport officials in Ndola said they received a radio message from the flight requesting permission to land at 11:35 P.M. But they never saw the plane. Ndola officials said later that they assumed the pilot must have decided to fly elsewhere. It wasn't until the next morning that a search was begun for the missing plane. At 3 P.M., fifteen hours after the flight's final message, the burned remains of the plane were found nine miles from the Ndola airport in a dense forest. Hammarskjöld, the only passenger not burned in the crash, apparently had been thrown from the plane and was killed by the impact, suffering a broken back and internal bleeding. Investigators believe, however, that Hammarskjöld hadn't died immediately. He was found half sitting up and clutching a clump of dirt.

There was only one survivor, Harold Julian, a U.N. security guard who was severely burned. He died five days later, but not before he told officials that a series of explosions had preceded the crash after Hammarskjöld had ordered the plane not to land at the Ndola airport. Rescuers had found watches on the dead passengers stopped at 12:11 A.M. Officials discovered later that three nearby villagers had been at the wreckage soon after the crash. They didn't seek help but did cart off the plane's coding machine, which they thought was a typewriter.

Investigators at first thought the pilot simply had mistaken his altitude and had crashed into a hill while approaching the Ndola airport. But with Hammarskjöld among the flight's victims, the world saw the crash in political terms. Even though no evidence of sabotage—which might have been burned in the crash—was found on the plane, several nations were accused of causing the U.N. leader's death. Belgium was blamed for allowing its mercenaries—who were accused of shooting down Hammarskjöld's flight—to fight in the Congo province. Great Britain was blamed because officials from its colony of Rhodesia reacted so slowly to search for the plane, which may have allowed more passengers, including Hammarskjöld, to die. Typical of the anger in some parts of the world, an Indian newspaper wrote, "Never even during Suez have Britain's hands been so bloodstained as they are now." Finally there were rumors of Soviet involvement based on Khrushchev's vehement opposition to Hammarskjöld.

The most thorough investigation of the crash, conducted by the U.N., turned up little conclusive evidence as to what actually had caused the plane to go down or even what had caused the explosions that Julian reported. U.N. officials did leave open the possibility of sabotage—from the ground, from another plane, or from a device planted inside the airplane.

Two days after the crash Tshombe signed a cease-fire. And a month later Hammarskjöld was posthumously awarded the Nobel Peace Prize.

WARREN HARDING
November 2, 1865–August 2, 1923

"MY GOD, this is a hell of a job!" Warren Harding said of his presidency. "I have no trouble with my enemies, I can take care of my enemies all right. But my damn friends, my goddamn friends, they're the ones that keep me walking the floor nights!" Harding was hardly the most capable man to live in the White House. The prominent Ohio newspaper editor and Republican got there in 1920 by being handsome and likable, which was just what voters wanted after the stormy years of Woodrow Wilson. Harding wasn't a strong leader, nor was he especially bright. He left much of his work to his aides, who would present him with simplified versions of the complicated problems of the nation. Still, Harding complained, "I never find myself done."

By the third year of his term, in the spring of 1923, it became clear that Harding had left far too much to his aides. His director of the Veterans Bureau, Charles Forbes, was caught selling government supplies illegally and fled to Europe. Shortly after, Charles Cramer, the Veterans Bureau's general counsel, who was in on the scam, shot himself in the head. Several weeks after that the Attorney General's private secretary, who ran his own racket selling liquor licenses during Prohibition, also shot himself in the head. At the time the scandals remained private, and the public was told the suicides had resulted from financial and health problems.

But Harding knew the real stories would get out sooner or later. Already weak from a severe flu the previous winter, and now depressed over his unruly aides, Harding that summer embarked on a major cross-country trip to Alaska. The President wanted to get away from Washington for a while (though he took with him an entourage of sixty-five) and also hoped to drum up support during his many train stops. The trip seemed to be going well, but Harding couldn't get over his anxiety about the simmering scandals. When his ship, returning from Alaska, rammed an escort vessel in heavy fog as it entered Puget Sound, Harding didn't leave his cabin but grumbled, "I hope the boat sinks."

Safely on shore in Seattle, Harding was giving a speech on July 27 when he seemed to become dazed. Later that evening the President collapsed. He was rushed to his train, which sped to San Francisco. The White House physician diagnosed the problem as ptomaine poisoning that Harding had gotten from eating crabmeat. But once the President arrived in San Francisco on July 29 and was examined in his suite at the Palace Hotel, doctors correctly diagnosed that Harding was suffering from heart trouble and pneumonia. Harding rested in bed and seemed to get better. But on August 2 at 7:30 P.M., as his wife was reading to him a highly complimentary article about him from *The Saturday Evening Post*, called "A Calm View of a Calm Man," Harding suddenly shivered and died.

Doctors said either his heart wall had ruptured or a blood vessel in his brain had burst. Either way, Harding's death stunned the nation, which had been told only that he had eaten some bad crabmeat. The suspicions about what really had killed the President began when it was learned that Harding hadn't even eaten any crabmeat. After Harding's wife, Flossie, refused to allow an autopsy, there were rumors that she had poisoned him. And after the Harding administration scandals began breaking a few months after his death, there were rumors that Harding had killed himself.

There wasn't a shred of evidence to support either claim, but the coming months and years provided plenty of motives. Within three months of Harding's death the real story of the Veterans Bureau broke, as did the more serious Teapot Dome scandal, in which Harding's men sold oil leases for bribes. Harding's Attorney General, Harry Daugherty, was deeply investigated by the Senate for improprieties that involved a group of

Harding's friends known as the "Ohio gang." Several of Harding's administration ended up in prison.

Closer to home, a woman named Nan Britton published a book in 1927 called *The President's Daughter*, in which she alleged that Harding was the father of her illegitimate child and that their affair had lasted well into the White House. Later it was revealed that Harding had carried on a long affair with the wife of a leading businessman in his hometown of Marion, Ohio. It also became known that Harding drank and served liquor in the White House during Prohibition.

Harding once said, "I cannot hope to be one of the great Presidents, but perhaps I may be remembered as one of the best-loved." Perhaps not, but at least he wasn't around to know it.

MATA HARI
August 7, 1876–October 15, 1917

MATA HARI had the world by its tail—until it turned around and bit her. How else to describe the Dutch officer's wife who fled to Paris in 1904, changed her name from Margaretha Geertruida Zelle to Mata Hari, and pranced naked onstage while convincing the capitals of Europe that she was an exotic Indian dancer? "I never could dance well," even she admitted. "People came to see me because I was the first who dared to show myself naked to the public."

Just a few years later Mata Hari was despised as the most notorious spy of World War I. Her trouble may have been that she was too popular, so that when war broke out the French and English immediately became suspicious of her German acquaintances. Those "acquaintances" included lovers who had kept her clad in jewels and furs—offstage—throughout her career, and one of them happened to be the German chief of intelligence in Spain. She was followed constantly throughout Europe, and finally, in February 1917, she was arrested at her hotel in Paris and charged with espionage.

There is much speculation as to whether Mata Hari really was engaged in passing secrets to the enemy. She had a gift for talking her way into things—it was the foundation of her career, after all—so it could be that she simply got carried away with her own imaginative tales. She claimed she actually meant to spy for the French, even though they hadn't requested her assistance. Whatever the case, France, on the brink of defeat, was not much in the mood to give her the benefit of the doubt. In a prison outside of Paris, Mata Hari was put in a padded cell to prevent her from committing suicide. Her many appeals were denied, even by her own Dutch government, to which she wrote, "Jealousy—vengeance—there are so many things that crop up in the life of a woman like me, once people know that she finds herself in a difficult position."

On October 15, Mata Hari was awakened at 5 A.M. and informed that she would be shot that morning. "It's unbelievable!" she said weakly, but otherwise remained composed. She put on a gray dress, a straw hat, and a white veil, then was driven to the Château de Vincennes, a military compound outside Paris. It was just above freezing and foggy when she was led in front of a firing squad of twelve soldiers. She refused to be tied to the pole and refused also to be blindfolded. It is said that as the soldiers raised their rifles, Mata Hari smiled at them, even winked.

After she collapsed an army surgeon walked over, checked her briefly, then fired a final shot—the *coup de grâce*—into her head to make sure she was dead. Her body, which had been no secret to much of Europe, was taken to a city hospital in Paris, where it was dissected for medical research.

JEAN HARLOW
March 3, 1911–June 7, 1937

"FAR FROM BEING a good actress," sniffed *Variety*, "Miss Harlow's appearance still counts with the boys." No kidding. With those tight-fitting gowns and that hair—the result of a bad rinse job—the original Platinum Blonde was boffo box-office in the 1930s regardless of whether she, or the picture, was any good. Both, in fact, got better in movies such as *Dinner at Eight, Bombshell,* and *Libeled Lady*. But the young star's health got worse.

The problem may have begun on her wedding night with her second husband in 1932. Movie executive Paul Bern, twice her age, beat her severely that night. A doctor told Harlow she had a bruised kidney, but Harlow, raised by a strict Christian Scientist mother, refused treatment. Two months later Bern shot himself, after leaving a note implying he was impotent. But Harlow did not get over the abdominal pains that she continued to suffer periodically.

In 1937, exhausted by almost constant film assignments from MGM, Harlow came down with the flu in February. After the illness didn't go away and her mouth swelled so that she couldn't chew, Harlow went into the hospital despite her mother's strong protests. Doctors treated the flu and a widespread infection. Two months later MGM demanded that she begin filming her next movie, *Saratoga*, with Clark Gable, even though she hadn't fully recovered.

Only her puffy face in her scenes in that movie hints at her weakness. But on Saturday, May 29, Harlow collapsed on the set. Her mother took the 26-year-old movie star home and banished all visitors from the house for the entire weekend while she prayed. Harlow, who had taken her mother's maiden name when she started making movies, spent the weekend vomiting and suffering severe pains in her stomach and back. It wasn't until Tuesday, after Harlow failed to show up on the set, that her agent forced his way past Harlow's mother and found the actress semiconscious. But still her mother refused to allow Harlow to be taken to a hospital, insisting that her religious faith was the better remedy. On Friday a doctor who visited Harlow at her home diagnosed her condition as uremic poisoning—kidney failure—and said she would die without surgery.

Finally on Sunday night, after MGM chief Louis B. Mayer telephoned, Harlow's mother relented and the actress was rushed to the hospital, almost in a coma. But by then she was too weak for surgery. Doctors gave her two blood transfusions and placed her in an oxygen tent, where she died the next morning with her mother and boyfriend William Powell at her side. Unlike most Hollywood funerals, Harlow's was private, and her casket remained closed. That, and the sudden announcement of her death when the public hadn't even been told she was ill, sparked rumors that she had died from a botched abortion. *Saratoga*, now long overdue, was completed with a double.

WILLIAM HENRY HARRISON
February 9, 1773–April 4, 1841

THE LESSON of William Henry Harrison is that if you hang around in politics long enough, you can be elected President. That, of course, says nothing of what happens after the election. The son of a signer of the Declaration of Independence and member of a distinguished Virginia planter family, Harrison was born to be President, though he spent most of his life ruining his chances. His military career in the Northwest Territory (now the upper Midwest) was heavily criticized, his terms in the U.S. Congress unnoteworthy. He failed to be reelected to Ohio's state senate and was recalled as the minister to Colombia after six months. By the early 1830s, Harrison was in such financial trouble from bad investments and trying to support his nine children that he got himself appointed county recorder.

"My maxim throughout life has been '*nil desperandum*,' " a beleaguered Harrison wrote to his debt-ridden son. Sure enough, when the Whig Party searched for a presidential candidate in 1836, Harrison looked awfully good. Clearly he was available, and he was tied to no strong stands at a time when all the issues, especially slavery, were extremely divisive. Harrison lost the election to Martin Van Buren, but got enough support that he immediately began planning for 1840.

The second time around, Harrison—called "Tippecanoe" in reference to a minor battle victory—was in a much better position, largely thanks to the Panic of 1837 and the economic troubles that followed. There were, however, nagging questions about his age. Harrison was 67 during the campaign and would turn 68 by his inauguration. The candidate insisted he was healthy, though in fact he became exhausted by the campaign. Even when he wasn't traveling there was a constant flow of visitors and office-seekers into his Ohio home. After he won his wife said, "I wish that my husband's friends had left him where he is, happy and contented in retirement."

The pace only increased once he arrived in Washington. He entered the city on February 9, 1841, a snowy day, though he declined an umbrella as he walked the streets lined with cheering crowds. Inauguration Day, March 4, was also cold and windy. Still, Harrison refused a covered coach and instead rode down Pennsylvania Avenue on his favorite horse. He wore no coat and his hat was off his head most of the time as he waved to the crowds. On the outdoor platform where the ceremony took place, Harrison stood without a hat, gloves, or overcoat and gave a speech that lasted one hour and forty minutes. Among his promises was that he would serve only one term.

Back at the White House, he continued to be besieged by office seekers. On March 26, Harrison got caught in a chilling rainstorm as he walked to deliver a letter of appointment to a diplomat. By the next day he had developed such a severe cold that he sent for his doctor, who decided not to let blood from the President because of his advanced age. Within a week Harrison was delirious. From his feverish mumblings he clearly was troubled by the demands of his office. "These applications, will they never cease? I cannot stand it. . . . I cannot bear this. . . . Don't trouble me."

While office seekers stood downstairs in the White House trying to figure out their own future, Harrison died after midnight early on April 4, one month after his inauguration.

JOSSLYN HAY, EARL OF ERROLL
1901–January 24, 1941

JOSSLYN HAY was the epitome of the decline of the British monarchy. He was the Earl of Erroll and the High Constable of Scotland, placing him directly behind the royal family in the traditional hierarchy of the throne. But in real terms all of Hay's titles meant nothing anymore politically. They simply granted him a well-off life. Not surprisingly, Hay, an extremely good-looking blond, grew up spoiled. He was expelled from Eton and showed little interest in pursuing a traditional life in public service.

Instead, he eloped to Kenya in 1924 with Lady Idina Gordon,

who divorced her second husband in favor of Hay. Kenya, at the time still a British colony, was developing a reputation as a fashionable playground for rich British subjects, as well as a suitable base for hunting safaris. Amid breathtaking vistas and rolling green hills near Nairobi, the white community settled in Tudor mansions with ever-flowering gardens. "Happy Valley," as it was dubbed, was especially popular among the British who had been socially ostracized back home.

Hay and Idina became the center of that crowd, as described in James Fox's fascinating book *White Mischief*. They hosted dinner parties at which, guests said later, they were expected to swap partners for the night and drugs and champagne flowed freely. Hay was well known for his many affairs with married women, one of whom he married in 1930 after she and he both divorced their current spouses.

By 1940 the again single 39-year-old Hay seemed to have settled down a bit. He became politically active in the colony and was responsible for organizing East African troops to attack Mussolini's army in Ethiopia at the start of World War II. Then in November 1940, Hay met Diana Broughton, a 27-year-old bored rich girl who less than a month before had married the very rich Sir Jock Delves Broughton, who was 57. Hay and Diana began a torrid affair and by January 1941 she asked her new husband for a divorce.

At first Broughton resisted, but on the night of January 23 he and Diana and Hay dined and drank together at the Muthaiga Country Club, the elite center of Happy Valley. Broughton even offered a toast to the happiness of his wife and her lover. Soon after Hay and Diana left to go dancing, while Broughton went back to his home with a mutual woman friend who had been staying with them. Shortly after 2 A.M. Hay delivered Diana back to her husband's home and then drove away.

An hour later two African dairy workers saw a large Buick sedan tilted in a trench at the side of an isolated intersection outside Nairobi. The headlights were still on, but the engine had been turned off. The two workers looked inside the car, where they saw a body slumped down under the dashboard. There was a bullet wound behind his left ear. The men sought British police, who left the body in the car until midmorning and only then did they realize it was their most famous resident, Josslyn Hay.

The police, who knew the town gossip as well as anyone, went immediately to Jock Broughton's home, where he was just finishing breakfast. Broughton went to identify the body and even took a handkerchief from his distraught wife to place on the corpse. A few weeks later, after telling police he had seen Hay earlier that evening but didn't know who killed him, Broughton and his wife, Diana, departed on a safari. But because of his obvious motive Broughton remained a prime murder suspect and finally was arrested March 10 after the bullet that killed Hay was traced to a pistol registered to him. Broughton had reported the gun stolen two days before Hay was killed.

Diana immediately became an intensely loyal wife. She hired a skilled barrister from South Africa who was able to poke several holes through the prosecution's case. Hay clearly had been shot by someone inside the car or on the running board, but the prosecutors had no evidence indicating how Broughton might have managed to hide in the car or meet Hay at the intersection. After deliberating for three and a half hours, the jury found Broughton not guilty. Broughton and Diana immediately left for Ceylon.

No one else ever was tried for the murder of the Scottish earl, though Happy Valley buzzed with rumors of many more suspects, mostly Hay's former lovers. Despite his acquittal, Broughton was shunned upon his return to Kenya and was banned from the Muthaiga Country Club. He finally returned to England, where he overdosed on morphine in December 1942. Diana remarried a month after Broughton's suicide, then divorced that husband in 1955 after she fell in love with another man.

ERNEST HEMINGWAY
July 21, 1899–July 2, 1961

"WE HAVE an obligation to kill cleanly, and if we would wound an animal, to follow it up all the way," Ernest Hemingway wrote in a letter in 1950. He was talking about hunting, but it seemed to be part of a broader philosophy of the great writer. Hemingway was macho, a ruddy hard drinker who survived more woundings than most. Unlike most writers, he was a celebrity in his own lifetime, wealthy, and the winner of the Pulitzer and Nobel prizes.

Periodically, Hemingway suffered from severe depression. As early as 1926 he wrote, "The real reason for not committing suicide is because you always know how swell life gets again after the hell is over." Two years later Hemingway's father, depressed over a diabetic condition, shot and killed himself. The writer speculated occasionally on how he would end his own life—whether he would jump off an ocean liner or pull the trigger of a shotgun with his toe.

Hemingway's depression grew worse in the late 1950s, partly because of complications from internal injuries he suffered in two airplane crashes while on an African safari in 1954. By his sixtieth birthday he had liver damage from drinking, hypertension, hepatitis, and high blood pressure. Much to their own shock, friends described the six-foot-tall, formerly 200-pound man as "frail." He stopped working on his latest novel, *The Garden of Eden*, and in the winter of 1961 was admitted to the Mayo Clinic for electric-shock treatments to combat his depression.

In April, after Hemingway had returned to his modern home in the Sawtooth Mountains near Sun Valley, Idaho, his wife, Mary, found him one morning holding a shotgun and staring out a window. He was put under heavy sedation and returned to the Mayo Clinic. By mid-June, Hemingway insisted he was well enough to go home. During the last week of June, Mary drove him from the hospital in Rochester, Minnesota, to Idaho. She had locked his guns in the basement.

But Hemingway knew where to find the keys. Two days after they arrived, Hemingway, wearing his pajamas and robe, picked the keys off the window ledge above the kitchen sink while his wife still slept. He unlocked the basement storage room, chose a shotgun he had used for pigeon shooting, then walked up to the oak-paneled front foyer. There he put the gun to his forehead and shot both barrels. Mary, who found him, at first claimed Hemingway had accidentally shot himself while cleaning his gun. But no cleaning materials were found in the room near Hemingway, a firearms expert.

Earlier in his final year Hemingway had written, "A long life deprives man of his optimism. [Better] to die in all the happy period of unillusioned youth, to go out in a blaze of light, than to have your body worn out and old and illusions shattered." Clearly the man who thirty-five years before had written "how swell life gets after the hell is over" no longer believed that was true.

JIMI HENDRIX
November 27, 1942–September 18, 1970

ROCK STAR Jimi Hendrix was called "the most pornographic of all performers," and that's hardly an exaggeration. His gyrating hips made Elvis Presley look inhibited. In tight black pants and a souffléed Afro, Hendrix played his electric guitar on his back, between his legs, and with his teeth, then would smash the instrument against his amplifiers at the end of his concert. To some it was unlistenable, but his hits like "Purple Haze," "Foxy Lady," and his classic distorted guitar version of "The Star-Spangled Banner" made the Seattle high school dropout a major star in the late 1960s.

Like many rock stars of the era, Hendrix popped drugs like candy. As he became more popular he stayed stoned all day and not infrequently would open his mouth and accept unidentified drugs from fans. Stunts like that occasionally caused him to break down onstage. In 1970 he was booed by an audience in West Germany, and at Madison Square Garden in New York he threw down his guitar in the middle of a song and told the audience "I can't get it together" as he walked offstage. If Hendrix realized where that would lead, he didn't seem bothered by it. "I tell you when I die I'm not going to have a funeral. I'm going to have a jam session," he said during one interview. "And knowing me, I'll probably get busted at my own funeral."

After a series of bad concerts Hendrix was in London in September 1970 with Mick Jagger's ex-girlfriend and groupie, Monika Danneman. On the night of the seventeenth they went to a party and a bar, then went to bed about 7 A.M. Danneman said she took one sleeping pill out of a package containing ten tablets. Apparently, soon after, Hendrix swallowed the other nine. Danneman woke up at 10:20 A.M., and after leaving the room for a few minutes, came back to find that Hendrix had vomited in his sleep. Danneman found his heart was beating but she couldn't wake him. Soon after an ambulance got the performer to the hospital, he died. Hendrix wasn't killed by the pills, but had suffocated on his own vomit.

Some suspected the 27-year-old Hendrix had committed suicide, in light of his recent rejection by his fans and some financial pressures. Others called it an inevitable accident. After Hendrix was buried in Seattle and a seven-foot floral guitar was laid on his grave, his fellow musicians did have a jam session. Of his death *Newsweek* wrote, "Who's next? Who else is good at han-

dling drugs until he isn't good at it?" Two and a half weeks later
Janis Joplin provided the answer.

WILD BILL HICKOK
May 27, 1837–August 2, 1876

AMID WIDESPREAD reports that he had been shot to death at Fort
Dodge, Kansas, in 1873, quick-draw lawman Wild Bill Hickok
wrote this letter to the St. Louis *Missouri-Democrat:* "Wishing
to correct an error in your paper of the 12th, I will state that no
Texan has, nor *ever will* 'corral William.' I wish you to correct
your statement, on account of my people. —P.S. I have bought
your paper in preference to all others since 1857."

Stories about James Butler Hickok were legendary in his own
time. As a deputy U.S. marshal over much of the Plains territory, Hickok developed such a reputation as a fast shooter that
other men would follow him around looking for a showdown.
Hickok, a tall, broad-shouldered man who carried two pistols
in his vest and a pair of .36-caliber Colt revolvers around his
waist, took to walking down the middle of the street and avoiding open windows. The former Union spy even sat in the bar-
ber's chair with his shotgun in his lap.

Still, Hickok relished his dangerous job. In fact, some say he
used his deputy's badge simply as a license to get involved in
gunfights. He once advised, "Young man, never run away from
a gun. Bullets can travel faster than you can. Besides, if you're
going to be hit, you had better get it in the front than in the
back. It looks better."

As the frontier towns grew more settled and hired their own
lawmen, Hickok was called on less and less. He performed in

some of Buffalo Bill's Wild West stage shows, but mainly he wandered the West in search of some action. In 1876, Hickok was in Deadwood Gulch, where gold had been discovered in the Black Hills of the Dakota Territory. He had gotten married that March and hoped to strike enough gold to settle down. But meanwhile Hickok pursued his passion for gambling.

On August 2, Hickok walked into the Number 10 Saloon just after noon to join a poker game. He always sat at the table with his back to the wall. But this time when he asked one player to get up and give him that stool, the other players just laughed it off, and Hickok finally took a seat that faced the front door but didn't give him a full view of the barroom.

At about 3 P.M. Jack McCall entered the saloon and walked to the end of the bar behind Hickok. Hickok had played against McCall the day before, and had even given him money for dinner after McCall went broke, so the former deputy continued to concentrate on his cards. Suddenly, McCall pulled a pistol and fired at Hickok, shouting, "Damn you, take that!" The bullet struck Hickok in the back of his head, exited through his right cheek, and then lodged in the wrist of the cardplayer across from him. Hickok, killed instantly, fell off his stool and slumped on his side on the floor.

McCall, who said later he shot Hickok for killing his brother, ran out of the saloon and jumped on a horse. But he was caught when the saddle fell over, and he later hanged. Hickok, meanwhile, left part of his legend on the poker table. The cards he was holding—a pair of aces and a pair of eights—are known as the "dead man's hand."

JIMMY HOFFA
February 14, 1913–July 30, 1975 (?)

FOR YEARS after the former Teamsters president disappeared 18-wheelers rolled down the highways with bumper stickers on the back that asked, "Where is Jimmy Hoffa?" So far, whoever knows ain't talkin'. Since the man who brought organized crime into organized labor vanished on a sunny summer day from a restaurant parking lot outside of Detroit, investigators have searched garbage dumps, swamps, cornfields, and even parts of the ocean to find his body. But to no avail. That Hoffa, long deposed from the truckers' union, could turn up permanently missing says a lot about his power and influence—of course it says even more about the muscle of the men who made him disappear.

James Riddle Hoffa, a Teamster since the union's violent beginnings in the 1930s, became its president in 1957 and kept his grip even when he went to prison in 1967 for jury tampering and mail fraud due mostly to the hounding of his nemesis, Robert F. Kennedy. In 1971, the Nixon administration commuted his sentence with the stipulation that Hoffa could not return to the union until 1980. But Hoffa soon began making moves to get his power back, angering not only the union bosses who had taken over after he went to prison but also some of the Mafia leaders whom Hoffa had brought into the union but who now saw him as a troublemaker and a potential threat.

That's where it stood on the afternoon of July 30, 1975, when Hoffa drove from his home in Lake Orion, Michigan, to the parking lot of the Machus Red Fox Restaurant in Bloomfield, where he was to meet Detroit Mafia figure Anthony Giacalone and Anthony Provenzano, a Teamster with whom Hoffa had been feuding. Hoffa apparently thought the meeting was to make peace. Giacalone and Provenzano later denied that there ever was supposed to be a meeting. Having waited in the parking lot for half an hour, Hoffa called his wife at 2:30 P.M. and said, "Where the hell is Giacalone? I'm waiting for him." After fifteen minutes Hoffa, who had been wearing dark blue pants and a casual blue shirt, was never seen again. His family, hoping to avoid publicity on the chance that he would show up, waited until late the next day to report the 62-year-old Hoffa missing. His 1974 Pontiac was found where he had left it in the restaurant parking lot.

Knowing Hoffa and his associates, the authorities immediately suspected he had been abducted. But by whom and for what? Take your choice: he had enemies in the Teamsters and the Mafia. Even his "foster son," 41-year-old Charles O'Brien, whom Hoffa had helped raise since he was three, became a suspect after investigators found blood on the seat of a car that O'Brien had driven the day Hoffa disappeared. O'Brien said the blood was from a 20-pound salmon, which turned out to be right, but police dogs later identified Hoffa's scent in the car as well.

There was speculation that Hoffa had been eliminated before he blew the whistle. He had been writing a book, which was hurriedly published after his disappearance, blaming his successor, Frank Fitzsimmons, for all the corruption. But if the point was to silence the charges before Hoffa levied them, his disappearance caused the opposite to happen. Officials not only dug around for Hoffa's body, they launched massive investigations into the Mafia and its ties to the Teamsters, which focused attention on many suspicious figures who before had managed to remain hidden. It got so bad that one mobster tried to help the FBI find Hoffa's body in a field in the hope that it would bring an end to all the inquiries.

But the body wasn't found in that field, nor was it uncovered in Brother Moscato's garbage dump underneath the Pulaski Skyway in Jersey City, New Jersey, where the FBI was hesitant to dig because it might release deadly methane gas. Nor did Hoffa turn up after CBS News paid $10,000 to a self-proclaimed psy-

chopathic killer and ex-convict who was supposed to lead a
television news crew to the body. The informant himself disappeared with the money, and CBS had no luck on its own
searching off the coast of Key West, where Hoffa supposedly lay
entombed in concrete.

After conducting thousands of interviews, federal agents believe they know what happened to Jimmy Hoffa, even though
they are unable to come up with enough evidence to arrest anyone. Agents believe Hoffa, thinking he was being taken elsewhere for the meeting, willingly was picked up in the restaurant parking lot by someone he knew. Instead, agents believe,
Hoffa was taken somewhere in the Detroit area and killed immediately by New Jersey Mafia men who had flown in for the
occasion. They believe Hoffa's body then was stuffed into a 55-
gallon oil drum and driven away in a Teamster truck. One mob
figure told investigators Hoffa had been crushed in a steel com-
pactor for junk cars.

There also was speculation, however, that Hoffa himself arranged his disappearance, perhaps to avoid further federal investigations or perhaps because he knew his life was in danger.
Whatever the case, whoever wanted Jimmy Hoffa to disappear
did a thorough job of it.

BILLIE HOLIDAY
April 17, 1915–July 17, 1959

"THE ONLY WAY she's happy is through a song" was how singer
Carmen McRae once described Billie Holiday. Heavyset but
strikingly beautiful, with white gardenias in her hair, "Lady

Day" cast a peculiar pose as she sang her melancholy hits like "God Bless the Child" and "Strange Fruit" in the 1930s and 1940s. It was after the Harlem-born singer had reached worshiped status that her life truly became tragic.

Holiday had used heroin for years with only an occasional lapse in her performance. But the drug did more immediate damage when she was arrested for possessing it in 1947. Holiday was sent to a federal women's prison in West Virginia for a year, but for years afterward she was refused a cabaret license, which she needed to sing in New York City, the foundation of her career. Holiday continued to tour and make records, but she also drank and smoked more and continued her heroin habit. She was arrested in San Francisco and Philadelphia on drug charges and her career dwindled further.

In 1959, at the age of 44, Holiday's health simply gave out. For the first time in her life she looked underweight, and occasionally she sang off-key. On May 25, Holiday agreed to sing at a small Greenwich Village club because she needed the $300 fee. She sang just two songs before she had to be helped from the stage, where she collapsed. A week later Holiday fell into a coma in her apartment. Broke, she was admitted to a city hospital in Harlem, suffering from cirrhosis and heart trouble.

As she lay in her hospital bed police arrived on June 12 and arrested her for heroin possession. A nurse said she had found a silver-foil package of the white powder near Holiday's bed. For several days police guards were posted outside her room even though the singer was too weak to get out of bed. Still, Holiday seemed to be looking forward to getting well enough to leave the hospital. She met with a writer to discuss a series of articles and possibly a movie about her life.

But before that happened Holiday died in the hospital at 3:10 Friday morning, July 17. Her lungs had become congested and her heart gave out. As nurses were removing her body from the bed they found fifteen $50 bills taped to one leg. It was what Holiday had been paid as an advance for the autobiographical articles. The singer was buried in her favorite pink lace stage gown, wearing pink gloves. She left no will, only an estate worth $1,000.

BUDDY HOLLY
September 7, 1936–February 3, 1959

CHARLES HARDIN HOLLEY was a most unlikely rock 'n' roll star. His thick-rimmed glasses and goofy grin made it look as if a nerd had taken over the bandstand. And offstage Holly (he dropped the *e* from Holley) didn't take drugs, didn't indulge in wild sex, and he didn't have a drinking problem. What this shy, wholesome Texas-bred kid did was create hits like "That'll Be the Day" and "Peggy Sue," setting the tone for guitar-driven sixties groups like the Beatles and everything that followed.

And he did it by the time he was 21, including appearances on *The Ed Sullivan Show* and tours of England and Australia. But despite flickers of national fame and glamour, selling records in those early days of rock 'n' roll still meant torturous tours of one-night stands. So it was that on February 2, 1959, Holly and other rock acts rode 350 chilling miles on an unheated bus from Green Bay, Wisconsin, to Clear Lake, Iowa, where they would perform that night in front of 1,000 teenagers at the Surf Ballroom for the Winter Dance Party. Afterward they were scheduled to get back on the bus for another all-night frigid ride to Moorhead, Minnesota, 430 miles away.

Holly, tired and possessing no clean clothes, decided to charter a small airplane so he could have more time to rest before the next night's show. Two other stars of the tour joined him: Ritchie Valens, a 17-year-old teen idol with the hits "Donna" and "La Bamba," and J. P. "Big Bopper" Richardson, who sang

"Chantilly Lace." About 1 A.M. the three young men boarded a four-seat Beechcraft, which took off in the midst of a mild Midwestern winter storm. There was a light snow, temperature of 18 degrees, and 35 mile-an-hour winds. The plane was piloted by a 21-year-old who was not certified to fly by instruments, something he would have to do on that cloudy night.

By dawn, when the plane hadn't arrived in Minnesota, an alert was issued. At 9:30 A.M. a search plane took off from the same airport to try to trace the missing flight's course. It was a brief mission, as the crashed plane was spotted eight miles from the airport. It had gone down in a cornfield several hundred yards from the nearest farmhouse and no one had heard the crash. The plane had hit the ground, bounced 50 feet, then skidded 500 feet before breaking apart and piling up against a fence. Holly and two others had been thrown from the wreckage. The speculation is that the young, inexperienced pilot had misread the instruments and—unable to see the stars above or the few scattered farmhouse lights below—thought the plane was ascending when in fact it was descending.

Buddy Holly was dead at 22, a year and a half after his first hit record. Because of rereleases, recordings by other singers, and movies, his music has stayed alive almost another three decades, so far.

HARRY HOUDINI
April 6 (?), 1874–October 31, 1926

HARRY HOUDINI was not a man to turn down a dare. But neither was he one to take a challenge lightly. The legendary escape artist allowed himself to be locked in handcuffs, bound into straitjackets, suspended off skyscrapers, or tossed into rivers while he was tied and stuffed in a locked, nailed-shut box. But before he wriggled free in public, Houdini would practice meticulously in private, studying the locks, measuring how long he could hold his breath, making sure that he was fully prepared to beat the dare. His unbroken success quickly turned his side show into a major worldwide attraction within a few years after he started in 1891.

In the fall of 1926 the 52-year-old short, stocky man still was packing them in by the thousands with a new show. One of his best tricks was the "Torture Cell," a glass-enclosed, water-filled booth in which Houdini would be suspended upside down in a straitjacket. Early in October in Albany, New York, a piece of the equipment fell over during a performance and broke Houdini's ankle. He completed the show and, against doctors' orders, continued his tour although he was weakened by great pain.

A few weeks later, in Montreal, three students who had heard Houdini lecture went backstage to meet him. One of the students, a husky youth over six feet tall, asked Houdini if he really could withstand hard punches in his stomach, which was one of Houdini's standard tricks. Houdini said he could as long as he had warning to prepare himself. Without giving Houdini that warning, the student slugged the older man hard. Houdini showed pain in his face, but the student hit him three more times before the other students pulled him away.

Houdini claimed he was all right. But by that night he was suffering intense pain. He struggled through the next day's performances, then took a train to the tour's next stop in Detroit. There a doctor diagnosed Houdini as having acute appendicitis. But the show-business veteran insisted on appearing for a sold-out performance that night. After the show he had to be carried to his dressing room with a temperature of 104. His wife finally forced him to go to a hospital at 3 o'clock the next morning.

There doctors removed his appendix—which they said had ruptured because of the punches—but by then the poison had been in his bloodstream for three days. The doctors gave him twelve hours to live. Houdini struggled for six days but finally died on Halloween. Before he passed away he made his ailing wife promise that whoever died first would try to come back and contact the other. It was an odd request, considering that part of Houdini's act had been to duplicate the tricks of psychics to expose them as hoaxes. The mediums got their own mileage out of the dead escape artist. For years afterward some of the same psychics he had discredited claimed that they had heard from Houdini.

LESLIE HOWARD
April 3, 1893–June 1, 1943

LESLIE HOWARD, the handsome, wistful actor who played noble Ashley Wilkes in *Gone with the Wind,* was regarded just as honorably off the screen. As early as 1939, when it was apparent that England might be headed for war, the British actor gave up his soaring Hollywood career as a romantic leading man to return home and help the war effort. He acted in and directed a series of morale-boosting war movies and conducted half-hour encouraging radio broadcasts. Just like the characters he portrayed in his films, in real life "he was a gentleman with guts," said one friend.

In the spring of 1943, Howard went to Spain and Portugal for a lecture tour on filmmaking and to explore the possibility of producing movies there. On his way back to England on June 1, he was one of thirteen passengers on a British Overseas Airways DC-3 that took off at 9:40 A.M. from Lisbon. More than an hour later, as the plane flew high above the clouds over the Bay of Biscay, it was attacked by six German fighter planes.

That was unusual, since the civilian plane was on what had been considered a neutral flight path. No planes had been disturbed along the route in three years of war.

The pilot radioed for help, and that was the last ever heard or seen of the flight. One of the German flyers said later that he saw the plane burst into flames and dive toward the sea. The back door of the plane was pushed open, and the German saw four men jump out. Only one parachute unfurled, and that caught fire, sending its carrier plunging with the rest.

Was Howard just another innocent victim of the war? That has never been made entirely clear. It is most widely believed that the plane was shot down because the Germans thought Winston Churchill was on board. The British Prime Minister was known to be in North Africa and presumed to be heading home soon. Another passenger on the flight, Alfred Chenhalls, an accountant and Howard's tax adviser, looked somewhat like Churchill and smoked equally large cigars, so some believe a German spy in Lisbon mistakenly thought he spotted Churchill boarding the airplane. Or it could simply have been that, knowing Churchill might be flying on that route, the Germans took no chances and attacked the plane—and two others unsuccessfully within a week.

But it is also possible that Howard was the real target. German leaders were known to be angered by his propaganda work. More mysterious are reports that Howard met with German spies while he was in Lisbon and that he was on some kind of British reconnaissance mission himself.

Whatever the cause, Howard's death shocked England like few others. One chronicler said the actor had been deeply popular because he characterized the "chronic disillusionment" between the wars. "He fitted well into the pause between battles and will be remembered not only because he was an accomplished actor but because he suited the mood of those moments." That he was dead was yet another reminder that the pause was gone forever.

HENRY HUDSON
d. 1611

ALTHOUGH HE discovered neither, Henry Hudson became immortal when they named the Hudson River in New York and the vast Hudson Bay in Canada. Hudson, a navigator for British and Dutch export companies, explored both waterways while trying to find a northern route to Asia. He failed, of course, because there was no way to sail through North America. But Hudson didn't know that, and it killed him.

Little is known about the navigator except that he probably was about 40 years old in 1610 when he embarked on the *Discovery*, his fourth voyage to try to sail atop the globe. Hudson had been forced back twice before by icy waters, and on this voyage his uneasy crew caused him to leave the cold sea north of Great Britain and instead search for a passage through Canada.

As the early winter arrived he persisted in poking along the coast of Hudson Bay, certain that he was close to discovering a new waterway and warmer waters. To his crew's dismay, Hudson continued his search until they were forced to settle in for the winter at the southern end of the bay, about 500 miles north of Toronto. The crew hauled the ship aground on November 1 and within ten days it was anchored by ice. During the long, harsh winter Hudson proved to be a less than able leader. He was accused of handing out unequal portions of the scarce food supply and of keeping too much for himself. Hudson dismissed some of his top officers, which angered the crew even more.

By the time the ice finally thawed enough for the ship to set sail on June 11, 1611, Hudson had alienated almost everyone. Eleven days later, when they finally found clear water, the crew mutinied. According to the mutineers who eventually returned to England, Hudson was tied up and put in a small boat with eight others, including his son and the sick crew members. Hudson guided the boat's small sail and followed behind his ship for half an hour before the unsettled mutineers unfurled their full sails and sped away.

Hudson and the others on his little boat were never seen again. At best, some speculate they made it to the nearby Danby Island, an isolated and barren plot where twenty years later explorers discovered a row of stakes driven into the ground. The mutinous crew, meanwhile, went ashore in Canada, desperate for food. They were attacked by Indians, who killed some of the ship's leaders. A few exhausted sailors finally straggled back to England, where they were put in jail. But their punishment lasted less than one year because, according to them, the mutiny had been led by those killed by the Indians. And no one was alive to tell differently.

IVAN THE TERRIBLE
August 25, 1530–March 18, 1584

IVAN THE TERRIBLE was as bad as he sounds. Still, as far as he's concerned, he made it into heaven. The Russian Czar tortured thousands of citizens, indulged in long drinking bouts, and had seven wives. But after each wild affair Ivan would atone by prostrating himself for hours in front of the church altar with such sincerity that he would bruise his forehead from hitting the stone church floor. Ivan believed he was divinely chosen to rule Russia, so any of his acts, no matter how terrible, were acts of God.

Ivan could be an eloquent and able executive, but his violent temper and cruelty also were lifelong attributes. As a child he amused himself by throwing cats and dogs from the roof of the Kremlin. As Czar, when a group of seventy citizens complained to him of injustices in their town, he ordered hot wine poured over their heads and had them lie naked in the snow. When it was rumored that the city of Novgorod was conspiring to defect to neighboring Lithuania, Ivan exterminated the city, torturing its citizens for five weeks and killing 60,000 people. In one fit of anger, in 1581, he struck his 27-year-old son in the head with his iron-tipped staff, killing him.

Early in 1584, Ivan saw a comet and, deeply religious man that he was, called together sixty astrologers who agreed that it was a sign that he would die soon. Sure enough, Ivan's body became extremely swollen by an unknown cause. Warm baths soothed him, making him feel well enough that on March 18 he was sitting up in bed and setting up chess pieces when he suddenly collapsed and died.

Following the custom of Russian rulers, Ivan died a monk, albeit the most murderous monk in history. He was shorn as a monk and buried in a monk's robes. It was said that he recanted his sins before he died and so fully expected that as a monk he would meet his Maker. Possibly, however, he died so suddenly that his aides had to recant for him. Only Ivan knows whether it made any difference.

JESSE WOODSON JAMES
September 5, 1847–April 3, 1882

JESSE JAMES is perhaps the most beloved murderer in American history. He and his gang shot bank clerks in cold blood, killed passersby who looked the wrong way, and derailed trains and robbed the passengers as they lay injured.

But none of that mattered. To many alive at the time James was a post-Civil War hero, satisfying the thirst of many defeated Confederates to get in a few last shots after the war. James, a handsome bearded man with blue eyes and a narrow face, was fashioned as a modern-day Robin Hood, though later historians were at a loss to find any evidence of charitableness.

As a Confederate guerrilla and later as a bank robber, James came close to a violent death several times. But as long as he had his own guns, he always seemed to survive. During the war he was badly wounded in the leg and his horse was shot out from under him. Just after the war federal soldiers shot James in the lung and left him for dead. He lay on the ground for two days until a farmer aided him. When he was ambushed robbing the Northfield, Minnesota, bank in 1876, three of his gang were killed, three were shot and captured, and only Jesse and his brother, Frank, escaped.

His luck ended in 1882, after a local sheriff got 21-year-old Robert Ford, a less notorious outlaw, to join James's gang to try to capture him. Ford and his brother easily joined up and were staying with James and his wife in St. Joseph, Missouri, that April, planning their next bank robbery. Early on the morning of the third, James, who had just come inside from feeding the horses, took off his jacket and, because he trusted his friends, his gun belt. He had climbed up on a chair to pull some cobwebs from a picture when he heard the cock of a pistol. As he turned, unarmed, Robert Ford shot James in the head with a .44-caliber pistol that James had given him as a present.

James's body was put in a $260 casket—paid for by the sheriff who had recruited Ford—and sent by train the few miles to his hometown of Kearney, in Clay County, Missouri. His open casket at the Kearney Hotel drew thousands, jamming the small town with their horses, and even passengers from trains that made unscheduled stops on their way through.

A collection to benefit James's wife and two children gathered less than $10, but that was only the beginning. Personal effects of the house were sold for about $250. The owner of the house, a St. Joseph city councilman who thought he had rented it to Thomas Howard (an alias of James's), sold bloody floor splinters for 25 cents apiece. A year later James's mother opened her home to visitors, also for a quarter. Of the more than twenty movies made about Jesse James, the first was financed by his descendants in 1920.

Meanwhile, Robert Ford was pardoned by the governor. Ford toured Eastern cities reenacting the shooting, but the show was booed in the Midwest. Later, in a mining camp in Colorado, Ford was shot in the neck and killed by a man with a sawed-off shotgun seeking revenge for the death of Jesse James.

THOMAS JEFFERSON and JOHN ADAMS
Born
April 13, 1743   October 19, 1735
Died July 4, 1826

PROBABLY NO TWO of the Founding Fathers were tied more closely than Jefferson and Adams. They served together in the Continental Congress, where Adams helped revise and fight for Jefferson's Declaration of Independence. Adams was an emissary to France during the American Revolution and was later joined and succeeded by Jefferson. After the war their friendship turned to rivalry, Adams siding with the conservative Federalists and Jefferson leading the then more democratic Republicans. Jefferson served uncomfortably as Adams's Vice President and then defeated him in a bitter campaign in 1800.

Adams retired to his home in Quincy, Massachusetts. Eight years later Jefferson retired to Monticello in Virginia. In 1811 a friend of Adams suggested he reestablish correspondence with his old colleague. Adams at first brusquely rejected the idea. "I have nothing to say to him, but to wish him an easy journey to heaven, when he goes, which I wish may be delayed, as long as life shall be agreeable to him. And he can have nothing to say to me, but to bid me make haste and be ready."

But a week later, in January of 1812, Adams did write his first letter in more than a decade to Jefferson, who responded with reminiscences of their days as "fellow laborers in the same cause. We rode through the storm with heart in hand, and made a happy port." Thus rekindled their friendship. In their letters they exchanged local gossip and discussed their daily lives—Adams his daily three-mile walks, Jefferson his daily three-hour horseback rides. The two men also debated the future of the new nation, still disagreeing on its direction. They were two of the last surviving Founding Fathers, and certainly the only two who together could recall so much.

Adams in particular also occasionally touched on the subject of their mortality. "It is of some comfort to us both, that the term is not very distant, at which we are to deposit in the same cerement, our sorrows and suffering bodies, and to ascend in essence to an ecstatic meeting with the friends we have loved and lost, and whom we shall still love and never lose again."

In 1826 a delegation of townspeople asked Adams to make an appearance at the upcoming celebration of the fiftieth anniversary of the signing of the Declaration of Independence, but the frail 90-year-old statesman was too weak to accept. On July 4, Adams sat in his armchair, barely conscious. He mumbled a few words, among them "Thomas Jefferson survives," then died at 6 P.M.

Adams had been wrong. Unknown to the second President, the third President had died five hours before in Virginia. Jefferson had suffered from a urinary disease and diarrhea for more than a year. By July 3 he was bedridden and in a stupor. That evening he awoke momentarily and asked, "Is it the Fourth?" He lingered until the afternoon of his most famous day.

KING JOHN
December 24, 1167–October 19, 1216

IN ALL RESPECTS but the manner of his death, history has not been kind to King John. The ruler, who was forced to sign the Magna Charta, pales beside the administrative skill and lust for

life of his father, Henry II, nor could he match the military genius of his older brother, Richard the Lion-Hearted.

John, who was self-indulgent, frivolous, and ill-mannered in
his youth, as King proved to be more so. He had a violent temper
and was a glutton for good food and wine. At Easter Mass, shortly
after Richard's death, John sent an attendant to the bishop three
times telling him to end his sermon because John wanted his
dinner. Among his first regal acts, John fixed the price of red
and white wine. During one battle John sent this message seeking aid: "Greetings. Be it known to you that we need wine.
Wherefore we command you, if you can find any wine for sale
at Sandwich, to buy it for our use and send it to Rochester at our
expense without delay."

As his excesses grew his lords' willingness to finance them les-
sened. They marched on London demanding certain liberties.
That led to the famous meeting at Runnymede in 1215, where
John signed the Magna Charta, the first time the power of the
British monarchy was formally restricted.

But the agreement was short-lived, and soon John and his
troops were on the run. He did a fair job of retaking some castles
and seemed to be getting the upper hand when he and his troops
came to the River Welland on October 12, 1216. John, always
impatient, refused to wait for the tide to drop. The river and its
sands were just as gluttonous as John, who lost several men as
well as his entire royal hoard—all his jewels, dozens of gold and
silver goblets, candelabra, and his coronation regalia.

John died a week later, but this is where history has been
chivalrous. For centuries the royal line was that John had been
poisoned by a disgruntled monk. The story went that the monk
squeezed the poison of a toad into a cup of cider. That, indeed, is
the tragic ending that Shakespeare gave to his play *King John*.

Ignoring the fact that toads hold no venom, it wasn't until
1653, more than 400 years after John's death, that Sir R. Baker
came out with the real story. John did lose his treasure, Baker
writes. "With the grief of which dysaster, and perhaps distem-
pered in his body before, he fell into a Feaver, and was let blood,

but keeping an ill diet (as indeed he never kept good), eating green Peaches, and drinking sweet Ale, he fell into a looseness and grew presently so weak, that there was much adoe to get him to Newark, where soon after he dyed."

In other words, King John died of dysentery, brought on by too much fruit and cider. A physician disemboweled the King and found no evidence of poison. The bowels were buried at Croxton Abbey, while the body was wrapped in a monk's cowl and placed under the high altar at Worcester. There he lay until 1797 when he was exumed and measured up in a way he never had in life. He measured five feet five inches.

CASEY JONES
March 14, 1864–April 30, 1900

YES, THERE REALLY was a Casey Jones. What was made up were the heroics surrounding the death of the legendary railroad engineer. And it all started with that famous ballad you might remember from summer camp:

> *'Twas round this curve he spied a passenger train.*
> *Rousing his engine, he caused the bell to ring.*
> *Fireman jumped off, but Casey stayed on.*
> *He's a good engineer, but he's dead and gone.*

Casey Jones was an engineer at a time when the job had the prestige of an airplane pilot in the 1920s or an astronaut today. John Luther Jones had left his small town of Cayce, Kentucky, at the age of 15 to work on the railroad as a telegraph operator, and finally fourteen years later, in 1893, became an engineer on the Illinois Central. Jones, a large, handsome man who stood six feet 4 inches, quickly gained a reputation for his speed on the rails and was rewarded with the best runs and the newest and fastest trains.

In February 1900, after the previous man was killed in a train wreck, Jones reached the peak of the line: engineer of the *Cannonball Express*. The line ran from Chicago to New Orleans, and Jones rode some of the most treacherous tracks, a hilly, curving stretch from Memphis to Canton, Mississippi, north of Jackson.

On the night of April 29, just after Jones pulled into Memphis, the engineer of the return run turned up sick, so Jones agreed to work a double shift. The train was already an hour and 15 minutes late, which Jones eagerly determined to make up. Normal speed on the route was 50 miles per hour. But Jones brazenly averaged 60 and sometimes pushed the powerful passenger train to over 100 miles per hour. Despite darkness and fog, by the time the train was 15 miles north of Canton, Jones was only two minutes behind schedule.

As he sped full-throttle, the tired Jones missed a flagman's signal that a freight train lay dead ahead on the tracks, waiting to move onto a second track to allow a northbound train to pass. Jones was no more than 150 yards away by the time he saw the red lights on the caboose. He pulled the air brakes, jammed the wheels in reverse, and, as the ballad says, blew the whistle just before he crashed, splintering the caboose and causing a thunder heard for miles. The steam engine plowed ahead, exploding a carload of hay and another loaded with corn before it jumped the track and fell on its side. None of the passenger cars was damaged, and the only fatality was Casey Jones, who lay dead in the engine with an iron bolt driven through his neck.

The ballad that followed is credited to Wallace Saunders, a black engine wiper and cinder-pit man who started singing about Jones's spectacular crash a week after it happened. Other trainmen picked it up and added their own stanzas as the song spread along rail lines throughout the country. A version was published on sheet music in 1909 and was popular in vaudeville.

A stone marker in Jones's Kentucky hometown commemorates the crash, which, it says, occurred "by no fault of his."

JANIS JOPLIN
January 19, 1943–October 4, 1970

"MAYBE I WON'T last as long as other singers, but I think you can destroy your now by worrying about tomorrow." What a "sixties" thing to say. But then Janis Joplin was the epitome of that decade, that culture. This sweet little girl from the Texas Gulf town of Port Arthur turned rebellious and headed for San Francisco in 1966, at the height of the flowering of Haight-Ashbury. A year later Joplin, backed by her band, Big Brother and the Holding Company, shrieked her way to becoming the nation's first female rock star at the Monterey Rock Festival.

Her image—the wild clothes and feathered boas, the psychedelic butterflies on her Porsche, her ratty flaming-red hair—grew wilder, but Joplin sang the blues for real. "Yeah, life's groovy," she said. "Sometimes it ain't groovy enough." Alcohol was part of her image—she demanded, and got, a fur coat from Southern Comfort for all the free publicity the distillery got from her drinking onstage—and drugs were part of her life. She admitted that heroin helped her dull the fear of her exploding fame. When Joplin, who predicted she wouldn't live to the age of 30, was asked to comment on the overdose death of rock star Jimi Hendrix—less than three weeks before Joplin herself would die—she said, "How about, 'There but for the grace of God . . .'"

Joplin was staying at the Landmark Hotel in Los Angeles in

the fall of 1970, working on a new album. Saturday afternoon, October 3, she called City Hall to find out about getting a marriage license with her latest boyfriend. She also made a call to get a fresh supply of heroin. That evening Joplin went to a recording session, then to a bar with friends for a couple of drinks. She got back to her hotel room after midnight, where she shot up with her new stuff, then dropped the plastic bag into a wastebasket and put the needle in a box in a drawer. She then walked down to the lobby and got a hotel clerk to change a $5.00 bill for cigarettes.

The time of her death was put at 1:40 A.M. Sunday. She wasn't found—collapsed on the floor of her room—until the next evening when her guitarist wondered why she hadn't emerged from her room all day. There was speculation that Joplin committed suicide. But it was unclear whether she used an unusually large amount of heroin or was given an unusually pure dose of the drug, which would have been stronger and more lethal.

In news reports of her death there was little indication of surprise, only sadness. As per her wishes, Joplin was cremated and her ashes were scattered by air along the Marin County coastline of California.

EDMUND KEAN
March 17, 1789 (?)–May 15, 1833

THERE ARE FEW juicier roles in the theater than the ones that require the actor to die onstage. The moment is so filled with drama that some actors even say that when their time really does arrive, they want it to happen in the middle of a performance. Such an act of bravado certainly would befit Edmund Kean, who still, more than 150 years after his death, is considered one of the greatest actors who ever lived. Kean, born a bastard in a London attic, physically was small and his voice was not deep and resonate. But he was intensely exciting to watch. Poet Samuel Taylor Coleridge said that watching Kean act was "like reading Shakespeare by flashes of lightning."

From his first major role at the Drury Lane Theatre in London, as Shylock in *The Merchant of Venice* in 1814, Kean was a star, breaking box-office records as he went on to conquer the roles of Hamlet, Othello, and Richard III. But he played the role of a star actor best of all. He was extremely arrogant yet paranoid that another actor would overshadow him. Having spent years in poverty, Kean performed to exhaustion in his effort to hold the spotlight and the money. At the same time he drank and caroused to excess. He founded the Wolves Club, which ostensibly was an organization for professional actors but actually was an excuse for heavy drinking and romps with actresses and prostitutes. With such a pace, Kean was spitting up blood by the end of his first season.

Kean remained successful, in both England and America, until 1825, when a jealous husband exposed the actor's long adulterous affair with the man's wife. Kean survived an attempt to send him to jail, but he was almost scandalized off the stage for good. He fled to America to avoid booing audiences, but when news of his sins caught up with him it caused a riot at a Boston theater. Back in London, Kean steeled himself against his unforgiving audiences by drinking large glasses of brandy offstage during the show. That, and the strain of his shattered career, often made him so ill that he collapsed before or after his performances. Though barely 40 years old, Kean sometimes was so weak that he would forget his lines. More tragic, he no longer had enough energy to sustain the illusion that his small— now emaciated—frame could fill the great stage.

"Fight for me," he wrote desperately to a London newspaper. "I have no resources in myself; my mind is gone, and body is hopeless. God knows my heart. I would do, but cannot. God damn ambition. The soul leaps, the body falls." Kean was able to perform less and less, finally ran out of money, and was forced to struggle through his demanding roles to support himself. On February 19, 1833, he fainted onstage. He recovered and on March 25 was playing Othello at the Covent Garden theater in London. His son, Charles, played Iago. Kean, pale and shivering, drank several glasses of brandy, then walked onstage to find the audience cheering him. He struggled through two acts. But in the third act, as he began one of the speeches that had made him famous—"Villain, be sure thou prove my love a whore!"—Kean threw his arms around his son and collapsed, gasping, "Oh, God, I am dying! Speak to them for me."

But Kean's death did not conform to the heightened reality of the stage. He lingered for several weeks, refusing to eat but continuing to sip brandy. Finally, on May 14, the 45-year-old actor lost consciousness, and the next morning, far from the stage and with no final dramatic speech, he died.

PRINCESS GRACE (KELLY) OF MONACO

November 12, 1929–September 14, 1982

IT IS INDICATIVE of the cool reserve of Grace Kelly—both on-screen and off—that she refused to provide the studio with her measurements. Hers was an elegance that shouldn't be sullied with such indecorum. How ironic, then, that her death filled the tabloids for weeks—partly, perhaps, because her privacy was guarded a little too closely.

The tragic accident occurred as the former movie star, who had given up her acclaimed career in 1956 after only eleven films for a fairy-tale marriage to Prince Rainier III of Monaco, was returning from the royal family's mountain retreat to the palace of the tiny Riviera principality on Monday morning, September 13, 1982. Normally a chauffeur would have been driving, since Princess Grace didn't like to navigate the steep, winding mountain roads. But for this trip she had laid out several dresses on the backseat of the Rover 3500 sedan, leaving room only for the Princess and her 17-year-old daughter, Stephanie. They were on a particularly difficult road, the Moyenne Corniche, just five miles from the palace when a truck driver following behind saw the car begin to swerve as it approached the final sharp turn on the road. It grazed the mountain on the left side and then drove straight off the curve. The car fell 45 feet down the tree-covered hillside and flipped several times before it landed upright in a flower garden.

As steam sprayed from the engine local residents pulled Stephanie from the driver's seat. Rescue workers later removed her mother from the rear seat of the car. Both were taken to Princess Grace Hospital. The 52-year-old princess, who suffered multiple fractures, including a broken thigh, broken ribs, and a shattered collarbone, never regained consciousness. She was placed on life-support equipment on Tuesday, but when the family was told she would never recover, they ordered the machines removed. She died of a cerebral hemorrhage at 10:30 P.M.

The news of her death shocked the world, not to mention the close-knit community of Monaco. But it wasn't just the suddenness of the loss. It was the unexpectedness of it. The initial report of the accident released by the palace gave no indication that Princess Grace's life was in danger. Princess Stephanie, the palace said, was only slightly injured, when in fact she had fractured a vertebra and been placed in a neck brace. The report also said the car had lost its brakes, when an inspection after the crash showed them to be in good working order. The misinformation occurred, simply enough, because the palace press officers were on vacation, so it was left to the family's personal staff to release news of the accident.

Their guardedness led the press to cry cover-up. The first speculation was that Stephanie had been driving, which even at the age of 17 would have been illegal in France, where the accident occurred. Stephanie had been pulled from the driver's seat, but neither she nor her mother had been wearing a seat belt— also an infraction in France—and the tumble down the hill could have thrown them anywhere in the car. Only after the false report was widely published was it determined that several witnesses had seen Princess Grace behind the wheel earlier on the drive toward the palace.

There also were rumors that the accident was caused by a fight between the Princess and her daughter, who were known to be at odds over Stephanie's new boyfriend. Such a sordid end for the regal star of Hitchcock films has never been proved. Stephanie told investigators she had tried to pull the hand brake as the car lost control. And according to Princess Grace's doctors, their examination before the Princess died indicated she had suffered a stroke before the accident, which might have caused her to become dizzy or confused and lose control of the car. Speculation then arose that the *stroke* had been caused by the fight with Stephanie.

All told, it clearly was not a storybook ending for one who seemed to have led so charmed a life.

SAINT LAWRENCE
d. 258

IF EVER a saint was known for his death, it is Saint Lawrence, the most celebrated martyr of Roman times. Lawrence was one of seven deacons under Pope Saint Sixtus II in the 3rd century when the Roman emperor Valerian was pursuing a periodic persecution of Christians. That really is all that is known for sure about Lawrence. But Christian writers soon after began telling a more detailed account of Lawrence's death, and here is the story that was adopted by the Catholic Church.

After Pope Sixtus was executed in 258, Lawrence believed he

would soon follow. Lawrence, who was the keeper of the church's treasures, began giving away valuable items to the poor until he was arrested and told to turn the rest of the riches over to the Roman court. Lawrence told the judge he needed three days to gather the treasures, and then proceeded to round up a crowd of poor and handicapped people. "These are the treasures of the church," Lawrence told the angry prefect.

The judge, believing a simple beheading was not sufficient, ordered that Lawrence be burned to death, slowly. He was stripped and strapped facedown on a gridiron that was propped above a bed of slow-burning coals. It is said that Lawrence maintained a cool smile as he roasted and seemed unaware of the searing heat. He even was quoted as telling the prefect, "Turn me. I am roasted on one side."

According to Catholic doctrine, the horrible event so moved those who witnessed it that several Roman senators converted on the spot and carried away Lawrence's body for burial. His death, in fact, is credited with inspiring a wave of conversions in Rome that ultimately turned the pagan city into the foundation of Catholicism. A church was built over Lawrence's tomb that stands as one of the seven principal basilicas of Rome.

But not all of Lawrence is buried there. A dozen other churches claim to possess relics of the saint and his martyrdom, including the gridiron, Lawrence's shoulder blade, arm, jaw, backbone joint, finger, foot, two ribs, and some melted fat.

BRUCE LEE
November 27, 1940–July 20, 1973

THE "FASTEST FIST in the East," the "King of Kung Fu," Bruce Lee was just beginning to attract Hollywood's attention as the oriental Clint Eastwood when he died. He had made three successful kung fu flicks in Hong Kong—*The Big Boss, Fists of Fury,* and *Way of the Dragon,* which he wrote and directed— when he starred in *Enter the Dragon* in 1973 and provided Warner Brothers with one of its most successful international releases. Trashy fight films, maybe, but together they grossed over $100 million and gave Lee a fanatically devoted following far beyond his previous American exposure as Kato on the *Green Hornet* television series in 1966.

Lee was half finished with his fifth film, *Game of Death,* which co-starred Los Angeles basketball star Kareem Abdul-Jabbar, when he died suddenly on July 20, 1973, at the age of 32. The official story was that he was in the Hong Kong apartment of actress Betty Ting Pei discussing a script. He complained of a headache and went to lie down in her bedroom after she gave him a prescription painkiller. A few hours later Pei was unable to wake him. He died at the hospital that night. The coroner said Lee had suffered a cerebral edema—swelling of the brain—caused by an allergic reaction either to the painkiller or to a drug he was taking for a back injury.

Lee's fans would have none of it. Some said he had died from being too healthy, that his body simply couldn't handle his rigorous fitness program and a diet that included raw beef, eggs, and occasional glasses of beef blood. More mysterious was the rumor that Lee had been murdered on orders from Chinese martial arts lords who were angry that he was giving away too many ancient fighting secrets in his movies. The speculation was that Lee either had been given an undetectable oriental poison or that he was the victim of "the vibrating hand," a mysterious death touch that kills two years after it is applied.

His funeral in Hong Kong drew an unruly crowd of 30,000. A second, quiet funeral in Seattle was held, with Steve McQueen among the pallbearers. But long after he was buried Lee reappeared on the screen more often than when he was alive. Producers of *Game of Death* salvaged 30,000 feet of fight footage and used a double to finish the movie. Noted one of the pro-

ducers, perceptively, "The fans are mainly interested in the
fight scenes and not whether Lee can recite Shakespeare." Other
movies were fashioned using any Lee footage their makers could
splice together, including childhood performances. His *Green
Hornet* episodes were turned into a feature film, while new
movies with Lee look-alikes were released with the bald claim
"Bruce Lee Lives!" One film featured three look-alikes. It at
least had the honesty to be called *The Clones of Bruce Lee*.

VIVIEN LEIGH
November 5, 1913–July 8, 1967

"I'M A SCORPIO, and Scorpios eat themselves out and burn themselves up, like me." Those words would never have crossed the
lips of Scarlett O'Hara, but they were very much in character for
the actress who played her. Because while Vivien Leigh may
have had the temperament of the famous belle from *Gone with
the Wind*, physically she could not keep up. As early as 1945
she was diagnosed as having tuberculosis, and for the rest of her
life she battled against persistent coughs and occasional delirium
even as she appeared in another twenty-five plays and five
movies, winning a Tony and a second Oscar.

The British daughter of a stockbroker, born in Darjeeling,
India, Leigh was always a driven actress. She was famous for
her scheming that landed her on the set of *Gone with the Wind*
as Atlanta burned, where her green-gray eyes and heart-shaped
face distracted producer David O. Selznick long enough to win
her her most famous role. And she astounded critics in 1951 by
appearing with her husband, Laurence Olivier, on Broadway in
two separate and successful portrayals of Cleopatra at the same

time, alternating nightly between Shaw's *Caesar and Cleopatra* and Shakespeare's *Antony and Cleopatra.*

Indeed, it was primarily her husband's career that Leigh felt driven to keep pace with, and that was no small feat considering that Olivier was already being called the greatest actor of the century. Despite her tuberculosis, Leigh would not slow down. She smoked heavily, aggravating her condition, she slept little and drank—not excessively, but even a little could send her into another period of sudden hysteria. Finally, on the Paramount lot in Hollywood during the filming of *Elephant Walk* in 1953, Leigh broke down. Soon it was no secret, after she conducted a wild screaming fit in front of the press as she was carried on a stretcher to an airplane that was to take her back to England to rest. A few months later she was back in rehearsal for a new play.

Leigh continued to work fairly steadily, though her erratic breakdowns finally led Olivier to end their twenty-year marriage in 1960. Seven years later, in May 1967, Leigh was in London rehearsing a new Edward Albee play, *A Delicate Balance.* She suddenly began to lose weight, her coughing became much worse, and she spat blood. She was diagnosed as having advanced tuberculosis, but she refused to go to the hospital and instead promised to rest at home. She continued to rehearse the new play in her apartment on Eaton Square and as late as July 2 she seemed unconcerned. "Isn't this a fair beast?" Leigh wrote. "So unexpected too. . . . Needless to say, I am far more worried about Larry [who also was seriously ill]. He writes me a lot but I think he is going through hell."

In the early morning six days later Leigh was found dead on her bedroom floor by Jack Merivale, her boyfriend since her divorce. Merivale had looked in on her fifteen minutes before and had seen her sleeping. Apparently soon after she had awakened in the midst of a choking spasm and her lungs had finally filled with enough fluid to suffocate her. She had knocked over the thermos on the nightstand, apparently groping for a glass of water.

Assessing her stunning performance in *Gone with the Wind* in 1939, *The New York Times* had called the 25-year-old actress "the very embodiment of the selfish, hoydenish, slant-eyed miss who tackled life with both claws and a creamy complexion, asked no odds of anyone or anything—least of all her conscience—and faced at last a defeat which, by her very unconquerability, neither she nor we can recognize as final." But in real life the role took its toll.

MERIWETHER LEWIS
August 18, 1774–October 11, 1809

THERE ARE ENOUGH suspects in the death of Meriwether Lewis—including the famous explorer himself—to fill an Agatha Christie mystery. How could the man who, with William Clark, was exalted for opening transcontinental passage to the Pacific Ocean wind up a few years later broke and dead on a well-traveled Eastern road? No one really knows, but theories abound.

Upon Lewis' triumphal return from his two-year expedition, President Thomas Jefferson, his friend and childhood neighbor, appointed him in 1807 governor of the upper Louisiana Territory. But Lewis was a better explorer than administrator. In office in St. Louis, he was plagued by unruly settlers, corrupt officials, and arduous negotiations with various Indian tribes. More and more distraught over his troubles by 1809, Lewis abruptly decided to go to Washington to try to straighten out some matters, including a dispute over unpaid expense reports that had left him in debt.

In early September, Lewis left St. Louis on a boat for New Orleans, from where he would take ocean passage for Washington. During the river voyage, he made out his will, leaving whatever estate he had to his mother. He apparently suffered a breakdown, and a few days later, when the boat reached Chickasaw Bluffs (now Memphis), Lewis was put ashore with a high fever and in a state of mental derangement. He had twice attempted to kill himself. The governor recuperated for a couple of weeks at Fort Pickering, then on September 29, after borrowing $100 to see him through his trip, left with two servants and an Army officer along the overland route called the Natchez Trace.

What happened after that has all been questioned by historians, but here is one version. On October 10, Lewis stopped for the night 72 miles southwest of Nashville in one of two log cabins owned by Mrs. Robert Grinder, whose husband was away. Mrs. Grinder said later that Lewis was clearly agitated. Well into the night he paced back and forth and mumbled, his muttering punctuated by occasional outbursts, about the unfairness of his problems in Washington.

During the night, Mrs. Grinder said, she heard a gunshot followed by a thud in Lewis' adjacent cabin. Then she heard him yell "Oh, Lord!," then another shot. Lewis staggered to her cabin and pleaded through the door, "Oh, madam! Give me some water, and heal my wounds!" But Mrs. Grinder said she was too frightened to open the door. Only the next morning did she send one of her children out to the distant barn to alert Lewis' servants, who apparently hadn't heard the commotion. They found Lewis lying on his bed, shot once in his side and once in his head, alive but with part of his forehead shattered and his brain exposed. Lewis begged them to kill him. His last words were "I am no coward, but I am so strong. It is so hard to die." Lewis was buried in a makeshift plank box near the cabin, alongside the Natchez Trace.

All indications from that story are that Lewis committed suicide. That's the version that made it to Washington and received the most attention. But local Tennesseeans believed otherwise. Speculation on foul play passed down through the generations, so that even on March 6, 1930, there was a headline in the *Lewis County Herald* that read: "Was Lewis Murdered?"

Was he? There was never an investigation to find out. But historians have pointed to several plausible suspects. The Army officer who had been traveling with Lewis had been separated from the group for a couple of days. When he arrived later on the day Lewis died, he didn't even examine Lewis' wounds for gunpowder burns to determine whether he had been shot at extremely close range. Given the political backstabbing rampant in the Louisiana Territory, the officer himself could have killed Lewis. So could Lewis' servants, who later complained that Lewis had never paid them enough. Lewis was found with only 25 cents on his body, although he had left Fort Pickering with more than $200.

Also suspect is Mrs. Grinder, who may have been so spooked by Lewis that she decided to kill him. Some say Mr. Grinder returned during the night and killed Lewis while robbing him. In fact, there were highway robbers all over the Natchez Trace who could be held in suspicion.

The verdict is forever suspended. Even the location of Lewis' grave is unclear. It was poorly marked until a national monument was established on the site in 1925, well over a century after the mystery was played out.

ALFRED LOEWENSTEIN
1877–July 4, 1928

AFTER ALFRED LOEWENSTEIN, called the richest man in Europe, fell out of an airplane over the English Channel on July 4, 1928, *The New York Times* reported it this way: "The plane in which he was a passenger was crossing from Croyden, near London, to Brussels when the financier disappeared. His valet, two stenographers as well as the pilot and mechanic of the plane were present but did not notice what happened." Didn't *notice* what happened? How could you not notice your employer falling out the rear door of a cramped six-passenger monoplane at 4,000 feet?

Especially when your employer was Alfred Loewenstein, known as "Croesus," or "the Belgian Santa Claus." He controlled steamship lines, European coal mines and steel mills, artificial silk factories, and African rubber plantations. So rich was he that he offered to lend Belgium $50 million interest-free to stabilize its currency. He had a castle in Brussels, eight villas in Biarritz, and a squadron of secretaries and aides, including a boxing instructor and a billiard expert. Loewenstein also owned twenty-two airplanes and had flown across the Channel hundreds of times.

So it would be truly freakish if Loewenstein died in the way his aides on the plane reported. They said their boss had been reading when he got up and, smiling, walked to the rear of the small plane, presumably to go to the bathroom. After he didn't return in fifteen minutes his valet went to look for him and found the rear exit door of the airplane unlocked and shut only by the force of the air pressure. The valet shouted to the pilot, but was drowned out by the loud engines. Finally he held a piece of paper up to the glass partition of the cockpit that said, "Captain gone." The pilot, unable to do anything about it, landed on a beach west of Dunkirk. He told French officials that Loewenstein apparently opened the wrong door on his way to the washroom.

Never mind that associates later agreed that Loewenstein, preoccupied with his business deals, had grown absentminded and had walked through wrong doors before. Tests by the airplane manufacturer soon after Loewenstein fell proved that the air pressure was strong enough to prevent any single individual from forcing open the door, let alone open it unintentionally.

When search crews found no body, and after a fisherman claimed he had seen a parachute descending over the Channel about the time the financier allegedly fell, there was speculation that Loewenstein had arranged his own disappearance because of recent business setbacks. One rumor had him eloping with "a pretty Yugoslav girl," another said he had entered a monastery. The European financial markets responded only to the most likely story—that he was dead. Two of his company's stocks plunged $30 million in value by noon the day after Loewenstein disappeared.

Loewenstein ended the rumors on July 19, when a fisherman found his body 10 miles off the French coast. His face was disfigured, but he was wearing a wristwatch inscribed with his name. He was dressed only in his underclothes, his socks, and one shoe.

So did the Belgian Santa Claus commit suicide or was he murdered? French and Belgian authorities, in rather perfunctory investigations at the time, apparently found no evidence of either. In 1987 author William Norris retraced the event and found plenty of people with a motive to kill the rich and powerful businessman, but no conclusive proof that any of them shoved him out the door. Most of those present are now dead themselves.

The rich widow is always a suspect, though in this case Madeleine Loewenstein found her husband to be worth far less dead than alive. He had bequeathed his entire fortune, estimated at $55 million, to her, but the collapse of his interests after his plummet left her with closer to $10 million.

CAROLE LOMBARD
October 6, 1908–January 16, 1942

WHEN MOVIE STAR Carole Lombard died suddenly at the age of 33, some said it was the end of an era—not just of her hilarious brand of screwball comedies like *My Man Godfrey* and *Twentieth Century* but offscreen, too, where her raucous and profane wit made her one of the most fun people in Hollywood. She was the type of star little girls dreamed of becoming: not only was she beautiful and glamorous, she was also married to Clark Gable, creating one of the most sensational love matches of Hollywood's golden days.

The pair were so well liked that it made perfect sense for them to be asked to headline the first war-bond drive after Pearl Harbor. The campaign would peak in Indianapolis, in Lombard's home state, so she decided to go anyway after Gable declined and took along her mother instead. On one night, January 15, 1942, Lombard helped raise over $2 million, four times what organizers had hoped for. Afterward, Lombard was eager to get back to California, so she instructed her press agent to book them on an airplane flight instead of the train. Lombard's mother was most reluctant. She had never flown before and her numerologist had told her that January 16 was an unlucky day for flying.

Lombard flipped a coin, and after the star called tails and won, the two women and the press agent took off at 4 A.M., Friday, January 16, on a flight that included several stops and was to take seventeen hours. One stop Friday afternoon was in Albuquerque, New Mexico, where several military officers wanted to board and displace civilian passengers. Four passengers got off the plane, but Lombard, pointing out that she had just raised

$2 million for the war effort, convinced the pilot to add three seats and let her and her companions continue the flight.

The plane made one last stop, in Las Vegas, to refuel, then took off at 7:07 P.M. headed for Los Angeles. About a half hour later workers at the Blue Diamond Mine south of Las Vegas reported seeing a bright flash atop a distant mountain and then heard an explosion. It seems the pilot, who had been reprimanded several times before for disobeying flight regulations, was flying off course over the mountains to try to make up for lost time from all the previous stops. The plane grazed a rocky projection then slammed into the wall of Table Rock Mountain near its peak at 8,000 feet.

It took rescue workers, led by a local 70-year-old Indian, almost a day to climb the steep cliffs and reach the crash site, surrounded by snow several feet deep. There was no snow near the destroyed plane. Many of the nineteen passengers and three crew members, including Lombard, were so badly burned, they couldn't be identified. It was several days before all the bodies could be removed from the mountain.

Gable, who had flown to the area and paced nervously until it was clear there were no survivors, soon afterward enlisted in the Army Air Force as a 41-year-old private.

HUEY LONG
August 30, 1893–September 10, 1935

To CALL Huey Long a dictator hardly does the man justice. Dictators usually have free rein over an entire country. Huey Long, a U.S. senator and—at the same time—governor of Louisiana, had free rein in a country full of laws written to prevent that sort of thing. When the governor was elected to the U.S. Senate in 1930, he called out the National Guard to block the lieutenant governor—an enemy who would have wrecked Long's powerful machine—from stepping up to finish his term. The siege lasted seventeen months, until Long could get his man appointed to replace him. The red-haired, chubby-faced "Kingfish," as he was affectionately called, also regularly relied on the National Guard and his own secret police force to oversee elections in Louisiana.

In fact, Long put the entire capital city of Baton Rouge under martial law for much of 1935 after he announced he had uncovered a plot to kill him. Long talked often of his belief that his enemies were conspiring to kill him and he always traveled with several armed bodyguards, though skeptics said his outspoken fears simply were an excuse to gain more power. Long's colleagues treated less than seriously his speech in the Senate chambers on August 8, 1935, when he read a transcript of a conversation that he said had taken place a few weeks before at a New Orleans hotel among several high-ranking politicians who were plotting to kill him. Long even implicated President Roosevelt, which most people took as Long's way of warming up his own anti-New Deal presidential campaign in 1936.

A month later Long sat in the chambers of the Louisiana legislature, which had been called into special session to consider several bills that would tighten Long's grip on the state and block New Deal money—and federal influence—from diluting it. About 9:30 that Sunday night, September 8, Long bounded up and walked briskly across the sparkling marble rotunda of his new $5 million, thirty-four-story state capitol and into the governor's office. He brusquely told Governor O. K. Allen that he wanted to see him early the next morning, then spun around and headed back out into the rotunda.

Long was just a few steps outside the governor's office when a man in a white linen suit came up to him, pressed a .32-caliber automatic pistol in his ribs, and fired. Long's bodyguards immediately forced the man to the floor as the senator staggered across the rotunda and down some stairs, where he fell into the arms of state official James O'Connor. "Jimmie, my boy," Long said, blood dripping from his mouth, "I'm shot." O'Connor hailed a taxi and sped to Our Lady of the Lake Sanitarium. Long's only words were "I wonder why he shot me."

Meanwhile, within seconds after Long was shot his body-guards pulled out their pistols and machine guns and levied a hail of gunfire on the man who had shot the senator. As bullets ricocheted and pockmarked the marble rotunda, the assailant was hit 61 times—30 bullet wounds in front, 29 in back, and two in his head. Governor Allen, upon hearing the gun pops, first ducked under his desk, then ran into his outer office, next to the rotunda, and yelled, "Give me a gun! Somebody give me a gun!"

The man who shot the 42-year-old Long turned out to be Dr. Carl Weiss, Jr., a 29-year-old noted eye, ear, nose, and throat specialist who lived with his wife and baby just a few blocks from the capitol. He was also the son-in-law of Judge B. H. Pavy, an opponent of Long's who, under a bill Long was pushing through the special legislative session, was to be gerrymandered out of his courtroom.

Doctors performed emergency surgery on Long to try to repair the damage of the bullet, which had pierced his colon twice, torn one kidney, and then exited out his back. The operation was only partly successful, and thirty-hours later, during most of which he was delirious, Long died at 4:10 A.M. on September 10 from severe internal bleeding. With Weiss dead, there was no substantial investigation of the shooting and Long's alleged conspiracy charges never were seriously examined. Some believed Long actually had been killed by a bullet from one of his own trigger-happy bodyguards.

Some 80,000 passed Long's casket in the capitol as state troopers patrolled Baton Rouge with orders to shoot anyone who tried to take pictures near the capitol or the hospital where he had died. In the day between Long's shooting and his death, Louisiana legislators passed the anti-New Deal measures that he had wanted. They did it surrounded by the National Guard, ostensibly for their own protection after the recent violence. But maybe it was just Long's way of letting them know he wasn't dead yet.

JEAN-BAPTISTE LULLY
November 29, 1632–March 22, 1687

"NEVER DID any man carry so far the art of playing the violin" was what one French journal wrote on the death of Jean-Baptiste Lully, a composer who so dominated the court of Louis XIV that his work monopolized French opera for a century afterward. Born Giovanni Battista Lulli in Florence, Italy, the son of a miller, Lully taught himself the violin and at the age of 13 caught the eye of the cousin of the King of France during a carnival and was invited to join her household. Within a few years the little operator was composing ballets for the young Louis XIV. By 21 he was "Instrumental Composer to the King" and at 30 "Music Master to the Royal Family."

Lully passed himself off as the son of a Florentine gentleman, which the King acknowledged, enabling Lully to marry extremely well. Musically, he was talented; he collaborated with Molière on a series of comedy-ballets that later led to French opera. But Lully's real talent lay in orchestrating his own career. He not only composed operas, he directed and produced them as well. By royal edict he created the Académie Royale de Music and attained a monopoly by prohibiting other theaters from employing more than two singers and six violinists.

On January 8, 1687, Lully was conducting 150 musicians and

singers in a performance of a new work, a *Te Deum*, to celebrate the recovery of the King after painful surgery. In those days the conductor didn't use a small wisp of a baton, but a large, heavy staff that he would bang on the floor to beat the tempo. As Lully vigorously conducted his new piece he accidentally stabbed his toe with the sharp point of the staff. At the time the injury didn't seem serious. But after he became feverish it was clear that gangrene had set in. The doctors wanted to amputate the toe, but Lully refused. A few weeks later the doctors told him they would have to amputate the entire leg for him to survive, but he again refused.

The 54-year-old Lully calmly put his affairs in order, leaving most of his vast fortune to his family, but also providing something for his servants, the opera workers, and the poor. Although he had never been religious, Lully fully repented his sins near his death. The priest had said that for Lully to prove his sincerity, he would have to destroy the opera he had been working on. Lully pointed to the unfinished manuscript on a table and the priest threw it on the fire. Always an operator, Lully later told a friend, "Don't worry. I knew what I was doing. I have another copy."

LYNYRD SKYNYRD
October 20, 1977

COINCIDENCE USUALLY is just that, but that doesn't make it any less eerie on occasion. Consider the story of the band Lynyrd Skynyrd, described as a "rhythm 'n' blues–based Southern rebel–macho rock outfit" and one of the hottest acts of the mid-

1970s. The group of seven Florida good ol' boys, who performed with a Confederate flag as a backdrop, sold over one million copies of their records, starting with their second album, and their biggest hit, "Sweet Home Alabama," was one of the decade's classics.

In mid-October 1977, Lynyrd Skynyrd released its fourth album, *Street Survivors*. The cover showed the band members surrounded by flames. One of the songs on the album was called "That Smell," which featured the chorus "Ooh, ooh that smell. The smell of death's around you." A week after the album was released the band was destroyed when its chartered propeller plane ran out of gas and crashed in a wooded swamp in southern Mississippi near Gillsburg. Two band members, including lead singer and songwriter Ronnie Van Zant, 28, were among the six killed. Twenty others, including the rest of the band and its crew, were injured.

One of the band's crew members who survived said later that the airplane hadn't been in good shape and the band was planning to vote on whether to keep on flying it. Earlier that week, which was the start of the group's biggest national tour, a six-foot flame had shot out of one of the plane's two engines en route from Miami to Greenville, South Carolina. And just before the crash, a survivor said, oil poured out of one engine. The pilot, who was killed in the crash, had told the band that the plane was to be worked on in Baton Rouge, Louisiana, which was where the plane was headed when it went down.

When the crash occurred 500,000 copies of the band's flame-covered *Street Survivors* album had already been sold. The remaining copies were pulled from the shelves and a different cover, simply showing the seven members standing against a black background, was substituted.

MANOLETE
July 5, 1917–August 29, 1947

IF THE NAME Manolete doesn't ring a bell, you are not from Spain or are not a fan of the bullfights. So revered was the bull-fighter Manolete that *Time* magazine described his death this way: "If Charlie Chaplin and Babe Ruth and General Mac-Arthur all died at once, Americans would not feel the loss as poignantly as millions of Spaniards and their cousins felt the death of Manolete."

Born Manuel Laureano Rodríguez y Sánchez, the son, grand-son, nephew, and great-nephew of bullfighters, Manolete grew up a skinny mama's boy who preferred reading to playing out-side. When he finally took an interest in the sport, he was cast as the comic of the event. He was lanky, with a long nose, bug eyes, and a sad face reminiscent of Woody Allen's. But he killed bulls deftly. He followed the classic style of standing straight, with his feet planted firmly in the ground, deflecting the charg-ing half-ton bull only by flicking his cape.

By the age of 22, in 1939, Manolete was hailed as the greatest bullfighter of his time. Statues were erected in his honor, a song about him was wildly popular, and a liqueur was named after him. He slew hundreds of bulls and toured Mexico and South America, adding to an estimated $1 million he earned in thirteen years in the ring. In that time Manolete was gored seriously twelve times.

In 1946 the 29-year-old veteran announced he was going to take some time off and possibly retire for good. Overnight the hero became a heel. His fans and the press accused him of fighting small bulls and of filing down their sharp horns. Manolete shrugged it off for a few months, until his nearest competitor, 21-year-old Luis Miguel Domínguín, challenged him to defend his reputation. Manolete met Domínguín in three matches in August 1947 and for the first time, no matter how skillfully he dispatched the bull, the crowd booed him and cheered for Domínguín, who was considered the underdog. Flabbergasted, Manolete exclaimed in a radio interview, "They're asking more than I can give. I only want to say one thing: I am very anxious for this season to end."

On August 28, Manolete and Domínguín met at a match in Linares, in southern Spain. They were to fight Miura bulls, a breed considered most vicious. Late in the afternoon, Manolete was first in the ring, and he killed his bull with little flair and little response from the crowd. Domínguín killed his bull with greater flourish and drew loud cheers.

Manolete's second bull clearly was more dangerous. Before Manolete began the bull gored a horse, throwing its rider and almost killing him before Manolete distracted the animal, which already was riled by swords jabbed shallowly in its shoulders. But instead of moving cautiously, Manolete grew bolder. He let the bull charge within inches of him, and, finally hearing the cheers of the crowd again, even turned his back on the angry animal. Finally, Manolete went for the kill. He chose the most dangerous move, thrusting his sword over the bull's horns and stabbing between its shoulders. Suddenly the bull lunged to the right, driving its right horn into the bullfighter's groin. Manolete was tossed high into the air and collapsed on the ground.

The bull rammed the lifeless body until officials could distract the animal and drag Manolete from the ring. Soon after, the bull collapsed, dead.

Manolete, wounded deeply, was rushed to the hospital, where he was given four blood transfusions. As the 30-year-old bullfighter lay in bed, complaining that he couldn't feel his right leg, he was presented with the bull's ears and tail, the traditional honor of a well-fought match. Early the next morning, as he was receiving his fifth transfusion, Manolete died. One newspaper summed up, "He killed dying, and he died killing."

JAYNE MANSFIELD
April 19, 1933–June 29, 1967

WHEN YOU'RE number two you have to try harder. So since Jayne Mansfield wasn't Marilyn Monroe, she had to show a little more cleavage, sigh a little deeper, and act a little dumber. She performed it with aplomb. Mansfield, who measured 40-18-35, would do anything for attention. She was Miss Queen of the Chihuahua Show, Miss Electric Switch—anything for a photo flash. In Hollywood, Mansfield showed up early to a press party for Jane Russell's new movie *Underwater* wearing a flimsy bikini that conveniently became unhitched after she fell into the pool. Mansfield got all the headlines, and she wasn't even in the movie. None of the dozen or so movies she did make were any good, but Mansfield lived in a big pink mansion and was a star.

And then along came the sexual revolution. Marilyn Monroe died a blond bombshell, but Mansfield lived on long enough for that image to be denounced by feminists and outdone by more explicit bodies. She bared it all for *Playboy* several times and dressed like a stripper for her bad nightclub act. But her bookings got more and more obscure. Still insatiable for attention, she even called a press conference on Christmas Day in 1966 when her six-year-old son came home from the hospital after being mauled by a lion.

The next summer Mansfield took her nightclub act to Gus Stevens Dinner Club in Biloxi, Mississippi. She finished the 11 P.M. show on June 28, then piled her luggage, boyfriend/manager, and three of her five kids in the car to drive 80 miles to New Orleans, where she was scheduled to make a television appearance at noon the next day. She sat up front with her manager and the 20-year-old driver provided by the supper club while the children slept on the back seat.

At 2:25 A.M. the highway was foggy from the recent spray of a mosquito-control truck. The driver didn't slow down in the smoke and apparently never saw the back end of the mosquito truck as the car slammed into it. The top of the car was sliced off by the trailer-truck, killing the three adults in the front seat. Mansfield was decapitated. Her three children were not seriously injured.

Needless to say, Mansfield got a lot of attention because of her violent death. Many stories tried to draw parallels between the car accident and the star's fast living and her lust for attention. But Mansfield didn't die from those things. She died because of bad driving.

FINIS.

JEAN-PAUL MARAT
May 24, 1743–July 13, 1793

JEAN-PAUL MARAT was the most radical and ruthless leader of the French Revolution—and that's saying a lot. He called for mob violence even after Louis and Marie lost their heads, and he was credited with, or blamed for, inciting riots that turned into massacres. As the revolution progressed, Marat turned against some of the less radical factions and had many of his former fellow patriots executed. A noted scientist and former physician to aristocrats, Marat believed France needed a dictator, as in ancient Rome, who would be subject to recall or assassination. Marat offered himself as a good candidate.

He got half his wish. By 1793, Marat's radical views had alienated him from most of his colleagues. His maintained his influence primarily through his newspaper, *L'Ami du Peuple*, which he edited in his Paris apartment. More precisely, he worked in his bathtub. Perhaps from years of hiding in damp cellars and sewers to escape arrest, Marat suffered from an excruciatingly annoying skin condition. To relieve the constant itching all over his body, the five-foot-tall, ugly man spent hours each day in a warm mineral bath, writing on a board placed over the tub.

He was thus situated at 8 P.M. on July 13 when he heard a woman's voice pleading to get past the guard to see him. The woman, who identified herself as Charlotte Corday, said she carried important information about a group planning a counter-coup against the revolution. But in fact, the 25-year-old woman had come to Paris to avenge the deaths of her friends whom Marat had executed. Marat, sitting in the tub, with a moist towel over his shoulders and a kerchief soaked in vinegar around his head, told the guard to let her in. Corday pulled up a chair near the tub and handed Marat a list of the alleged conspirators. He read the list and said, "They shall soon be guillotined!"

Corday then suddenly pulled a sharpened six-inch kitchen knife from her dress and stabbed the full length into the left side of Marat's chest, pushing the blade through his lung and piercing his heart. "*A moi! Mon amie!*" he called to his common-law wife as he tried to stand up before he collapsed and died. Corday was grabbed as she tried to run out of the room, and was executed four days later.

Despite Marat's growing unpopularity, a radical group put his heart on display and thousands lined up to view it. He hadn't gotten his wish to be dictator, but then again, perhaps he had met the same end.

CHRISTOPHER MARLOWE
February 26, 1564–May 30, 1593

THOUGH HIS PLAYS are rarely performed, Christopher Marlowe is alive and well on the stage. His style is believed to have had a strong influence on his contemporary, one William Shakespeare, who also borrowed some of Marlowe's plots. There are those, even, who insist that Marlowe, author of *Doctor Faustus* and *The Jew of Malta*, actually also wrote some of the plays credited to Shakespeare.

As if "Kit" Marlowe didn't have enough intrigue in his life already. The son of a shoemaker, Marlowe rose to an Oxford education before, historians believe, he became a spy for Queen Elizabeth. This being the late 16th century, shortly after England's break with the Catholic Church, the Queen vigilantly was persecuting those of her subjects who continued to follow the Pope. Marlowe is believed to have been sent to France to report on the heretical religious practices of British citizens there.

It is probably through those activities that Marlowe met the three men with whom he spent the last day of his life. In 1593 the well-established playwright himself was facing the paranoid religious persecutions of anti-Catholic England. On May 18, 1593, he was informed that the Queen's Privy Council wanted to talk to him about charges that he was an atheist. Marlowe had reason to be worried. He had spoken too loosely about his unorthodox religious views and his plays were called blasphemous by some.

Perhaps seeking advice—though no one is sure exactly why they got together—Marlowe met three men for dinner on May 30. All three had suspicious reputations. One, Ingram Frizer, had been involved in many business swindles. The other two, including notorious spy Robert Poley, were members of the Queen's secret service. They met at the private home of Eleanor Bull, a widow, who lived just outside of London at Deptford. The four men shared a big dinner and a leisurely afternoon together. Then after a light supper at 6 P.M., Marlowe lay down on a bed in the room while the other three men played backgammon. Somehow, Marlowe and Frizer began arguing about the dinner bill. Marlowe was not one to back down from disputes and twice had been hauled into court for dueling illegally.

This time Marlowe attacked Frizer from behind as he sat at the game table. Marlowe grabbed Frizer's dagger from his belt and began beating him in the head with the heavy handle, cutting him two or three times. One contemporary writer described what happened next: "Hee [Frizer] quickly perceiving it, so avoyded the thrust, that withall drawing out his dagger for his defence, he stabd this Marlow into the eye, in such sort that, his braynes comming out at the dagger point, he shortly after dyed."

Only later recognized as a great Elizabethan dramatist, the 29-year-old Marlowe was buried in an unmarked grave in a churchyard in Deptford. Shortly afterward some blasphemous letters that he had purportedly written surfaced at the Privy

Council's hearings. Marlowe, of course, never got a chance to answer whether or not he was an atheist, which has served to enlarge the issue in countless analyses by historians. On the brighter side, given the mood of the Privy Council, it may well be that Marlowe's untimely death prevented a more deliberate beheading.

SENATOR JOSEPH McCARTHY
November 14, 1908–May 2, 1957

IF EVER SOMEONE proved the fickleness of political fads it was Joe McCarthy. It was just four years from his "I have here in my hand" speech, in 1950, to a vote to censure him for his scare tactics by his fellow senators. In between, McCarthy smeared hundreds of Americans but never firmly proved even one of them was a Communist. But that wasn't clear at the time, and neither was the crusade's personal toll on McCarthy.

McCarthy, a Republican who was elected to the Senate from Wisconsin in 1946, had always been a drinker, but he began to drink much more once he became famous. By 1952, at the height of his inquisition in the Senate committee chambers, a few were whispering that McCarthy suffered from alcoholism. Even before he was publicly humiliated on national television during the Army hearings, McCarthy's speech was occasionally sluggish, and his mood swings grew more abrupt.

After the Senate voted to condemn him in 1954, McCarthy fell into despair and bitterness. Though still a senator, he would sit at home watching TV soap operas and drinking. Once he returned to his familiar Senate hearing chambers as part of a committee investigating the Teamsters union. But this time, far from lording it over the proceedings, McCarthy stared blankly. When he spoke he rambled and was repetitive, much to the visible annoyance of his colleagues. He also limped, and his skin was described as "ghastly," slightly yellow.

The ailments were described as old troubles—a nagging stiff knee, an elbow injury. In fact, by the summer of 1956, McCarthy was hospitalized periodically for detoxification and treatment for his already damaged liver. He suffered fits of delirium, screaming that snakes were attacking him. He broke down with one friend, saying, "No matter where I go they look on me with contempt. I can't take it anymore." McCarthy's wife, his former office aide, arranged to adopt a baby girl early in 1957 to try to cheer her husband. It helped, but he did not stop drinking. He would gulp full drinking glasses of whiskey, or whatever. His face grew bloated, his body drawn, and his skin more yellowish.

McCarthy was again admitted to the U.S. Naval Medical Center in Bethesda, Maryland, on April 28, 1957. His wife said he was undergoing treatment of a knee injury. There were reports of a mental breakdown or cancer. Probably as much as anything, McCarthy had just given up. When the 48-year-old senator died four days later, the hospital said it was from "acute hepatitis," origin unknown. Only later was it acknowledged that McCarthy was being treated in the neurology ward for alcohol abuse, which caused his liver failure.

Upon his death, flags at the Capitol were lowered to half-mast, but remembrances were restrained at best. President Eisenhower, who had been so annoyed with McCarthy's harassments that he had announced he wouldn't support his fellow Republican if McCarthy sought reelection in 1958, issued a statement extending his "profound sympathy to Mrs. McCarthy in the grievous personal loss she has sustained." McCarthy left behind only the legacy of his name. Webster's defines "McCarthyism" as "personal attacks on individuals by means of widely publicized indiscriminate allegations, especially on the basis of unsubstantiated charges."

ALESSANDRO DE' MEDICI
1511–January 5, 1537

ALESSANDRO DE' MEDICI gave his family a bad name the way Caligula did the Caesars. For more than a century the powerful Medici banking family had financed much of the Italian Renaissance. But by the time Alessandro stepped up to rule Florence, the family flourish was wilting fast. Officially, Alessandro was the son of a Medici duke. But historians later came to believe he really was the second bastard son of Guilio de' Medici, who became Pope Clement VII. Alessandro, an obnoxious child, never was well liked, and his dark features caused speculation that his mother was a Moorish maiden.

Nevertheless, the 20-year-old Alessandro was the last one left in the ruling Medici branch when Pope Clement—either his uncle or his father—named him Duke of Florence in 1531. At first, much to everyone's surprise, Alessandro handled his responsibilities just fine. But when Clement died in 1534, Alessandro regressed beyond anyone's wildest imagination. He organized sexual orgies, raided convents and invaded private homes in search of new women, and murdered those he considered to be his opponents. Exiled Florentines pleaded with Holy Roman Emperor Charles V to do something, but he didn't, as his illegitimate daughter Margaret was betrothed to Alessandro.

Alessandro's partner in all of this was another Medici, a poor distant cousin named Lorenzino. Unlike Alessandro, this younger Medici was well educated. In fact, Lorenzino considered himself more worthy of the wealth and power that Alessandro abused and he plotted to befriend his unruly cousin so he could someday replace him. Lorenzino went along with all of Alessandro's terrorizing deeds until another Medici cousin, a Catholic cardinal, dropped dead on his way from Rome to confront Alessandro.

When Lorenzino learned that Alessandro in all likelihood had ordered his cousin to be poisoned, Lorenzino began plotting another way to steal Alessandro's power.

It happened during the New Year's carnival of 1537. Lorenzino took the very drunk duke to his rooms adjacent to Alessandro's palace, then promised to return with his attractive cousin. Alessandro was asleep when Lorenzino returned, not with his cousin, but with a professional assassin. The two men quietly entered, and as the stuporous duke slept, Lorenzino stabbed his sword into Alessandro's back. The duke groaned and rolled over and tried to grab Lorenzino, who stuck two fingers down Alessandro's throat to prevent him from screaming. Alessandro bit down to the bone before the assassin stepped in, jabbing his dagger into Alessandro's throat.

The two men wrapped the dead duke in his sheets, and Lorenzino pinned a note that read, "Love of country and unbounded desire for glory shall conquer." Lorenzino locked the door behind him, and Alessandro, who everyone assumed was enjoying the New Year's carnival, was not discovered until the next evening. Lorenzino, meanwhile, fled to Venice. He never got the power or the wealth. That went to yet another Medici cousin, Cosimo, who in 1547 assassinated Lorenzino.

GLENN MILLER
March 1, 1904–December 15, 1944

As GLENN MILLER boarded a single-engine, nine-seat Norseman airplane on December 15, 1944, he looked around and said, "Hey, where the hell are the parachutes?" "What's the matter, Miller?" replied a colonel, already seated. "Do you want to live forever?" Not forever, perhaps, but at least through the war. And for someone who was used to being in control, an "uptight" perfectionist, World War II was unnerving even behind the front lines.

Miller, tall and slim and wearing his characteristic professor's spectacles, had been one of the most popular big-band leaders before the war, with hits like "In the Mood," "Tuxedo Junction," and his signature song, "Moonlight Serenade." Once the United States joined the war, Miller volunteered for the Army and took his music on exhaustive national fund-raising tours and, in June 1944, to Europe to entertain the Allied troops. Bombs were still falling when Miller and his Army band arrived in London, and the band leader had several narrow escapes. Even worse, for Miller, were airplane flights, where he also experienced some close calls.

Although he talked about his plans after the war—he wanted to form a new band with war veterans, he planned to invest in motels and a Coca-Cola distributorship, and he and his wife had recently adopted a boy and a girl—Miller also said, one night after a recording session outside London, "Christ, I don't know why I spend my time making plans like this. You know, I have an awful feeling you guys are going to go home without me, and I'm going to get mine in some goddamn beat-up old plane."

That plane was the Norseman he boarded on December 15. The Army band was scheduled to entertain troops that recently had liberated Paris. Miller was to fly ahead on December 13 to make arrangements. The flight was delayed two days because of rain and fog. When the plane finally took off on the fifteenth, conditions still were miserable. The temperature hovered around the freezing point, and since the plane had no deicing equipment, there was a danger of ice building up on the wings. To avoid that the pilot would have to fly low across the English Channel where it was slightly warmer.

The band landed in Paris three days later, unaware that Miller had never arrived. It took several days to determine that his plane was unaccounted for, and even Miller's wife wasn't told he was missing until December 23. The Army finally concluded that the plane probably crashed in the Channel due to the bad weather, but no proof was ever found.

Then in 1984 a former British Royal Air Force navigator said Miller might have died under different circumstances. Fred Shaw said his plane, along with 150 others, was returning to England over the Channel on December 15, 1944, after an aborted bombing raid in Germany. As was standard practice, the planes exploded their unused bombs over the Channel before they landed. Shaw, whose account was corroborated later by the pilot of Shaw's plane, said that as one of their bombs exploded a few feet above the water, they saw a Norseman aircraft fall into the sea. The plane hadn't been hit by the bomb but was actually shaken out of the sky by the force of the blast. Shaw said he had completely forgotten about the mission until a few years ago when he saw the movie *The Glenn Miller Story*.

SAL MINEO
January 10, 1939–February 13, 1976

SAL MINEO had a taste for the bizarre. His almost-over-the-edge performances won him two Academy Award nominations: first in 1956 when he was 17, as a switchblade-flashing juvenile delinquent opposite James Dean in *Rebel Without a Cause*, then five years later as a homicidal Israeli freedom fighter in *Exodus*. In 1969, he directed and acted in a controversial Broadway play, *Fortune and Men's Eyes*, which featured an onstage nude homosexual rape scene. A sagging career left him playing an ape in *Planet of the Apes*, but by 1976 the Bronx-born son of a Sicilian coffinmaker was trying hard to make a comeback. He had agreed to pose nude for *Playgirl* magazine and was rehearsing a new play, "*P.S. Your Cat Is Dead*, in which he played a bisexual burglar.

One night after a rehearsal, Mineo was returning home to his West Hollywood apartment, located in a middle-class neighborhood just below the kinky Sunset Strip. As he walked away from the carport, someone stabbed him through the heart with a knife. He cried out, "Help! Help! Oh, my God!" as a man whom witnesses could only vaguely describe ran away. A neighbor, who found Mineo lying on his back with his feet in the air, gave the actor mouth-to-mouth resuscitation for five minutes, then gave up. Mineo's wallet wasn't taken, but police said the stabbing could have been the result of a failed robbery attempt. After a several-month investigation, the murder remained unsolved.

Mineo's choice of acting roles, as well as the location of his apartment, sparked many rumors that his deviance had gotten him into trouble. But film director Peter Bogdanovich said, "Sal had some strange tastes, but he was totally unaffected by it. The murder was so shocking because as a person he was so innocent."

MARGARET MITCHELL
November 8, 1900–August 16, 1949

MANY PEOPLE found it hard to believe that Margaret Mitchell, a four-foot-eleven, modest Atlanta housewife, could be the author of *Gone with the Wind*, a robust, panoramic novel that has outsold every book except the Bible. But in fact much of the voluminous manuscript that she delivered in a suitcase to a publishing talent scout was based on her own life. Born in Atlanta and

raised on its fashionable Peachtree Street, Mitchell could remember her grandmother recounting the actual burning of the
city by Sherman and describing how Confederate troops re-
treated through her backyard. And though she would never
admit it, Mitchell based the recalcitrant Rhett Butler on her
husband from her failed first marriage.

What with a Pulitzer Prize and an Oscar-winning movie, the
first-time author found herself overwhelmed by her book. She
became Atlanta's favorite daughter and was forever besieged by
curiosity-seekers who knocked on her front door or drove slowly
by her home, just a few blocks from the Peachtree mansion
where she had grown up. "Being the author of *Gone with the
Wind* is a full-time job," she said, and for nine years after the
book was published in 1936 she didn't even think about writing
another one. She joked that her ambition was to become "fat
and amiable" and grow old gracefully. When Mitchell finally
was ready to think about another story in 1945, her second husband, a retired advertising executive, suffered a heart attack and
she spent three years nursing him back to health.

By the summer of 1949 her husband was well enough for
them to go out. So on August 11, a hot, sticky night, they drove
a few blocks to the Peachtree Arts Theatre in downtown Atlanta
to see a new movie, *Canterbury Tales*. They were in a hurry to
make the start of the show, so Mitchell quickly parked the car
on the street across from the theater and helped her husband
out of the car. Peachtree was a busy thoroughfare and was especially dangerous where they crossed because the street curved
nearby in both directions.

When Mitchell and her husband, arm in arm, were just across
the center line, a car suddenly sped toward them. Mitchell, in a
panic, left her husband in the middle of the street and ran back
toward the curb they had left, which was the farther side of the
road. The car swerved and skidded 60 feet before it hit the petite
woman, dragging her a distance of seven feet. The 48-year-old
author, lying by the side of the street where she had grown up,
suffered a skull fracture and a broken pelvis. She never fully re-

gained consciousness and died five days later. The driver, a 29-year-old off-duty cabdriver who had 23 prior traffic violations and had been traveling at 50 miles per hour, later was convicted of involuntary manslaughter.

Mitchell had ordered that all of her letters and much of her manuscript be burned after she died. She did want some documents preserved, and specifically had asked one friend, book reviewer Edwin Granberry, not to destroy the letters she had written him. Among those letters she had written, "I'm going to die in a car crash. I feel very certain of this."

MARILYN MONROE
June 1, 1926–August 5, 1962

PERHAPS NO DEATH in this century—oddly enough, other than John F. Kennedy's—has inspired such an undying legacy of analysis and speculation as that of Marilyn Monroe. Did she commit suicide? Was she murdered? Scarcely a year goes by when some new book doesn't try to answer those questions or nominate new ones. As late as 1982—twenty years after she died—the Los Angeles district attorney's office reopened her file, then four months later determined there wasn't enough new information to warrant a full investigation. And all of this because of a waify, dark-haired foster child who blossomed on the screen into a bleach-blond, blue-eyed, breathless bombshell.

Ironically, by the time Monroe died at the age of 36, it wasn't clear how much longer her sex-symbol image would last. Her last two releases, *Let's Make Love* and *The Misfits*, had been flops, and she had been dismissed from the picture she was working on because of repeated absences. The movie was called *Some-*

thing's Got to Give, and Monroe loudly protested how she felt she was being mistreated. "We're what's okay with the movie business," she told a reporter. "Management is what's wrong with the business. To blame the trouble of Hollywood on stars is stupid. These executives should not knock their assets around."

Less than two months later Monroe was found dead in the bedroom of her modest home in the Brentwood section of Los Angeles. She had overdosed on sleeping pills, but everything else about the event has been disputed. The initial story was that her housekeeper was the last person to see her alive when Monroe went into her bedroom about 8 P.M. on Saturday, August 4. The housekeeper said she saw a light in the movie star's room at 3:25 Sunday morning. When she found the door locked she went outside and peered in through the French windows, where she saw Monroe lying across her bed with one arm extended and her hand draped over the telephone. The housekeeper called Monroe's analyst, who had prescribed a bottle of about 40 sleeping pills three days before and had spoken to Monroe earlier that evening. The analyst arrived at the house and broke a windowpane to get into her room, where he found Monroe dead. Beside her bed was an empty bottle that had contained the sleeping pills he prescribed, as well as 14 other bottles of medicines and pills. Monroe had left no note.

Or had she? Of course she wouldn't have left a note if she had been murdered. But evidence of that is based on who might have had a reason to kill her, not any proof that someone did it. The allegations—like much about Monroe's death—center on President Kennedy and his brother Bobby, who was the Attorney General. There have been substantial claims that Monroe had affairs with both men and that Bobby was trying to break it off when she died. The murder theory is that Monroe was killed to frame the Kennedys or at least cripple them politically. During Bobby's later campaigns right-wingers even accused him of ordering her killed to prevent a bigger scandal. Even if she did kill herself, it is alleged that Bobby Kennedy was in her home before police arrived and cleared out any damaging evidence, including a suicide note. But the only firm link between Bobby Kennedy and Monroe near her death was telephone records indicating that Monroe had called Kennedy's office at the Justice Department several times in the days before she died.

It certainly is more plausible that Monroe killed herself, though possibly the overdose was accidental. Monroe had been treated in mental institutions twice in 1961. She spent much of her last year doped on pills and alcohol, getting medicines from at least two doctors without telling each of the other's prescriptions. On May 19, 1962, Monroe caused a sensation with her breathy, seemingly sensuous purring of "Happy Birthday" to President Kennedy in a celebration at Madison Square Garden, when in fact her dazed performance was no act.

Two days before she died *Life* magazine quoted Monroe as saying, "It might be kind of a relief to be finished. It's sort of like I don't know what kind of a yard dash you're running, but then you're at the finish line and you sort of sigh—you've made it! But you never have— You have to start all over again." In her final days Monroe was distraught over her dismissal from the film and, allegedly, over Bobby Kennedy's refusal to return her phone calls. She spent much of Saturday, August 4, on the telephone, sounding distressed to her friends and trying to decide whether to attend a party that night at the home of Peter Lawford, the Kennedys' brother-in-law. She was visited by her analyst and her hairdresser.

Amid a gathering storm of rumors, Monroe received a quiet funeral in Westwood, California, near Hollywood. Among the 500 guests, few stars were invited and the press was banned. Joe DiMaggio, the former Yankee baseball star and the second of Monroe's three husbands, kissed her just before her coffin was closed. Revered acting instructor Lee Strasberg, with whom Monroe had studied, wept before he delivered the eulogy. "In her own lifetime," Strasberg said, "she created a myth of what a poor girl from a deprived background could attain. For the entire world she became a symbol of the eternal feminine." The eternal flame remains fueled by how she died.

MARIA MONTEZ

June 6, 1920–September 7, 1951

TRITE BUT TRUE, Maria Montez's death could have been a scene out of one of her B movies. The daughter of a Spanish government official, Maria Africa Vidal de Santo Silas left the Dominican Republic to pursue modeling in New York. A talent scout at a party suggested a screen test and soon the exotic beauty was a star of sorts. Her first year in the business, 1941, Maria was in seven movies. During the decade she made twenty-eight films, starring in movies like *Gypsy Wildcat, Cobra Woman*, and *South of Tahiti*. Critics said the "Queen of Technicolor" couldn't act, but audiences thought she looked good doing it.

Offscreen, Maria remained a star. She was married to French movie star Jean-Pierre Aumont. As a present Jean-Pierre bought her a palatial home in the Paris suburb of Seresnes. One morning, with her husband on location and her two sisters scheduled for lunch, Maria took her daily weight-reducing bath, a three-hour production in extremely hot water spiced with reducing salts.

Her sister found her there, unconscious. Maria, "proud that her figure never topped 125," had drowned in the tub after suffering a heart attack, probably caused by the hot water. *The New York Times* solemnly reported, "The firemen used artificial respiration in a vain effort to resuscitate the auburn-haired, brown-eyed actress." Fade out.

JIM MORRISON
December 8, 1943–July 3, 1971 (?)

"I wouldn't mind dying in a plane crash," Jim Morrison, the lead singer of The Doors, said in 1969. "It would be a good way to go. I just don't want to die of old age or O.D. or drift off in my sleep. I want to feel what it's like. I want to taste it, hear it, smell it. Death is only going to happen once, right? I don't want to miss it." If it was experiences Morrison was looking for, he found plenty. Three years after he dropped out of UCLA film school, he was a rock star by 1967, known for his loud, sexually suggestive lyrics and writhing leather or snakeskin pants. With hits like "Light My Fire" and "Hello, I Love You," he and The Doors were the most popular American band in the late 1960s.

From the beginning Morrison's experience was colored by drinking and drugs. At first it was an integral part of his image in concert, but by 1969 the concerts were getting out of hand. He spit at his fans and verbally abused them. He was arrested repeatedly for drunkenness and allegedly exposing himself on-stage. A particularly riotous performance in Miami in 1969 led the city to organize a "Rally for Decency," which drew 30,000. Through it all Morrison just smirked and went on doing what he wanted to do. He never owned a home, just lived out of cheap motel rooms or on friends' couches. During tours he had a habit of hanging off the balcony of his hotel room, just because he felt like it.

The only thing Morrison seemed to take seriously was his poetry. So when, in March 1971, he got fed up with all the legal hassles and pressure from the record company for a new album, Morrison took his longtime, sometime girlfriend and went to Paris to write poems. He was supposed to stop drinking and work seriously, but he didn't. He often stayed out all night in bars where, referring to the drug overdoses of Janis Joplin and Jimi Hendrix the year before, he would say, "You're drinking with number three."

On Friday, July 2, after Morrison and his girlfriend, Pamela Courson, had dinner at an outdoor cafe, he took her home and said he wanted to go to a movie by himself. The rest of the story is a mystery. On Monday, July 5, the press began calling to confirm rumors that Morrison was dead. Neither his record company, Elektra, nor the American Embassy in Paris knew anything about it. The record executives, in fact, weren't surprised by the rumors, since Morrison's wild behavior had inspired almost weekly reports of his death. Finally, Elektra representative Bill Siddons called Courson, who said he should come to Paris. When Siddons arrived on Tuesday at the flat where Morrison had been staying, he found Courson, a sealed coffin, and a death certificate stating that Morrison had died of a heart attack. The coffin was buried the next day in a Paris cemetery that also contained Edith Piaf and Oscar Wilde. The official announcement of Morrison's death didn't come until Thursday, July 8.

What had happened that weekend? Courson said Morrison returned to their apartment early the next morning, though it isn't clear whether he actually had gone to a movie or instead went drinking or elsewhere. Courson said she woke up at 5 A.M. Saturday and found Morrison lying in a bathtub full of water, dead. But many have never been satisfied with that story, partly because it was six days before his death was officially announced. Some said he died of a heroin overdose, though Morrison wasn't known to use the drug. Others say he was killed as part of an antileftist conspiracy.

But most intriguing, some insist Jim Morrison isn't dead. There was an unconfirmed report that he was seen boarding a plane that weekend. And during The Doors' popularity the prank-ridden Morrison had joked about staging his death as a publicity stunt. Also, say his devotees, Morrison had gone to Paris to get away from the rock-music world. Maybe, they say, Paris wasn't far enough. If that's true, then perhaps Jim Morrison is off writing poetry somewhere. And perhaps death remains one experience he has yet to try.

WOLFGANG AMADEUS MOZART
January 27, 1756–December 5, 1791

How's THIS for a child prodigy: Mozart began composing at the age of 5. He performed in public at age 6, delighting his royal audiences with his astounding abilities to sight-read difficult music perfectly, improvise upon the melodies, and play an entire tune from memory after hearing it once. He composed his first symphonies when he was 9 and was named court *Konzertmeister* in Vienna when he was just 16. "The committing to paper is done quickly enough," Mozart wrote of his composing. "For everything is already finished, and it rarely differs on paper from what it was in my imagination." He was overwhelmingly prolific, and when he died at 35 it was almost as if his creative mind was so highly charged that it couldn't keep from burning out early.

For all his musical genius, Mozart struggled with daily life. Slight of frame and with a pale complexion, he was exhausted by his work, which he would often accomplish in feverish bursts of twelve hours or more. When he wasn't working he partied just as feverishly, blowing his money on extravagant nights out or foolish gifts for his wife. His finances, already depleted from frequent periods out of favor with the royal family, were further drained by doctors' bills, primarily from his wife's six childbirths. Four of the children died in infancy.

Through all these pressures Mozart was able to compose his great operas—*The Marriage of Figaro, Don Giovanni,* and *Così*

Fan Tutte—during his last years, until his body finally gave out in 1791. He had been commissioned to compose a *Requiem* for an anonymous patron, and he seemed haunted by the prospect. Even after he was confined to his bed in November, suffering from blinding headaches, fainting spells, and swollen hands, Mozart continued to work on the piece. On December 4 he became partially paralyzed and the last rites were given. He sent for a few friends and weakly joined them in singing strains of his unfinished mass for the dead. That night, as cold compresses were applied to his forehead to reduce the fever, he fell unconscious. He died at 1 A.M.

Because his wife could afford no more, his body was buried in a pauper's grave with other bodies. A skull claimed to be Mozart's is displayed in Salzburg, but some historians say there is no evidence that it actually is the one that once contained more music than it could handle.

AUDIE MURPHY
June 20, 1924–May 28, 1971

THE MOST DECORATED American war hero in World War II, Audie Murphy returned home with no place to go but down. What could top his spectacular battle feats? After lying about his age to join the army at 17, he had been wounded three times and credited with killing 240 Germans. Of 235 men in his company, Murphy was one of two who survived. Not yet 21, he won twenty-seven medals, including three from the French and one from Belgium.

After the war, Murphy was recruited to Hollywood by James Cagney, and in 1955 he starred in a movie version of his autobiography, *To Hell and Back*. He said it was "the first time, I suppose, a man has fought an honest war, then come back and played himself doing it." Murphy joked about his lack of talent, but in twenty years his boyish face and freckles appeared in forty movies, mostly war films and Westerns in which he played eager fighters. It was a far cry from his youth as one of eleven children of a Texas cotton sharecropper—and from the battle-fields of Europe—and the transition was not smooth. Murphy said the war left him with nightmares for years. He slept with a loaded automatic pistol under his pillow, and when he was asked how people survive a war, he said, "I don't think they ever do."

One of Murphy's friends, cartoonist Bill Mauldin, said, "Murphy wanted the world to stay simple so he could concentrate on tidying up its moral fiber wherever he found himself." Murphy became a quasi law-enforcement officer in the 1960s. He was made a special officer of a small California police department and rode around with police during drug busts. In 1970, he and a bartender friend beat up a dog trainer in a dispute over treatment of the friend's dog. Murphy was acquitted of attempted murder.

Though he had earned more than $2.5 million in his film career, Murphy was forced by too many bad business ventures to declare bankruptcy in 1968. Three years later, hounded by creditors and still trying to rebuild financial security for his wife and two teenage sons, he became interested in a company in Martinsville, Virginia, that manufactured prefabricated homes. He was on a small charter flight from Atlanta to see about making an investment when the plane crashed in a wooded mountain area during a light drizzle. The region, northwest of Roanoke, was so isolated that the wreckage, including the bodies of Murphy and five company officials, was not found for three days. The war hero was laid to rest in Arlington National Cemetery.

PRIMMIE NIVEN
1918–May 21, 1946

PRIMULA ROLLO was living the dream of many a moviegoer. As
a 22-year-old member of the British Women's Auxiliary Air
Force in 1940, she met movie star David Niven in a London art
gallery while he was on leave from the British Rifle Brigade. A
few weeks later, as bombs rained on the city, they were married.
"There was never a shadow of doubt in my mind that this was
the one," Niven wrote later. They survived five years of war,
during which Niven fought in perilous battles and Primmie
gave birth to two sons.

After the war Niven moved his family to sunny Hollywood.
Primmie had never even been to America, and she was enchanted by the entire movie-star life-style. She immediately set
about remodeling the home Niven had bought, next to that of
Douglas Fairbanks, while they rented a huge Spanish-style home
nearby. A few weeks after Primmie arrived, in mid-May 1946,
Niven had just finished his latest light comedy, *The Perfect*

Marriage, and the couple spent the weekend at Clark Gable's retreat in Monterey. From there Primmie wrote to her father that she had never been happier.

They returned to Hollywood Sunday to find an invitation for a party at Tyrone Power's. They arrived to eat barbecue with Gable, Lilli Palmer, Rex Harrison, and Gene Tierney, among others. As was the custom at those informal affairs, someone suggested a party game. It was called "Sardines," and all the lights were turned out while one person hid. The others had to grope in the dark, find the hidden player, and join him or her in hiding until soon just one lonely person was wandering around looking for the giggling cluster.

The game was under way for only a few minutes when they heard a crash. When the lights were turned on they found Primmie at the bottom of the basement stairs. She apparently had opened a door in the hallway thinking it was a closet. Primmie, carried upstairs by Cesar Romero and Oleg Cassini, wasn't bleeding at all but she was unconscious. They applied cold compresses, and as her head rested in the lap of Lilli Palmer she finally opened her eyes. "Lil," she murmured, "I feel so, strange. Even when I had babies I never felt so . . ." Primmie tried to smile and said, "We'll never be invited again."

Niven took her to the hospital, then stopped by the party an hour later to report that it was nothing serious, just a concussion. The next day he went to the set of his next movie. That night her condition worsened and doctors decided to operate. Later that night the movie star's 28-year-old wife, who had arrived in Hollywood seven weeks before, died of a fractured skull and brain lacerations. The coroner's report listed "death by misadventure."

NOSTRADAMUS
December 14, 1503–July 2, 1566

SOME SAY the French prophet Nostradamus really did see the future. Even as late as World War II, almost 400 years after he had died, his cryptic quatrains were credited with foreseeing not only that war itself but dozens of specific battles and diplomatic events. But perhaps his real talent lay in being obtuse. Nostradamus, who ascribed his prescient powers to "Divine Virtue and Inspiration," didn't bind himself to names or dates. And he wrote his hundreds of vague predictions in no chronological order, so latter-day followers have been free to pick whatever prophecies seem to match current events, including the French Revolution and the rise and fall of Napoleon.

The fame of Michel de Notredame—which was his name before his college buddies recognized his broad knowledge of Latin —really began with this ditty:

> *The young lion will surpass the old one*
> *in natural field by a single duel.*
> *He will pierce his eyes in a golden cage,*
> *two blows at once, to die a grievous death.*

Nostradamus already was known in several towns for his "plague powder," a concoction of cyprus sawdust and rose juice that seemed to heal some of its users. But after he wrote that quatrain in 1556 he was summoned by the French King Henri II, whose seriously superstitious wife, Catherine de Medici, was afraid that the prediction applied to the King. Sure enough, in 1559, Henri was killed in a tournament when his younger opponent's lance pierced his visor and jabbed one of his eyes. He died painfully after ten days.

A few years later Nostradamus retired to Salon, where he continued to forecast the future despite bouts of gout and dropsy. In June 1566 he wrote his will. And one evening soon afterward, as his assistant got up to leave, saying, "Tomorrow, master," Nostradamus replied, "Tomorrow, at sunrise, I shall no longer be here."

Among his quatrains, Nostradamus had written:

> *Upon the return of the Embassy, the King's*
> *gift put in place, Nothing more will be done.*
> *He will have gone to God: Nearest relations, friends,*
> *blood brothers, Found quite dead near bed and bench.*

Believers say the prophet had foretold his own death. At the time King Charles IX recently had returned from a trip and had sent some money to Nostradamus, which he had safely put away. The morning after Nostradamus had bade his assistant goodbye, he was found dead of a dropsy attack, lying on his bench at the foot of his bed.

RAMON NOVARRO
February 6, 1899–October 31, 1968

WHEN RAMON NOVARRO, who had been second only to Valentino as a 1920s silent-movie heartthrob, announced his retirement in 1935, he said, "I am much happier, believe me, now that I am free from the insincerities of Hollywood. What a place! You know, I had no time to fall in love and get married. The career must always come first and love must go by the way. But it is different now. I am an author. I can express myself."

Novarro never did marry. Nor did he ever leave Hollywood. But neither was the faded star ever able to reignite the passions of female filmgoers that he had fueled as a second-string Latin lover or as the star of the 1925 epic *Ben-Hur*. The Mexican-born actor failed to make the transition into talking pictures and, after directing a few films and an attempt at an opera career, spent the 1940s and 1950s showing up in small character parts in movies and later in television series like *Bonanza*.

Less and less was heard from Novarro, except for occasional interviews in which he would reminisce about the golden days. "Now they kick a woman, pull her hair," he said once. "They are less of the gentleman. Our lovemaking was sexier, but it was subtle, a sentimental courtly variety. There is more vulgarity in love scenes now."

Indeed there was. On Halloween 1968, Novarro was bludgeoned to death in his elegant Hollywood Hills home by two male hustlers. He was found naked on his king-size bed in the master bedroom the next morning by his male secretary. Police determined he had died of suffocation caused by massive bleeding from the severe beating about his head and upper body. There were no signs of forced entry into his home, but the small-framed 69-year-old man clearly had fought for his life, as furniture was overturned and vases were broken in the den, living room, and bedroom.

Six days after his murder—and two days after more than 1,000 people passed by his open coffin—two brothers from Chicago were arrested in Los Angeles and charged with the killing. Police said the young men, ages 22 and 17, had been guests in Novarro's home the night they killed him. Both were convicted a year later and sentenced to life terms.

SIR HARRY OAKES
December 23, 1874–July 8, 1943

HARRY OAKES, born in Sangerville, Maine, searched the world for his fortune and wound up the richest man in the Bahamas. He had dug for gold for fifteen years—in the Yukon, the Philippines, the Congo, and Death Valley, Nevada—before he struck the mother lode in 1912 in Ontario, Canada, where he developed the second-richest gold mine in the western hemisphere. By the time he moved to Nassau in 1935 to escape Canada's high taxes, he was worth an estimated $200 million. Soon after Oakes became a British citizen and promptly bought himself a title.

Sir Harry was gruff, even boorish, but he was extremely well liked in his new country. The island's largest property owner and one of its biggest employers, he and his wife also were close friends of the British island's new governor and former King, the Duke of Windsor. In fact, one of the morbid little details of Oakes's death was that, while their governor's residence was being renovated, the Duke and his wife had slept in the very same bedroom at Oakes's mansion in which Oakes was brutally murdered on July 8, 1943.

The 68-year-old multimillionaire was found in his bed early that morning by a houseguest. He had been bludgeoned in the head, then his body had been put on his bed, which had been set afire with gasoline. Detectives said later they believed Oakes was still alive when he was placed on the burning bed. An electric fan apparently blew out the flames before Oakes was burned beyond recognition. Feathers from the bed and pillows rested over much of his body. The houseguest, a real estate promoter named Harold Christie who was sleeping two bedrooms away, later testified that he found the body still warm. He put a pillow under the bloody head and tried to pour water in Oakes's mouth before he called the house staff.

The Duke of Windsor, who was notified immediately, ignored the island's police and summoned two detectives from Miami to investigate. There seemed to be plenty of clues. Blood splattered on the walls showed several fingerprints and dirty footprints were visible on the stairs. But during the first days of the investigation the house remained open. Between the visitors who trekked in and out and the humidity that quickly faded most of the prints, the detectives were able to come up with little evidence of who had been in Oakes's bedroom after he had gone to bed at 1 A.M.

No matter for the detectives, who thought they knew who had killed Oakes. In two days they arrested his son-in-law, Count Marie Alfred Fouquereaux de Marigny. The 33-year-old native of an Indian Ocean island had been at odds with Oakes ever since he defied the gold baron and married his 17-year-old daughter the year before. Unlike his father-in-law, de Marigny wasn't well liked in the Bahamas, where many believed his "Count" title was phony. The detectives said they had found a fingerprint of de Marigny on a Chinese screen next to Oakes's bed. De Marigny, loyally supported by his wife, said he hadn't seen his father-in-law since they had had a bad argument four months before in March.

At a sensational trial that fall Oakes's daughter testified on behalf of her accused husband, while Oakes's widow, who had been summering in Bar Harbor, Maine, at the time of the murder, took the stand against him. The prosecutors painted a perfect motive for de Marigny to kill his father-in-law, but the detectives' measly evidence didn't hold up in court. The jury deliberated less than two hours before acquitting de Marigny, though the jurors did recommend that he be deported.

The investigation into Oakes's murder was never reopened after de Marigny was declared not guilty. But since then writers have come up with others who had reason to kill the wealthy miner. The Mafia, which controlled gambling in Cuba, was trying to expand its operations into the Bahamas, and Oakes, as a major land and hotel owner, was making himself a stubborn stumbling block. One writer claims Oakes actually was murdered on a mobster's yacht and then was dragged back to his burning bed to try to destroy the evidence.

As for de Marigny, he was a free but ruined man. He left the Bahamas for Cuba, then wandered among several countries before he wound up nearly broke in South America. In what was perhaps Sir Harry's final grace note, de Marigny and his wife had their marriage annulled in 1949.

THOMAS PAINE
January 29, 1737–June 8, 1809

IT IS PERHAPS telling that Thomas Paine, whose *Common Sense* more than anything else may have galvanized the American colonies to revolt, lost money on the best-selling treatise. Paine, who didn't even arrive in America from England until late in 1774, got his moment of glory. But it soon was overshadowed by a host of later controversies so damning that even a century later Teddy Roosevelt referred to him as a "filthy little atheist."

Paine's problem was that he was a rebel to a fault. Considered too abrasive, he wasn't offered a position in the new American government so he returned to England, where he wrote *The Rights of Man* in support of the French Revolution. He soon had to flee to France after he advocated a similar uprising in England and was banished. In France, Paine was imprisoned during the Revolution for being an Englishman. But his real trouble came with *The Age of Reason*, which later was to become a classic argument for rational thought but at the time got him branded an atheist.

Paine's declining reputation only made him more stubbornly outspoken. His delight in a good argument turned combative. He started drinking much brandy and rarely bathed or washed his clothes. He wrote vicious attacks against President Washington that caused Americans to forget about *Common Sense*, to the point that when Paine returned to the United States in 1802, he was an outcast. President Jefferson was loudly attacked for entertaining his old friend. A minister was ousted after he shook hands with him.

Paine continued to write at length but was ignored. In 1806, staying in a spartan rooming house in New York, he suffered a stroke and fell down a flight of twenty stairs. Requiring some care from then on, he lived in a series of rooming houses, usually moving out after he offended each proprietor. In 1809 he was bedridden in the home of his longtime friend, Marguerite de Bonneville. Near the end his doctor asked if he wanted to profess his religious faith. Though weak, Paine said adamantly, "I have no wish to believe on that subject." He died in his sleep three days later.

Paine had asked to be buried in a Quaker cemetery, following the religion of his parents. The Quakers refused. He was buried elsewhere, but ten years later William Cobbett, who had been one of Paine's harshest critics, dug up his bones and took them back to England, intending to build a monument. The statue never was built, and after Cobbett died in 1835 the probate judge refused to include Paine in Cobbett's estate. His bones and casket were bought by a furniture dealer and haven't been seen since.

Paine's reputation received even a less restful fate. Long after Teddy Roosevelt, the mayor of Providence, Rhode Island, in 1955 blocked a proposed statue of the revolutionary hero because, he said, Paine was too controversial.

CHARLIE PARKER
August 29, 1920–March 12, 1955

"WHEN BIRD was 16 he looked 38. He had the oldest-looking face I ever saw." That memory from a Kansas City jazz-club owner sums up Charlie Parker's life perfectly. Because even as a teenager "the Yardbird" already was blowing jazz that musicians twice his age couldn't match. In his twenties he was regarded as a master, playing Carnegie Hall and touring Europe. Had he been born twenty years later Charlie Parker might have been a rock star. Given his fate, the parallels go beyond the music.

Parker grew up in Kansas City in the 1930s, when gangster-run nightclubs made the city flush with jazz. At 16, Parker and his alto saxophone were regular features in the progressive music scene. And almost from the beginning, some say, Parker gained his extra edge from drugs. "From nutmeg, Bird went to Benzedrine inhalers," said the Kansas City nightclub owner.

"He'd break them open and soak them in wine. Then he smoked tea [marijuana] and finally got hooked on heroin. He was the only man I knew who could drink with heroin."

In 1946, only 26 years old and long since one of the hottest jazz musicians on Fifty-second Street in New York, Parker suffered a breakdown. He set his hotel room on fire and was committed to a mental hospital for six months. That made him cut back on heroin, but he began drinking more heavily as a substitute. By 1948 a doctor told him he had six months to live if he didn't rest for a few years.

The message, though slightly ahead of its time, did not sink in. Parker's reputation began to match his talent, so that in Paris in 1950 he was showered with gifts of free drugs and alcohol—much as would happen to Janis Joplin and Jimi Hendrix twenty years later. That worried him enough to cancel the performance, fly back to New York, and check into a hospital for several weeks for the treatment of ulcers. "The doctor told me if I don't quit drinking, I'll die," Parker said. "I've had my last drink." Well, for a few months, anyway. In 1954, his career in shambles, Parker tried to commit suicide by swallowing iodine. The following winter, in Chicago, he refused to put on an overcoat. "I don't want to see another winter," he said. "Pneumonia's next for me."

Parker was back in New York for a gig that March. On the ninth, before leaving for Boston for his next performance, he felt ill and went to the home of a friend, the Baroness de Koeningswarter, a daughter of the Rothschild international banking family who lived in the Hotel Stanhope on upper Fifth Avenue. Parker refused the advice of the Baroness's doctor to go to a hospital, but he agreed to rest in her apartment, where he was cared for by the Baroness and her daughter.

Three days later, and forty-five minutes after the doctor examined him at 7:30 P.M., Parker collapsed, dead. He had been watching the Dorsey Brothers on television. The doctor said Parker had died of a heart attack, cirrhosis of the liver, and pneumonia. Parker, who looked 38 when he was 16, was 34 when he died. The doctor estimated the condition of his body as that of a 53-year-old man.

LIEUTENANT GENERAL GEORGE S. PATTON
November 11, 1885–December 21, 1945

GEORGE PATTON was a soldier's general. "Old Blood-and-Guts," as he was affectionately called by his men, was ruthless and crude, but those attributes on the battlefield enabled him to drive his troops to sweeping victories in World War II in North Africa, Sicily, and the western front of Europe. "Kill every one of the goddamn bastards," he roared as he stood on the front lines in the invasion of Sicily, his two pearl-handled revolvers holstered on his hips. He came close to being killed in the war three times, but continued to push so hard that he had to delay his advances because supply crews couldn't keep up.

Off the battlefield, Patton's boldness got him in a lot of trouble. His military victories sometimes seemed more like maneuvers to get ahead of his fellow generals, which didn't sit well in the methodical Army. After Germany surrendered Patton's command over Bavaria was stripped away after he publicly criticized denazification policies. Patton was so angered by his lack of a good position after the war that he seriously considered retiring, but decided to delay the matter until after his Christmas vacation, for which he was scheduled to fly to the United States on December 10, 1945.

The day before, with nothing to do on a Sunday afternoon, Patton decided to go pheasant shooting with his chief of staff.

North of Mannheim, Germany, Patton's limousine driver apparently didn't see that a two-and-a-half-ton Army truck coming the other way on the two-lane highway was signaling to turn left across the road. The general's large sedan, unable to stop, smashed into the truck's side, crushing the front end of the car. Neither driver was hurt, nor was Patton's chief of staff or his hunting dog. Patton himself didn't seem badly injured. "My neck hurts," he said, completely conscious as he was rushed to a makeshift hospital. But he complained of a lack of feeling in his lower extremities, and when they arrived at the hospital Patton had to be lifted from the car. "Relax, gentlemen," the general said. "I'm in no condition to be a terror now."

In fact, he had broken his neck. The crash had thrown him forward in the back seat, tearing the top of his scalp on a sharp-cornered ceiling light and slamming his face into the driver's partition. He had fractured one vertebra and dislocated another, which squeezed his spinal cord and paralyzed him from the neck down. With visitors the stalwart general was cheerful and optimistic. But in private, at night, he was depressed. He asked his doctor what were the chances that he would ever ride a horse again. "None," the doctor said. "In other words, the best I could hope for would be semi-invalidism," Patton said.

Doctors put him in traction, for a while his condition seemed to improve, and he began to regain some movement. Within a week plans were being made to return him to the United States for treatment. But on December 20 a blood clot moved to his lung, causing congestion that couldn't be cleared because his paralysis prevented him from coughing. Late the next afternoon, less than twenty-four hours after his condition began to deteriorate, and though he had been awake and comfortable earlier in the day, Patton died in his sleep. His heart, pressured by the congestion, gave out.

The general was buried on Christmas Eve at an American military cemetery in Luxembourg. The simple white marker over his grave matched thousands nearby, many of which stood over some of the men he had commanded.

BISHOP JAMES PIKE
February 14, 1913–September 2, 1969

WHEN BISHOP PIKE was reported missing in the wilderness of the Israeli-occupied West Bank, the fourth chapter of Matthew was cited as a poignant parallel. The wilderness where Jesus fasted for forty days and was tempted by the devil traditionally was believed to be the same area where the controversial and best-known Episcopal bishop had last been seen. And just as Jesus had roamed those barren hills at the start of his ministry, so, too, did Bishop Pike seem to be on a religious search of his own.

Pike had gone to Israel in August 1969 with his new wife, Diane, to study the origins of Christianity. He recently had announced he was leaving the Episcopal Church, which had barred him from preaching after he entered his third marriage without the church's approval. It was the end of a stormy tenure. At his height Pike had been dean of the Cathedral of St. John the Divine in New York City and later the bishop of the Diocese of California. But in the 1960s the animated preacher began challenging fundamental Christian doctrines, such as the belief in the virgin birth, and attacking the church for moving too slowly on civil rights and the Vietnam War. In 1966 a group of bishops sought to have Pike tried for heresy after he claimed he had made psychic contact with his 20-year-old son, who had committed suicide earlier that year in a New York City hotel room. Pike further embarrassed church officials by writing a book called *The Other Side: An Account of My Experiences with Psychic Phenomena*. Pike recently had formed the Foundation for Religious Transition, and his wife was the executive director of the New Focus Foundation, which conducted research into life after death.

On Monday morning, September 1, the 56-year-old Pike and Diane, 31, decided to drive their rented Ford from Bethlehem east to the Dead Sea. It was only 10 miles or so, but much of the terrain was extremely rough, pocked by deep canyons and sand traps. There was no road, but Pike, who had been to Israel five times before, and his wife thought their map would help them find their way. Although the desert temperature would rise well above 100 degrees, they didn't take a jug of water because they didn't plan to be gone very long. "We wanted to get the feeling of the wilderness because the Bible says that whenever Jesus wanted to be alone He went out into the wilderness to pray," Diane said later. "We wanted to find out what it was like. God, we found out!"

At about three that afternoon the car got stuck. The couple tried for more than an hour to heave it out of its rut, but to no avail. Sometime after 4 P.M. they began walking. Within an hour Pike said he was too exhausted and thirsty to go on. "He lay down to sleep," Diane later told reporters. "I lay down next to him and I said we would die together." But she woke up about 6 P.M. and decided to seek help on her own. She left the map for Pike and told him to follow her when he was rested. Ten hours later, early Tuesday morning, Diane, badly bruised and cut, stumbled into a work camp on the shore of the Dead Sea where Arab workers were building a road.

Israeli soldiers, trained to track down Palestinian guerrillas, immediately mounted a search for the missing minister. A helicopter soon found the stuck car, but there was no sign of Pike. The search continued on Wednesday and the map was found, but officials believed Pike could have survived the intense heat only if he had managed to find a cave. Indeed, after several soldiers were hospitalized from the heat, the search was called off on Thursday.

Minutes later Diane received a call from California reporting that a psychic medium there had seen a vision of Pike alive in a cave. The medium was Arthur Ford, who some years earlier had gotten notice by claiming he had received a message from

Houdini. Still, Diane insisted her husband was alive. She said that she and Pike were able to communicate with each other through extrasensory perception. "I'm sure if he were dead I would get something," she told reporters. "I'm sure of it. I don't think he's dead."

The search resumed on Friday, with officials taking their directions from two mediums. They found underwear that Diane identified as her husband's. Then on Sunday they found Pike, dead, in a kneeling position on a rocky ledge 70 feet below the top of a steep cliff. He was two miles from the Dead Sea. Officials believed he had fallen as he tried to climb the cliff to get out of the canyon. They believed he had been dead for three or four days. The day Pike was found searchers also discovered Pike's glasses and a contact-lens case that he apparently had placed as clues to his whereabouts. He apparently had found a pool of water, but had moved on to try to find his wife.

Diane was with the searchers when Pike was found. She joined the group after she said she had a feeling her husband was dead.

PONTIUS PILATE

d. A.D. *37*

PONTIUS PILATE, the Bible tells us, played one of the crucial roles in the history of religion—he ordered the crucifixion of Jesus Christ. But the Bible never says what became of him afterward.

Pilate, as procurator of Judea, ruled the region on behalf of the Roman Emperor Tiberius for ten years, from A.D. 26 to 36. He was considered a harsh ruler and incited trouble among his

Jewish subjects from the start. After he installed symbols of the Emperor the Jews complained to Rome that the emblems represented false idols and got Pilate to remove them. He turned around and issued coins with pagan symbols, and caused riots when he took money from the Jewish temples to build an aqueduct.

By the time the Jewish priests pressured him to execute Christ, some say, Pilate obliged them in order to avoid further confrontation. If so, his acquiescence didn't last long. In A.D. 36 Pilate finally was recalled by Rome to answer charges of cruelty and oppression after he massacred a group of Samaritans. Pilate arrived in Rome to find the Emperor Tiberius dead and Caligula in his place.

Soon after, according to the fourth-century writer Eusebius, Pilate committed suicide. It is unclear whether Caligula ordered Pilate to kill himself or whether Pilate did it in anticipation of the vicious Emperor's sentence. There is a legend that Pilate's body was thrown into the Tiber River, where it caused such great floods that he was pulled out of the water. Pilate then, according to legend, was thrown into the Rhone River, where he caused the same trouble. His body finally was put to rest, it is said, in a deep pool in the Alps.

Among some early Christians, Pilate's suicide was seen as repentance for his execution of Christ. They regarded both Pilate and his wife as saints. But in fact if Pilate actually ever thought twice about the role he played in the Bible, it has been lost to the ages.

PLINY THE ELDER
A.D. 23 or 24–August 24, A.D. 79

MUCH OF WHAT we know about daily life in the ancient Roman Empire we know because of Pliny the Elder's incurable curiosity. The historian and scientist couldn't take a bath without having some servant read to him so he could learn something new to record in his journals later in the day, perhaps as he was being shuttled about Rome on a chair so he could write along the way. As a Roman military officer, he traveled the known world and recorded its geography, physics, botany, anatomy, and its minutiae.

Some of his works, including *On Throwing a Javelin from Horseback*, have been lost. But his major achievement, his 37-volume *Historia Naturalis*, has survived. "My purpose," he begins humbly, "is to give a general description of everything that is known to exist throughout the earth." Among the 20,000-odd facts he recorded are: that you can prevent baldness by getting your hair cut right after a full moon; an herb that will keep dogs from barking at you; a cure for swollen lymph nodes, given here in its 17th-century translation. "If one come to a fig tree, bend a bough or branch thereof downward to the ground, and bearing up his head without stooping, reach and catch hold of a knot or joint with his teeth, and so bite it off, that no man see him when he is doing it." The volumes weren't all old wives' tales. In fact, some of Pliny's observations are the only surviving source of what the Romans knew, or thought they knew, at the time.

In A.D. 79 Pliny was confronted with perhaps the most extraordinary event he had ever had the chance to record. As an admiral in the Roman Navy, Pliny was stationed with his fleet at the northern end of the Bay of Naples. He was doing some reading one afternoon, following his midday nap, when his sister alerted him to a huge cloud of smoke rising over some nearby mountains. Parts of the cloud were white, but other plumes were dark and heavy, as if from an explosion.

Pliny ordered up his ship and sailed toward the smoke. He of course couldn't know that he was sailing toward Mount Vesuvius on the day its volcano spewed one of the most violent eruptions ever recorded, burying Pompeii and killing thousands. As the locals fled away from the mountain, inquisitive Pliny sailed toward it even as he was showered with stones from the eruption. The next morning, on the shore of the bay near the volcano, a choking cloud of sulphurous gas began to descend and darken the sky. His companions fled, but not Pliny, and he was asphyxiated. His body was recovered a day later, collapsed on the beach. His death, he would have been proud to know, did not go unrecorded. The account was written by his nephew, Pliny the Younger.

EDGAR ALLAN POE
January 19, 1809–October 7, 1849

THAT HIS LIFE was as tormented as his writing is part of the macabre appeal of the nightmarish tales of Edgar Allan Poe. His death could have been another of those stories.

"I was never *really* insane, except on occasions where my heart was touched," Poe wrote in a letter to his aunt, who was also his mother-in-law. He was writing after the death of his young wife, Virginia, his cousin, in 1847. It was for her that he wrote "For the moon never beams, without bringing me dreams of the beautiful Annabel Lee . . ."

Though Poe had had problems with alcohol and opium before, after his wife's death they grew worse, as did his hallucinations and paranoia. In 1848 he pursued women with a passion.
He visited a woman in Providence, Rhode Island, who had
written him about his work. He called on her daily for four
days, then proposed. He tried to convince another woman in
Lowell, Massachusetts, to leave her husband for him. He attempted suicide by swallowing a form of opium, but wound up
retching the poison on a sidewalk.

In 1849 he went back to where he had grown up, Richmond,
Virginia, to court a childhood sweetheart, now a widow. He
continued to suffer sudden mood changes, but after a delightful
party in September he proposed to Mrs. Sarah Elmira Royster
Shelton and she accepted. He told her he had to go to New
York City to tie up some business, and early the next morning,
September 27, he boarded a steamboat for Baltimore, where he
would catch the train north.

Six days later, in the early Wednesday afternoon of October 3, Poe was discovered lying in a Baltimore street by a printer
for the Baltimore *Sun* who knew him. Poe was wearing a torn
black coat and ill-fitting trousers that probably were not his
own, and a tattered hat lay next to him. In a hospital, Poe
wandered in and out of consciousness, mumbling and occasionally bursting out mad shouts. But he was never coherent enough
to remember, or say, what had happened during those six missing days. Sunday, October 7, he died. The cause of death was
presumed to be alcoholism, but historians have speculated that
Poe may have suffered from a disease not known at the time,
such as diabetes or a brain tumor.

Poe's funeral drew four mourners, as his relatives in the area
considered him the same kind of alcoholic disgrace as his father.
Partly because of his erratic behavior, Poe was not well liked
in the literary community. One of the more charitable reports
of his death came from the *Journal of Commerce*. That obituary
said, "We hope he has found his rest, for he needed it."

JACKSON POLLOCK
January 28, 1912–August 11, 1956

COMBINE THE brooding power of Hemingway and the jeans, T-shirt, and cigarette-dangling of James Dean, and you'll have a rough sketch of abstract painter Jackson Pollock. Born on a Cody, Wyoming, sheep ranch, the handsome and athletic Pollock brought a violent intensity to the New York art world with his "controlled accident" style of painting. His replaced brush strokes with a series of splatters, spills, and drippings so radically different from what everyone else was doing that by 1949 he was anointed the leading painter of his generation. Renowned arts patron Peggy Guggenheim called him "the greatest painter since Picasso."

Pollock had a harder time controlling what happened off the canvas. "Painting is no problem," he often said. "The problem is what to do when you're not painting." A heavy drinker since he was a surveyor near the Grand Canyon at the age of 15, Pollock was treated for alcoholism from the time he was 25 and received extensive psychiatric counseling throughout his adult life. All the acclaim and attention only made him more self-conscious, almost to the point of artistic paralysis. Even his studio near East Hampton, Long Island, no longer was a refuge, as many artists followed Pollock to the area. By the early 1950s he was downing beer all day long with an occasional shot of whiskey. The painter was in a series of "uncontrolled" accidents on Long Island, the most serious of which occurred in 1952 when his Cadillac left the road while he was making a turn and he hit a tree.

In 1956, 44-year-old Pollock was involved in one of his many affairs, with 25-year-old artist's model Ruth Kligman. That August, Pollock's wife had gone to Europe to allow the couple some time apart, but Pollock was supposed to join her in a few weeks. Kligman went out to Pollock's home near East Hampton the second weekend in August, bringing along a friend, Bronx beautician Edith Metzger. The three of them went out Saturday night, August 11, to attend a charity concert.

They went to dinner, then, instead of going to the concert, for some reason drove back toward Pollock's home on Fireplace Road. At about 10 P.M., just a few hundred yards from his house, Pollock missed a sharp curve and lost control of his car. The green 1950 Oldsmobile convertible swiped an embankment, then bounced across the road and skidded through the brush before hitting four trees and flipping upside down. Kligman's friend was found dead, forced by the crash into the trunk of the car. Kligman was thrown from the car and seriously injured. Pollock also was thrown and hit his head against a tree, killing him instantly.

CHARLES PONZI
1877–January 18, 1949

CRIME DIDN'T PAY for Charles Ponzi—no matter how hard or how often he tried. His biggest scam was in Boston in 1920 when he promised to "Double your money in 90 days," or gain you "50 percent in 45 days." Eager investors—businessmen as well as widows and children—sent him more than $15 million in just a few months. When his cashboxes got full, the five-foot-tall Italian immigrant stuffed money in his desks, then in wastebaskets. The profits from his miracle scheme were supposed to come from the purchase of International Postal Union coupons throughout the world, with an immediate gain from fluctuating exchange rates.

Needless to say, this collapsed. It turned out the entire issue of postal coupons was never more than $500,000 a year. Ponzi began paying earlier investors with the new money that came in, and by the time he was arrested and charged with mail fraud he had $4 million in assets and $7 million in debt. He served only four months in prison on the federal charge, but when he got out, Massachusetts sentenced him to seven to nine years for larceny. Out on bail, Ponzi got involved in a bogus Florida land deal that earned him another year in jail. Meanwhile, he jumped bail and was captured in New Orleans. Ponzi also was convicted of smuggling aliens across the Canadian border, and in Canada for forgery. After he served all his time, Ponzi was deported to Italy in 1934. Before World War II he went to Brazil, where he taught English and received Brazilian unemployment compensation.

Ponzi's health failed in the 1940s. He was partly blind in his right eye, his arteries hardened, and a blood clot formed, leaving him unable to move his left arm and leg. But even as an invalid, the swindler had fond memories. He said in 1948 that he had once planned to bilk the Soviet Union out of $2 billion by promising to smuggle gold to the country, then renege on the deal. "What a joke on the Communists that would have been!" he said with a grin.

But Ponzi never got his chance. The next year he died of the blood clot in his brain in a hospital charity ward in Rio de Janeiro. According to *The New York Times*, "He was flanked in the ward by an old man with a hacking cough and an aged Negro who spent most of his time staring quietly at the ceiling." Ponzi's burial was paid for with $75 he had managed to save from his Brazilian pension.

COLE PORTER
June 9, 1892–October 15, 1964

IF LIFE is a party, Cole Porter was the perfect host. His songs, like "Night and Day," "Begin the Beguine," and "You're the Top," were urbane and witty, and so was he. He furnished his home on the Left Bank in Paris with platinum wallpaper and zebra-skin chairs. One of his parties featured fifty gondoliers and a troupe of high-wire acrobats. Porter wrote songs for Broadway and Hollywood while sailing on round-the-world cruises and jaunts down the Rhine and he claimed he could work anywhere. "I've done lots of work at dinner, sitting between two bores," the trim, small, well-tailored man said drolly. "I can feign listening beautifully."

Porter made it all seem so easy, like mixing martinis. But the party crashed early. In 1937, while riding on a Long Island estate, Porter was thrown from his horse, which then fell on top of his right leg. As the horse frantically tried to stand, it fell again, crushing Porter's left leg as well. The injuries were so severe that both legs nearly had to be amputated. As it was, the accident left the 45-year-old composer in constant, great pain. He tried to mask it, naming his plaster-casted legs Geraldine and Josephine and joking about what he thought was a temporary faux pas.

In fact, the composer never really recovered. Over the next twenty years Porter underwent more than thirty operations to keep his legs alive and reduce the sharp pains. He developed a bone-marrow infection, but ultimately was able to walk again with braces. In between—and during—his medical treatments Porter also created some of his best work. From 1939 to 1944 he wrote five hit Broadway shows, often sitting at his piano in his wheelchair. The biggest success of his career, *Kiss Me Kate*, came in 1948. Even in the 1950s, when he was in and out of the hospital more frequently, Porter wrote the film classics *High Society* and *Silk Stockings*. Socially, as well, Porter maintained his charm, hosting elegant, sought-after dinner parties and riding on the arms of his valets into the theater and affairs hosted by others.

But in 1958, Porter's right leg was amputated almost at the hip, and he stopped writing and refused to appear in public. The once bon vivant became almost a recluse, traveling quietly from his memorabilia-filled nine-room apartment at the Waldorf in New York to a 350-acre weekend estate in the Berkshires and a summer home in California. Still, the composer kept his hair dyed and spent a daily session under a sun lamp. He continued to host small dinner parties, but as he substituted martinis for his own plate even some of his close friends began declining his invitations.

The 72-year-old Porter entered a Santa Monica hospital in October 1964 with a bladder infection and on October 13 doctors successfully removed a kidney stone. Two days later Porter's heart stopped beating and he died. His body was racked with severe pneumonia, degenerated kidneys, hardening of the arteries, and emphysema. Finally the host called an end to a party long since over.

FRANCIS GARY POWERS
August 17, 1929–August 1, 1977

UNTIL HIS U-2 airplane was shot down over the Soviet Union on May 1, 1960, Gary Powers would hardly have fitted the description of a classic cloak-and-dagger spy. But once he was captured, publicly tried, and sentenced to ten years in a Soviet prison, pilot Powers was thrust into the center of one of the most explosive espionage events of the Cold War. Soviet Premier Khrushchev abruptly canceled a summit meeting with President Eisenhower after the Soviets recovered photographic and electronic surveillance equipment from the downed plane.

Powers was in fact merely a technician, a CIA staffer who overflew Soviet military installations on command. In a few years, the job would be performed by satellites. Powers had been flying a routine mission at 60,000 feet—thought to be out of Soviet firing range—when his plane was sent out of control by a missile over the city of Sverdlovsk. Despite the violent spinning and quick plunge of the aircraft, Powers managed to eject himself before the plane crashed and parachuted safely down to awaiting Soviet officials. After spending less than two years in a cell with a Soviet dissident, Powers was freed in exchange for a high-ranking Soviet spy.

He returned home to less than a hero's welcome. While a Congressional investigation praised his actions and his loyalty, hard-liners said it had been his duty to swallow a poison pin he carried on every mission and thus prevent capture. Powers, a soft-spoken man, said later he had trouble reentering American life knowing that some thought he should have committed suicide.

Powers returned to the CIA only briefly. He divorced his first wife to marry an agent and kicked around at various jobs, finally becoming a traffic-watch helicopter pilot at a Los Angeles radio station. He later flew for an L.A. television station and was returning to the airport after filming a typical hot-summer-afternoon brushfire when he crashed near a Little League baseball field in the San Fernando Valley suburb of Encino. Both Powers and the cameraman were killed. Powers had radioed ahead to the airport, saying his helicopter was low on fuel and requesting priority clearance to land, just before he crashed.

Powers was buried at Arlington National Cemetery, where grounds are reserved for those who lost their lives in the service of the United States.

ELVIS PRESLEY
January 8, 1935–August 16, 1977

THE ONLY THING remarkable about the death of Elvis Presley
is that it didn't seem to slow up his career at all. What with
repackaged collections of his hit songs, tours of Graceland, Elvis
conventions and club meetings, and paraphernalia like ashtrays
and combs, "Elvis Inc." makes more money after he died than
some years when he was alive. It probably isn't much of an
exaggeration to say that, of all the superstars who have died,
Elvis's death—the when and how of it—made the least difference to the legend.

After all, his leading edge in rock 'n' roll was dulled almost
twenty years before, when he was drafted in 1958. But his following was so fanatical that when a sagging "Elvis the Pelvis"
labored his way through the same old concerts in the 1970s,
doped on dozens of pills, way overweight, and dripping with
sequins and sweat, they didn't care. Hell, when he complained
of stomach pains during one concert, fans in the front rows
waved antacids for him to swallow. Even after the press turned
against him, roasting his concerts and publishing photographs
of the 250-pound performer bulging out of his white, gold-
studded jumpsuit, his shows still regularly sold out before he
hit the road.

On August 16, 1977, Elvis was scheduled to leave for another
sold-out tour of the East Coast. At 10:30 the night before, his
dentist paid him a visit at Graceland in Memphis and filled two
cavities. At 4 A.M., partly because of his insomnia and mostly
because of his years of addiction to prescription medications that
confused his system, Elvis woke up a couple of friends and
played racquetball. About 6 A.M. he retired with his fiancée,
Ginger Alden. She fell asleep, but Elvis swallowed another

round of pills, put on his pajamas, and took a book to read in his cushiony chair in his lavish bathroom. When Alden woke up at 2 P.M. she found the 42-year-old singer slumped in a fetal position on the floor, where he had fallen out of his chair. Neither his Graceland aides nor the hospital staff could revive him.

The autopsy indicated that Elvis had died of an erratic heartbeat. Later, more thorough tests found ten drugs in his blood, including codeine, morphine, and Quaaludes. The levels were enough to kill most people, but Elvis's long addiction had so increased his tolerance that doctors said the drugs did not directly cause his death. His personal doctor later was tried and acquitted of illegally prescribing drugs after it was learned that he had prescribed 5,000 pills for the star in the last seven months of his life, 19,000 in the last two and a half years.

But Elvis's fans didn't much care about those details. Within an hour of the announcement of his death that afternoon, more than 1,000 people crowded around the gates of Graceland. By the next day, when Elvis's reconstructed, post-autopsied body was laid out in his mansion, some 80,000 had made the pilgrimage. Hundreds fainted, one man had a heart attack, a woman went into labor, and the National Guard was called out. T-shirts were sold outside the gates for $5.00.

That, of course, was only the beginning. The near-riot crowds were compared to those who swooned over the death of Valentino in the 1920s. But even the great silent screen lover never had anything like the 200 Elvis impersonators who performed at the Statue of Liberty celebration in 1986. There have been scores of biographies, to be sure, including accounts by his uncle, his karate instructor, and one of his hospital nurses. The list goes on and on. Suffice it to say the king may be dead, but long lives the king indeed.

SIR WALTER RALEIGH
1554–October 29, 1618

SIR WALTER RALEIGH, whose name is associated with tobacco and the city in North Carolina, actually never set foot in North America. The British nobleman did organize some of the early settlements in the New World in the 1580s, but none of the colonies he supported survived. No, in his own time, Raleigh's American endeavors were overshadowed by his activities closer to home. (He is, in fact, credited with popularizing tobacco and potatoes in England.) Handsome and dashing, Raleigh was Queen Elizabeth's "favorite." He reportedly caught the Queen's eye by laying his cloak over a muddy puddle for her. She lavished him with expensive gifts, including many revenue-generating licenses, and he flaunted her affection by wearing big jewels, even on his shoes. Outside the Queen's circles, however, Raleigh, who was more than a little arrogant, was hated as an upstart.

That left him in a very bad position when Queen Elizabeth died in 1603. Already Raleigh had damaged his relationship with the Queen by marrying one of her "maids of honor," but now, under James I, his limited charm turned unlucky. He was stripped of his titles and sent to the Tower, accused of plotting to overthrow the King. Raleigh was imprisoned for thirteen years. Finally he negotiated his release in 1616 by promising the King that he could find gold in South America. He had led a similar unsuccessful mission twenty-two years earlier, but this time Raleigh was desperate. "If I bring them not to a mountain of gold and silver ore," he vowed, "let the commander have commission to cut off my head."

Raleigh got no financial support from the crown and had to invest what was left of his fortune to launch the voyage. Once under way, the ships ran into a hurricane, then later were stranded for forty windless days in the doldrums. Many of the crewmen died of scurvy and fever, and when they finally reached Guiana in South America, Raleigh himself was too sick to press inland toward the gold deposits. Instead, his assistant led the exploration and promptly ruined it by burning a Spanish settlement. They found no gold.

Faced with the prospect of returning to England empty-handed, Raleigh implored his men to help him attack some foreign vessels at sea so he could at least take home some booty. But his men refused, and Raleigh slunk home with nothing in June 1618. He was not arrested immediately, so Raleigh began writing an apology and a long explanation that he hoped would save his head. When it became clear that that wouldn't be good enough, Raleigh secretly arranged for boats to slip him down the Thames and off to France. But one of the boat owners, bribed by the government, betrayed him.

On October 29, Raleigh was led to the scaffold, where he suddenly became more humble and more quotable than ever before in his life. "Of a long time my course was a course of vanity," Raleigh told the crowd. "I have been a seafaring man, a soldier, and a courtier, and in the temptations of the least of these there is enough to overthrow a good mind, and a good man." As he lay his head on the chopping block, someone said he ought to face east. "What matter how the head lie," Raleigh replied, "so the heart be right?"

Raleigh refused to be blindfolded. He felt the sharp edge of the ax and said to the executioner, "Dost thou think that I am afraid of it? This is that that will cure all sorrows." Finally, Raleigh lay against the block. The axman hesitated, and Raleigh demanded, "What dost thou fear? Strike, man, strike!" It took two blows. Raleigh's remains were turned over to his wife. His body was buried in a London church, but his wife had his head embalmed. She kept it near her in a red leather bag for the last twenty-nine years of her life.

GRIGORY YEFIMOVICH RASPUTIN
1872–December 30, 1916

THE SUPERMARKET tabloids couldn't have written a better history of Rasputin. This wandering miracle healer, who got much of the blame for the fall of czarist Russia, inspired books with titles such as *Rasputin, Saint or Devil*, *Rasputin: Prophet, Libertine, Plotter*, and *Rasputin, the Rascal Monk*.

Rasputin, a semiliterate Siberian, preached that the best way to be near God was to intensely desire forgiveness. And the best way to intensely desire forgiveness was to sin intensely. Often his religious sessions would turn into wild, drunken sexual orgies. His big break came when he performed his healing powers on the hemophiliac son of Czar Nicholas II and his wife, Alexandra. Rasputin became, unofficially, the most powerful man in the empire outside of the royal family. Even Czar Nicholas was advised to comb his hair with Rasputin's comb before making any decisions.

Rasputin's power angered many in the palace at St. Petersburg, among them Prince Felix Yussupov, husband of the Czar's niece, and Vladimir Purishkevich, a conservative adviser to the

Czar. Yussupov invited Rasputin to his house at midnight on December 29, 1916. Rasputin, who knew there were plots against him, apparently saw no danger from this young man, whom he called "the Little One." Besides, Rasputin hoped to meet Yussupov's beautiful wife, as he had met so many other noblemen's wives.

Yussupov had prepared the basement room of his home with bottles of wine and chocolate cake that contained potassium cyanide. He also sprinkled cyanide in the wineglasses for good measure. Yussupov said later that Rasputin ate and drank freely but showed no ill effects. Either he was lying or Rasputin was correct in his claim that his experience with heavy drinking had given him a thick stomach lining. Yussupov, understandably nervous, went upstairs, where his co-conspirators gave him a revolver and told him to finish the job.

Back downstairs, Rasputin finally said he felt ill and his throat was burning. Rasputin suggested they go see the gypsies, "With God in thought, but with mankind in the flesh." Yussupov pointed to a crystal cross and said, "Grigory Yefimovich, you had better say a prayer before it." Rasputin glanced at Yussupov, then looked at the cross as Yussupov shot him in the back. Rasputin groaned loudly, then collapsed on his back with his eyes closed. The co-conspirators rushed in, and a doctor nervously pronounced that the Czar's closest adviser had been pierced through the heart and was dead.

Everyone left, but a short while later, well aware of Rasputin's legendary mystical powers, Yussupov and Purishkevich went back downstairs just to make sure they had completed their task. Yussupov shook the body, which at first remained still. Then an eyelid twitched. Then Rasputin rose to his feet and tore an epaulette from Yussupov's shoulder. The two conspirators raced up the stairs, locking the basement door behind them. Rasputin crawled after them and burst through the door and out into a courtyard. Purishkevich fired his revolver, missing twice before hitting Rasputin twice more, causing him to collapse. Purishkevich continued the assault by kicking the bloody body in the head while Yussupov beat it with a steel rod.

Still not satisfied, they bound Rasputin's hands, loaded his body into a car, and took him to the Neva River, where they dumped him through a hole in the ice. Rasputin did not resurface. But it turns out that their last efforts were not in vain. After the body was recovered, an autopsy revealed that Rasputin had not died of poison or gunshot wounds, but from drowning. The cold water, in fact, apparently had revived him once more, because one hand was free from the ropes.

Rasputin was buried in the Imperial Park as the royal family watched. But he was not allowed to rest there either. After the revolution a few months later, the Bolsheviks dug him up and burned the coffin on a bonfire.

In keeping with his predictive powers, Rasputin had written a letter earlier in the month he was murdered, saying, "I feel that I shall leave life before January 1. . . . If I am murdered by nobles, for twenty-five years they will not wash their hands from my blood. Brothers will kill brothers . . . and for twenty-five years there will be no nobles in the country."

Rasputin may have had foresight, but even he was short-sighted.

GEORGE REEVES
April 6, 1914–June 16, 1959

"FASTER THAN a Speeding Bullet" was a catchy phrase for a comic-book hero, but to George Reeves, the actor who played Superman on television, it was a death sentence. In standard Hollywood fashion, Reeves was a well-trained actor who got no satisfaction out of his blue-tights role that delighted children but didn't give him the respect he sought from adults. Yet until the 104-episode TV series that was syndicated from 1952 to 1957, the Iowa-born actor was probably best remembered as one of the Tarleton twins who vied to fetch dessert for Scarlett O'Hara in *Gone with the Wind*.

When *Superman* ended the six-foot-two-inch, broad-shouldered Reeves could find no one willing to cast him outside his superhero mold. On Monday, June 15, 1959, Reeves had gone to bed in his Los Angeles home. His fiancée, Lenore Lemmon, and writer friend Robert Condon also were asleep in the house. At 2:30 A.M. two friends dropped by and woke everyone up. Reeves was angered by the lateness of the visit, but soon he apologized and said, "I'm tired. I'm going to bed," and went upstairs.

Lemmon, who was to marry Reeves on Friday, said, "He's going to shoot himself." The others thought she was joking. Then Lemmon said, "He's opening the drawer to get the gun." Then they heard a shot. "See there—I told you!" Lemmon said.

Reeves was found dead on his bed, a bullet from a .30-caliber Luger pistol in his head. He left no note.

ZACHARY SMITH REYNOLDS
November 5, 1911–July 6, 1932

INITIALLY THE DEATH of Zachary Smith Reynolds, heir to the R. J. Reynolds tobacco fortune, was uniformly reported as a suicide. After a big party at the family's 600-acre estate in Winston-Salem, North Carolina, on July 5, 1932, the 20-year-old had walked out onto the sleeping porch and fired a .32-

caliber bullet into his head, officials said. He died a few hours later without regaining consciousness. His new wife, Libby Holman, the famous Broadway chanteuse who introduced the song "Body and Soul," was said to be bedridden with grief.

Barely mentioned was the fact that one official, Sheriff Transou Scott, said his investigation wasn't finished yet. The sheriff got more attention three days later when he ordered Holman and the heir's lifelong friend Albert Walker held for questioning in what now was a possible murder investigation. And before Reynolds was even in the ground his death became one of the most sensational cases of the decade.

The events of the evening began to be pieced together by a coroner's jury. Reynolds and his 26-year-old wife had hosted a raucous dinner party at which everyone got very drunk. Guests told of nude swimming and various couplings, possibly including Holman and Walker. The tall, raven-haired Holman, who was especially flirtatious that night, at one point stood drunkenly on a tree stump and, wearing revealingly torn pajamas, sang her famous torch songs. Reynolds clearly was upset by his wife's behavior. It was after midnight when the few remaining guests, who were bedding down for the night, heard a shot and then heard Holman say, somewhat disgustedly, "He's shot himself!" An ambulance was called, but Holman and Walker, both still drunk, dragged Reynolds's body into a car and drove to the hospital.

Holman, who testified before the coroner's jury from her bed, said she didn't remember anything about that night. In fact, she didn't remember anything from Monday night, two nights before, until after the party, when she said she woke up in a strange bed, saw her husband with a pistol, heard him say "Libby," and then saw him shoot himself. She said it was the first time she had ever blanked out like that. Holman also testified that Reynolds was a "sensitive person with an inferiority complex." She said he had threatened to kill himself several times and often held a gun to his head. Recently, she said, he had been upset because he thought he had hurt Holman's Broad-

way career and because he had "suffered a lapse of virility."
Holman produced suicide notes that Reynolds had written as a
teenager and testified that a strange entry in the family Bible—
"Born November 5, 1911, died shortly thereafter of old age"—
had been written by her late husband a few days before he shot
himself.

All of that made it reasonable to conclude that Reynolds had
indeed committed suicide. But it didn't match the evidence.
Doctors said the bullet had entered above Reynolds's right ear
and traveled sharply downward, exiting below his left ear. It
was thought that Reynolds was left-handed, so it didn't make
sense for him to hold his gun in his right hand. But more puz-
zling, the angle of the wound made it practically impossible for
him to have pulled the trigger himself. Further, doctors had
found no powder burns to indicate that the barrel of the gun
had pressed against Reynolds's head.

The coroner's jury didn't charge Holman or Walker. But it
did decide on July 11 that the fatal bullet had been fired by
"a person or persons unknown," which meant someone other
than Reynolds. Holman left town as soon as she was released.
A few weeks later she surrendered in black mourning clothes
after a grand jury indicted her and Walker for first-degree murder, punishable by the electric chair. Because the grand jury
met in private it has never been clear what evidence led them
to charge the pair.

It also has never become certain why the prosecutor abruptly
dropped the charges two months later. There was speculation
that the Reynolds family, which lorded over Winston-Salem and
already had had its share of scandals, pressed for the charges
to be dropped to avoid a messy trial. But the fact was that apparently no one witnessed the shooting except Holman, and
much of what she said about Reynolds's suicidal tendencies was
confirmed by others. The case quietly faded after the Reynolds
family settled the heir's estate by giving Holman $500,000 and
providing $2 million for her unborn son, Christopher, even
though some believed the baby wasn't Zachary's. Had Reynolds

lived to 28 he would have received the bulk of his inheritance, $20 million.

Even after the publicity died down Holman's career was never as bright as it had been. Her second husband, depressed over his brother's death in World War II, overdosed on sleeping pills in 1944. Christopher, Holman's and probably Reynolds's son, was killed climbing Mount Whitney in California in 1950. Holman, who drank heavily, took up with Montgomery Clift, the brooding movie star who drank himself to death in 1966. And in 1971 Holman was found dead in the garage of her home in Connecticut, asphyxiated by carbon monoxide fumes from her car.

ARTHUR RIMBAUD

October 20, 1854–November 10, 1891

"WITH INSTINCTIVE rhythms I have invented a poetry that touches all the senses," wrote French poet Arthur Rimbaud. "I have noted the inexpressible. I have deliberately sought hallucination. I consider sacred the disorder of my mind." Like a modern rebellious teenager, Rimbaud at the age of 15 broke all the rules and went down in history as one of the greatest French poets of the late 19th century. With works like *Sonnet des Voyelles, Une Saison en Enfer*, and *Illuminations*, Rimbaud would be called a master of Symbolism and one of the cornerstones of Surrealism. All this though his literary career ended when he was 19.

The young writer's disorder and rebelliousness stretched beyond his poems. The son of an army captain who abandoned his family when Rimbaud was six, the poet began running away from his strict mother when he was 16 and rarely returned for the rest of his life. He spent a couple of years traveling Europe with Paul Verlaine, an older French poet who divorced his wife in favor of Rimbaud. Their relationship ended when Verlaine drunkenly shot the still teenage boy in the wrist. Afterward, Rimbaud completed *Une Saison en Enfer* (*A Season in Hell*) and never wrote again.

Rimbaud wandered Europe on his own for another five years, working on farms and in a rock quarry, before he traveled to Ethiopia as a trader. He spent more than a decade there, buying African goods and gunrunning. He wrote no poems and wouldn't say why. Finally, in his mid-30s, Rimbaud talked of saving enough money to return to France and find a wife. He had planned to make the trip in 1890 but ended up putting it off.

By the next February it was too late. The 36-year-old man developed a pain in his right knee, which he ignored for several weeks until his entire leg was so swollen that he couldn't walk. Finally, in April, he hired sixteen men to carry him on a stretcher across 300 kilometers of desert to where he could board a boat and get to a doctor. After an agonizing two-week journey on land, Rimbaud sailed for three days to Aden in northern Africa. Doctors there sent him to Marseille, where his leg was amputated.

He returned to his mother's home in northern France to recuperate, but his condition worsened and his relationship with his mother did not improve. After a month Rimbaud returned in August to the Marseille hospital, where doctors finally diagnosed cancer. Cared for by his sister, Rimbaud weakened and grew paralyzed. As he lay dying he described hallucinations to his sister that were reminiscent of poems he had written almost twenty years before. On November 9, barely conscious, he told his sister to write a letter to a steamship company. "I am entirely paralyzed and so I wish to embark early," Rimbaud dictated. "Please let me know at what time I should be carried on board." He died the next day.

PAUL ROBESON
April 9, 1898–January 23, 1976

I heard a Black Man sing last night,
I heard the thunder roar.
I heard a man, a towering man;
And I never can hear more.

Poet Earl Conrad was moved by more than Paul Robeson's voice. Because when Robeson sang he didn't just make music. He made a statement. Robeson will forever be remembered for his version of "Ol' Man River," the song that, in the musical *Show Boat*, is sung by a stereotype lazy black man but which Robeson transformed into a battle cry. "But I keeps laughing instead of crying, I must keep fighting until I'm dying," boomed the six-foot-three, 240-pound former All-American football player who also had a law degree from Columbia University, and people around the world were moved.

Many, however, moved against him. When the Cold War set in, Robeson's outspoken support of civil rights and his previous trips to the Soviet Union overshadowed his theatrical career, which had flourished since the 1920s. He had earned $100,000 in 1947. But by 1952 he made just $6,000 as concert halls refused to book him. In 1949 an outdoor concert in Peekskill, New York, was disrupted by violent bands of anti-Communist agitators.

Robeson repeatedly denied he was a member of the Communist Party and stubbornly refused to soften his stand. When he testified before a subcommittee of the House Un-American Activities Committee in 1956, he was asked why he didn't just move to the Soviet Union. "Because my father was a slave," Robeson snapped. "And my people died to build this country, and I am going to stay right here and have a part of it, just like you. And no Fascist-minded people will drive me from it. Is that clear?"

After finally winning an eight-year battle to retrieve his passport, which had been revoked because of his Soviet sympathies, Robeson left the country almost immediately in 1958. He sang in Europe, then celebrated New Year's Eve at the Kremlin. He had found his cheering audiences again. But soon after his concert tour frequently was interrupted by bouts of the flu and dizziness. He finally was forced to stop performing after a last major tour of Australia and New Zealand in 1960.

There was nothing seriously wrong with Robeson physically, but friends believed the strain of his struggle finally caught up with the 60-year-old man. Robeson spent many months in Soviet hospitals, where he suffered a nervous breakdown in 1962. The following year, frail, severely depressed and bitter, Robeson returned to the United States and settled in Harlem. After his wife died in 1965 he moved in with his sister to live in a twelve-room house in Philadelphia. There he became a virtual recluse. He refused almost all visitors and would spend days upstairs in his room in his pajamas, with the blinds drawn throughout the house.

Over the next decade he was hospitalized several times because of his nervous condition. On December 28, 1975, Robeson suffered a stroke, and more than three weeks later, at the age of 77, he died in a Philadelphia hospital.

By then, at least, his reputation had been restored. He declined to appear at a Carnegie Hall celebration in 1973 honoring him on his seventy-fifth birthday, though the event must have given him a certain sense of victory. "What I wanted to do I did," he wrote to acknowledge the invitation. "What I wanted to say I said, and now that ill health has compelled my retirement I have decided to let the record speak for itself." Although it had been eighteen years since his last American performance, and almost thirty years since the height of his fame, more than 5,000 attended his funeral in Harlem, mostly working-class blacks who, like Earl Conrad, had heard the black man sing.

JOHN D. ROCKEFELLER III
March 21, 1906–July 10, 1978

As MUCH AS it could be said of any member of the family, John D. Rockefeller III was unpretentious. His namesake grandfather had founded Standard Oil, and two of his brothers, governor Nelson and bank president David, were constantly in the spotlight. But the third John D. preferred to work quietly in the family business and a wide variety of philanthropies, such as the construction of Lincoln Center and the restoration of colonial Williamsburg. The oldest and most cautious of his generation, John D. III jokingly referred to himself as "unemployed." He eschewed limousines and often walked to work from his Beekman Place apartment in New York City or took a crosstown bus. At his weekend country estate in Westchester County, he enjoyed chopping wood and tending his rose bushes.

After one such day at Fieldwood Farms, as his estate was called, Rockefeller got a ride from his secretary in her 1965 Mustang so he could catch the local train for the trip back to Manhattan. They were about a mile from where Rockefeller and his brothers had grown up at the family's 3,200-acre estate in Pocantico Hills, driving along a curving stretch of the winding, shaded road shortly before 6 P.M., when they were hit head-on by a Volkswagen Dasher.

Driven by a 16-year-old honor student, the speeding car had veered into oncoming traffic and sideswiped another car before it plowed into the one in which Rockefeller was riding. The

72-year-old Rockefeller and the youth, the nephew of a U.S. ambassador, were killed instantly. Rockefeller's secretary was seriously injured.

MICHAEL ROCKEFELLER
May 18, 1938–November 19, 1961 (?)

As the son of Nelson Rockefeller and great-grandson of John D., Michael Rockefeller had every opportunity to enjoy a charmed, adventurous youth. He grew up at the family estate outside New York City, spent his summers in Puerto Rico or working on his father's ranch in Venezuela, and graduated from Harvard in 1960. Then, not quite ready to begin work at the offices of the family dynasty, Michael enlisted in the Army. Having enough of that after six months, he joined a group of friends on a filmmaking expedition to New Guinea.

"It's a desire to do something adventurous at a time when frontiers, in the real sense of the word, are disappearing," said the young Rockefeller, who was the crew's sound technician. New Guinea was certainly beyond the edge of civilization. There still were tribes on the South Pacific island that had never come in contact with modern man. Some tribes practiced cannibalism and head-hunting, and only recently had the Dutch colonial government succeeded in putting a stop to much of it. Rockefeller and his friends witnessed tribal battles during their six-month visit.

Rockefeller was so taken with New Guinea that within a week after he returned to New York in September 1961 he flew back to the island. This time he intended to collect artifacts for the Museum of Primitive Arts in New York, which his father had founded and of which he was a trustee. He returned to the southern coast of Dutch New Guinea, the "Asmat" coast, which was called by natives the "land of lapping death" because of the muddy rivers and swamps laden with sharks, crocodiles, and mosquitoes, and the turbulent tides from the Arafura Sea.

Within a month Rockefeller and his traveling companion, ethnologist René Wassing, had amassed a vast collection of primitive carvings, which the two men acquired by trading knives, tobacco, and cloth. Dutch officials were uneasy about Rockefeller's visit, particularly about his desire to get some of the decorated heads that had been trophies among the headhunting tribes. Rockefeller was offering ten steel hatchets for one head. One area administrator said tribesmen had asked permission to go head-hunting again, "for one evening only, please, sir."

Rockefeller seemed to relish the daily struggles of the primitive region. "Our living since our arrival has been out of a Marx Brothers movie," he wrote. He brushed off warnings from the missionaries about unfriendly tribes and the dangers of the natural environment. On November 18, against the advice of local officials, Rockefeller, Wassing, and two native guides set out from one outpost, Agats, on a 25-mile water journey to the village of Atsj. They traveled in a 40-foot catamaran, consisting of two dugout canoes lashed together to support a tin-roofed shelter where they stored their gear and artifacts. They had been warned that the boat was top-heavy because of the shelter and that the 18-horsepower motor was too small against the tides of the coast.

Three miles offshore, rough seas drenched the boat and killed the motor, leaving the four men helplessly tossed about by the tides. After the boat capsized the two native guides swam for shore, which was barely visible. Rockefeller and Wassing clung to the overturned boat throughout the night. When no help arrived the next morning Rockefeller decided he would swim for shore before they were swept into the coastal stream and carried farther out to sea. The six-foot-one, lean, strong swimmer stripped to his shorts, tied his much-needed glasses around his neck, and strapped on two gas cans as floats. He told Wassing, "I think I can make it," and dove in.

Eight hours later Wassing was rescued by a Dutch patrol boat 20 miles offshore. The two guides had made it safely to land, but it had taken them almost a day to walk 11 miles through the tropical jungle back to Agats. Rockefeller remained missing. A massive search was launched, employing Australian helicopters, Dutch ships, and more than 1,000 native canoes after tribesmen were offered "250 sticks of tobacco" if they found the young man.

Because of the remoteness of the search, it took three days for word to get to Michael's father, Nelson. The New York governor immediately flew 10,000 miles down to New Guinea with Michael's twin sister, Mary. For ten days the Asmat coast and seas were combed. The governor declined the aid of a U.S. Seventh Fleet aircraft carrier, but spent hours flying overhead with Mary in a DC-3, peering out the windows with binoculars for the son believed to be his closest. Finally, with no sign of Michael after ten days, Nelson Rockefeller held a· press conference for the sizable corps of reporters that had descended on the remote jungle. He said there was nothing more he could do there. Then he and Mary flew back to New York.

Michael Rockefeller was never seen again—at least not according to any confirmed report. A book published in 1972 told the story of a sailor who claimed he had seen Michael alive in 1968, held captive by a New Guinea tribe and suffering intense pain from never-treated broken legs. The book, *The Search for Michael Rockefeller* by Milt Machlin, made the case that Michael had been rescued by a friendly tribe only to be captured almost immediately during a battle with a rival tribe as revenge for an earlier death. Machlin had investigated on his own in New Guinea, but found no trace of the young heir.

NELSON ALDRICH ROCKEFELLER
July 8, 1908–January 26, 1979

ANY MAN whose birth was announced on the front page of *The New York Times*, who served every President since FDR except Kennedy, who sought the presidency three times and was Vice President under Ford and governor of New York for fifteen years certainly would expect to receive substantial attention when he died. What Nelson Rockefeller, also grandson of the founder of Standard Oil, probably didn't expect was the sloppiness of the event.

The first report, emblazoned with a three-column headline on the front page of *The New York Times* Saturday morning, announced that Rockefeller had died of a heart attack at 10:15 the night before while working at his desk on the fifty-sixth floor of 30 Rockefeller Plaza in midtown Manhattan. According to longtime family spokesman Hugh Morrow, Rockefeller had had dinner with his family at their Fifth Avenue duplex before he went to the office. A bodyguard had been unable to revive him, Morrow said.

Later Saturday, Morrow recanted his first statements. Rockefeller hadn't died in his main office but in his town house at 13 West Fifty-fourth Street, which adjoined another of his offices. And he hadn't suffered the heart attack at 10:15 P.M. but after 11 P.M., just before 911 emergency medical services was called at 11:16. Morrow said police had found Rockefeller lying unconscious on the living-room floor. Also present, he said, were a bodyguard and a 31-year-old woman with whom Rockefeller had been working, Megan Marshack.

That was grist for Sunday's newspapers. By Monday, along with solemn accounts of the funeral, they were publishing the transcript of Marshack's frantic call to 911. "It's death! It's immediate! Please!" the transcript said. Marshack, the stories said, was 25, not 31. She had been a reporter for the Associated Press before joining Rockefeller's staff in Washington in 1975 when he was Vice President. She was one of the few who had been kept on when he returned to private life in New York in 1977. Marshack and Rockefeller had been working on a book about his modern art collection when he died, the stories said.

The revisions continued. It turned out Rockefeller's heart attack did occur at 10:15 P.M.—an hour before 911 was called—and Marshack hadn't made the call. A voice analysis of the tape confirmed that help had been summoned by Ponchitta Pierce, hostess of a weekend NBC television show who owned a co-op in the same building as Marshack a few doors from Rockefeller's town house. Pierce had gone to the town house after Marshack called her, then returned home after calling 911.

Also it turned out there had been no bodyguard in Rockefeller's town house, only Marshack and the former Vice President. Although Morrow said Marshack was wearing a long black hostess gown, the New York *Daily News* called it a housecoat and said there were no papers to indicate that they had been working on a book, only food and wine on a table.

Whether there was more to the story or not was never published, though it certainly has been the subject of much speculation and rumor. The final note came at the reading of the will. Rockefeller had forgiven a $45,000 loan he had given to Marshack so she could buy her co-op.

J. I. RODALE
1899–June 7, 1971

JEROME IRVING RODALE was a health-food nut before the term was invented. He began extolling the virtues of chemical-free foods in 1942 when he founded *Organic Farming and Gardening* magazine. It lost money for sixteen years, but in the 1960s the ecology movement finally caught up with Rodale and made him rich. With other magazines, including *Prevention* and *Compost Science*, Rodale Press grew into a major publishing company.

The son of an immigrant grocer on the Lower East Side of New York City, Rodale was a cheerful eccentric. He swallowed seventy food supplement tablets a day and spent ten to 20 minutes a day under a machine that gave off short wave radio waves that he said boosted the body's supply of electricity. As he lived and exercised on his 65-acre farm in Emmaus, Pennsylvania, Rodale welcomed wandering youths of the sixties generation who stopped by to learn his organic techniques.

By the end of the decade Rodale had gained national attention as a leader of the health-food movement. In 1971 he was featured on the cover of *The New York Times* Sunday magazine, which called him the "Guru of the Organic Food Cult." "I'm going to live to be 100," said the *Newsweek*-dubbed "Don Quixote of the Compost." "Unless I'm run down by a sugar-crazed taxi driver."

The day after the *Times* story was published Rodale appeared as a guest on a taping of the *Dick Cavett Show* in New York. Clearly relishing his new legitimacy, Rodale repeated his old themes, opposing wheat, milk, and sugar. The publisher had just finished explaining the benefits of bone meal when he slumped in his chair, dead of a heart attack. ABC substituted a rerun when the show was scheduled to air.

PAUL ROGERS
1936–September 13, 1984

AFTER BEING rejected by ten publishers, Paul Rogers finally got his first novel published in 1982 and found it widely praised. *Saul's Book* is the story of Sinbad the Sailor, a Times Square male hustler who is abused all his life until he meets Saul, a middle-aged intellectual who becomes the boy's lover and protector. The book was graphic. A reviewer in *The New York Times* said, "It offers scenes of degradation so devastating that to read them makes you tremble. To have written them must have been excruciating, and to have lived them nearly unspeakable."

Rogers offered little insight into whether there was any truth in his fiction. He wouldn't tell even his publisher about his past and simply wrote on the book jacket that he was a schoolteacher and former social worker. "With my love and devotion, now and forever," Rogers dedicated the book to Chris, a boy he had adopted three years before. *Saul's Book* sold so well that it was issued in paperback in 1984.

On September 23 of that year Rogers was found beaten to death in the closet of his apartment in the Rego Park neighborhood of Queens. He had been dead about ten days. Police immediately arrested 19-year-old Chris and Nicholas Ondrizek, 27, a drifter who also had been living in the apartment for a few weeks. The two men admitted to police that on September 13, as Rogers lay drunk on his bed, Ondrizek had clubbed the 48-year-old author with a two-by-four board and then covered the body with a sheet and put it in the closet. Ondrizek burned the wooden plank in the building's incinerator. Chris was unable to help Ondrizek because he had a mangled right leg from a suicide attempt earlier that year. The two said they took Rogers's wallet and bank card, then began raiding his $37,000 bank account to buy drugs. In October 1985 both men pleaded guilty to murder, conspiracy, and robbery.

In Rogers's book, Sinbad the hustler says, "I gotta rip everything out of me—weakness, pity, sentiment—so that there's nothing left for somebody else to come along and rip out."

WILL ROGERS
November 4, 1879–August 15, 1935

"IT LOOKS LIKE the only way you can get any publicity on your death is to be killed in a plane. It's no novelty to be killed in an auto anymore." Will Rogers had the knack to turn anything into a joke and get away with it. Part Cherokee, Rogers took his lariat tricks from Indian territory in Oklahoma to Broadway, where his shy grin and classic drawl—"All I know is what I read in the papers"—made him the most popular folk hero of his time. He wrote a nationally syndicated newspaper column starting in 1926 and would file it six times a week no matter where he happened to be—which was likely to be anywhere in the world.

In August 1935, Rogers happened to be in Alaska, casually flying around the territory with Wiley Post, a famous globe-trotting aviator. "Was you ever driving around in a car and not knowing or caring where you went?" Rogers wrote in his column August 12. "Well, that's what Wiley and I are doing. We sure are having a great time. If we hear of whales or polar bears in the Arctic, or a big herd of caribou or reindeer, we fly over and see it." The two men also had plans to fly over the Arctic to Siberia and on to Moscow to explore the possibility of making it a regular air route. But they kept that mission secret. "Me and Wiley are just a couple of Oklahoma boys trying to get along," said Rogers, who so loved to fly—he said it was safer than riding a train—that he already had logged over 300,000 miles at a time when air travel was relatively new.

The two men took off from Fairbanks on August 15 for a 500-mile trip to Point Barrow, a barren outpost at the northern tip of Alaska. Post was flying a new single-engine airplane, since he had retired his record-breaking Winnie Mae to the Smithsonian. Actually his new plane wasn't new. Low on money, Post had bought a plane that had been assembled out of two damaged crafts. The different parts were not aerodynamically designed to fit together, and Post had discovered that the plane was heavy in front and had a tendency to pitch forward at low speeds.

But their more immediate concern on August 15 was the weather. They had been warned of dense fog along their route but Post just said, "I think we might as well go anyway." Rogers agreed and pointed out, "There's lots of lakes we can land on." About 50 miles from Point Barrow the fog got bad enough that Post did indeed land the pontooned plane on a lake. They soon took off again but, unsure of their route, they landed on a shallow river 15 miles from Point Barrow to ask directions from some Eskimos who were camping nearby.

At 5 P.M. they took off, again. About 50 feet in the air, before they had even reached the end of the water, the engine sputtered. Post turned sharply to the right, then the plane plunged nose-first into the edge of the stream into about two feet of water. The right wing was torn off and the plane came to rest upside down. Both men were killed instantly. Post was crushed by the engine, which had been forced back into the cockpit. Rogers was also killed by the impact, though he had been seated farther back in the plane, probably to try to counterbalance the front-end heaviness. It was unclear why the engine misfired, but some have speculated that the plane was out of gas.

After the crash an Eskimo who had given them directions ran 15 miles to Point Barrow to report what he had seen. It took him three hours. It was dark by the time a U.S. Army sergeant set out in a whale boat through the icy waters. He towed the bodies back to Barrow in a skin boat.

"When I die," Rogers had said in a speech in 1930, "my epitaph, or whatever you call those signs on gravestones, is going to read: 'I joke about every prominent man of my time, but I never met a man I didn't like.' I am proud of that. I can hardly wait to die so it can be carved. And when you come around to my grave, you'll probably find me sitting there proudly reading it."

The epitaph stands over his grave in his hometown of Claremore, Oklahoma.

JOHN ROLFE
May 6, 1585–1622

JOHN ROLFE is credited with doing two things that ensured the permanence of the early English settlements in Virginia. First, he developed a strain of tobacco that could be exported to England and soon became the economic foundation of the New World's southern colonies. Second, he married Pocahontas, the daughter of the Indian chief Powhatan, which inspired eight years of peace and allowed the settlers time to get settled.

Rolfe fell in love with Pocahontas after she was captured by the English in 1613 as ransom for prisoners and stolen tools held by the Indian princess's father. She was treated very well by the colonists, who remembered her legendary act of 1608 when she prevented the death of Captain John Smith, head of the Virginia colony, by throwing her body over his head to block his beating. But no one in the strict Christian colony had yet married an

Indian girl, and even Rolfe was troubled by his love for "one whose education hath bin rude, her manners barbarous, her generation accursed, and so discrepant in all nurtriture from myself."

Nevertheless, Rolfe, whose first wife had died soon after they arrived in the colony in 1610, and Pocahontas married in 1614, with the blessing of both sides. In 1616 the couple went to England, where Pocahontas—christened Rebecca—was greeted warmly and was even presented to King James and Queen Anne. But the next year, before Rolfe could take her back to the more temperate climate of Virginia, Pocahontas caught a chill and died, leaving one son.

Rolfe returned to the colony and married a third time. Meanwhile, Opechancanough, Powhatan's brother, had become impatient over the growing intrusion of the English settlements. On Good Friday in 1622 the Indian leader and some of his tribe joined the colonists for a breakfast celebration. During the meal the Indians massacred all the English settlers. It is believed that Rolfe, father of Powhatan's grandson, was among the victims.

MARK ROTHKO
September 25, 1903–February 25, 1970

ABSTRACT EXPRESSIONIST Mark Rothko said of his paintings, "They are like my children. I cannot send them away." For Russian-born Rothko, who came to the United States when he was 10, painting was a spiritual experience and he refused to sell his works to anyone, including museum curators, whom he considered unworthy. "A picture lives by companionship," he said, "expanding and quickening in the eyes of the observer. It dies by the same token. It is therefore a risky act to send it out into the world. How often it must be permanently impaired by the eyes of the unfeeling and the cruelty of the impotent who would extend their affliction universally." How ironic, then, that Rothko, who hated to sell his paintings, would be one of the few major Abstract Expressionists to live long enough to see the prices of his works soar.

By the late 1960s, Rothko faced increasing pressure from art dealers to sell more of his paintings. Painfully, he would agree to part with a select few of his choosing, while his warehouse continued to expand with his recent works. At the same time the artist, in his late sixties, developed a serious heart condition that often left him too weak to paint. He drank and smoked heavily and was treated with antidepressants.

On February 24, 1970, the day before he was to sell more paintings to a dealer, Rothko's doctor told him his health was improving. That evening he had dinner with a woman he had been seeing since he had separated from his wife the year before. The next morning the 66-year-old Rothko was found by his assistant lying in a pool of blood on the floor of his studio in New York on East Sixty-ninth Street. The artist had slashed his veins on the insides of his elbows. He also had taken an overdose of barbiturates, possibly to dull the pain of the razor blade, which he had taken care to wrap partly with a tissue so as not to cut his fingers.

His wife died suddenly six months later, which left his estate, including several hundred paintings, to his teenage daughter and a young son he had fathered when he was 62. It was then that the paintings Rothko spent his life protecting touched off one of the most sensational legal battles the art world had ever seen. Within three months of Rothko's suicide the three executors of his estate had quietly sold or promised 798 of the artist's paintings to an art dealer for much less than they were worth—especially now that the artist was dead. The dealer proceeded to resell many of the works at up to ten times the price he had paid.

A widely covered lawsuit, filed on behalf of Rothko's children, lasted six years and ended with the dismissal of the executors of Rothko's estate, who also were fined, along with the art dealer, a total of $9 million. Control of the estate, valued at $30 million, was turned over to Rothko's daughter.

It seems that when Rothko hadn't wanted his paintings to get into the wrong hands, he wasn't just being stubborn.

SERGE RUBINSTEIN
1909–January 27, 1955

AFTER SERGE RUBINSTEIN's death *Time* magazine eulogized, "He was a crook—who called himself an international financier—and he got away with it because highly placed people were impressed by his spending and his line." It was an apt summary of a pre-modern corporate raider who was banned from France for endangering the franc, was sued by his own brother for defaming his own mother (Rubinstein said he was illegitimate), and yet was entertained by President Roosevelt and hosted nine ambassadors at his wedding reception.

The Russian-born financier seemed to elude capture. Even after he spent thirty months in a federal penitentiary for draft evasion during World War II, Rubinstein simply draped his operations, which included oil, mining, and real estate properties, with an intricate and suspicious web of dummy corporations. He was repeatedly sued and the subject of several government investigations, but the stocky, not handsome financier threw it back at his enemies by maintaining a high profile, always armed with an array of beautiful women.

So the problem that confronted the police—after Rubinstein

was found strangled to death with a curtain cord in his Fifth Avenue mansion bedroom—was not determining who might have had a reason to kill him but who didn't. "They've narrowed the list of suspects down to 10,000," *Time* quipped. Within a few days investigators had questioned more than 500 friends and business associates that they culled from six loose-leaf notebooks that Rubinstein kept. But none of the leads led anywhere.

Rubinstein spent his last night alive in typical fashion. On that Wednesday night, January 26, 1955, he dined at a chic Manhattan restaurant with one of his latest girlfriends, a cosmetics salesgirl. About 1:30 A.M. Thursday morning they returned to his home, but she left after about fifteen minutes. Rubinstein called another girlfriend about 2:30 A.M., but she said it was too late for her to come over. At 8:30 A.M. the butler found the 46-year-old man in his blue silk pajamas lying dead on his back in the third-floor bedroom of his five-story mansion. His hands and feet were bound with curtain cord, adhesive tape covered his mouth, and there were abrasions and bruises on his throat.

Rubinstein's 78-year-old mother, Stella, who lived on the fifth floor of the mansion, had been in her room all night after she returned from the opera. She told police she heard men's voices sometime after 1 A.M. His 82-year-old aunt was staying on the fourth floor, just above his bedroom. She told police that a woman entered her room briefly at about 1 A.M., flicked the lights on and off, then left. Neither lady looked to see if there was any trouble because they said they were used to Serge having late-night guests.

Investigators believed Rubinstein was killed by some mob figures who perhaps had bungled a kidnapping plot. He had been a target a few months before, when he was roughed up on the street, and later a rock with a threatening note was thrown through his window in an attempt to extort $535,000. Even after they caught that guy police recommended that Rubinstein hire a bodyguard. But he declined, saying it would interfere with his personal life.

Now, perhaps because Rubinstein's life had been so checkered, police were at a loss to pinpoint who killed him. In February 1957, more than two years after the murder, a team of twelve investigators were still working on the case full-time with no success. If he really had been as wealthy as he lived, Rubinstein managed to elude his creditors and business partners even after he died, leaving a traceable estate of just $1.3 million against claims of over $6 million.

At Rubinstein's funeral even the rabbi found it hard to be charitable. "He possessed a brilliant mind but was utterly lacking in wisdom," the rabbi said. "He had a genius for acquiring wealth, yet never learned the simple lesson that money is a good servant but a harsh master."

BABE RUTH

February 6, 1895–August 16, 1948

"THE BAMBINO," "the Sultan of Swat," "Wizard of Wham," "Bazoo of Bang." Sportswriters stretched further and further to tag baseball's greatest legend, owner of 54 major league records including 714 career home runs and 60 home runs in one season, both of which stood for more than 30 years. The stocky, pugnosed New York Yankee fielder was always affable but also knew his worth. At the height of the Depression, in 1931, he was pressured to take a $10,000 pay cut in his $80,000 salary. "Root," said Yankees owner Colonel Ruppert, "last year you earned more money than President Hoover." "Hell," replied Ruth, "I had a better year than Hoover."

The adulation of his fans didn't stop when Ruth retired in 1935 at the age of 40. In fact, when he became critically ill in

1948, even though he had been off the field more than a decade, "his condition became a matter of nationwide concern exceeding that usually accorded to the country's most important public officials, industrialists and princes of the church," declared *The New York Times*.

It was in 1946 that Ruth began suffering severe headaches and hoarseness in his throat. In November he checked into a hospital when the left side of his face became so swollen he couldn't swallow food. Doctors removed a tumor in his throat but were unable to excise the source of the growth, lodged in the air passage behind his nose. Ruth apparently never knew he had cancer. News accounts of his illness never mentioned the disease until after he died. But he did know he was very sick. Bob Considine, who helped Ruth write his autobiography, said, "It was damn hard to work with a man who was dying, dying as resentfully as Babe was. He was often in incredible pain."

The bitterness stemmed from Ruth's years of retirement. The occasional cheers at old-timers' baseball games couldn't fill the daily routine of his twenty-year career and he was frantic for something to do. After a series of misguided ventures, including a stint as a wrestling referee, Ruth tried to get a job—any job— with the Yankees a couple of months before he became ill. His old team turned him down. Just after his major surgery he jumped at the opportunity that spring to promote baseball leagues on a national tour and logged 50,000 miles. That summer, despite a painful relapse, he gladly appeared to accept several awards around the country.

At the same time he grew weaker and his voice more gravelly. on June 13, 1948, Ruth returned to Yankee Stadium to celebrate the twenty-fifth anniversary of "The House That Ruth Built." To thunderous cheers, the drawn, white-haired idol walked slowly from the dugout to home plate, using a bat as a cane. His wife said he cried that night and most of the next day.

Ten days later Ruth was admitted to Memorial Hospital. He asked why he had been taken to a cancer hospital, and doctors convinced him that other patients were treated there as well. On July 21, Ruth was so ill that a priest administered the last rites. But five days later he showed up at the premiere of a movie, *The Babe Ruth Story*. He was supported on both arms and was so weak that he had to leave halfway through the film.

On August 12 the story of Ruth's condition—which had been followed regularly in the press for a year and a half—moved to the front page with the announcement that the ball player was critically ill. Medical updates were released three times a day and hundreds stood vigil outside the East Side hospital, including dozens of children who weren't even old enough to have seen their idol play ball. Taxi drivers would stop in front of the hospital, leave their passengers waiting, and run inside to get the latest word. More than 15,000 messages and telegrams poured in. Many were from people Ruth had visited when they were in the hospital, like 17-year-old Margie Reardon of Paterson, New Jersey, who wrote, "Dear Babe, you told me to put up a good fight. Now, I hope you'll do the same thing. You are in all our prayers."

On the morning of August 16, Ruth, who had grown less bitter and more resigned, told one visitor, "Don't come back tomorrow. I won't be here." That evening, at 6:45, he suddenly got up out of bed and started to walk across the room. The doctor led him back to bed and asked, "Where are you going, Babe?" Ruth replied, "I'm going over the valley." At 7:30 P.M. he fell into a coma and a half hour later he died.

An estimated 77,000 people passed by his closed coffin at Yankee Stadium. A few days later 75,000 lined Fifth Avenue in the rain for his funeral at St. Patrick's Cathedral, while another 100,000 watched the procession to Westchester County, where the Babe was buried in Gates of Heaven Cemetery.

CHARLES SCHWAB
February 18, 1862–September 18, 1939

CHARLES SCHWAB, who in 1901 was the highest-salaried executive in America as the first president of U.S. Steel, admitted in 1935 that he had a fundamental disagreement with his mentor. "I disagreed with [Andrew] Carnegie's ideas on how best to distribute his wealth. I spent mine! Spending creates more wealth for everybody," said the industrialist who, after he left U.S. Steel, built Bethlehem Steel into its major competitor.

Schwab, worth an estimated $25 million in his prime, practiced his idea of economic reform by building two of the most palatial homes in the country. In his small hometown of Loretto, Pennsylvania, he had his mother's house moved to make way for Immergrun. There were a respectable forty-four rooms in the main house, but that was just one of eighteen buildings on 1,000 acres, which also included a nine-hole golf course and French cottages to house the chickens. In New York City, Schwab in 1905 built Riverside, which turned out to be the last and largest of the city's mansions. Modeled on Chenonceaux, it cost $3 million and took four years to build, including ninety bedrooms and its own power plant.

Self-indulgent, surely, but the big spender did have his

generous side. When the Depression hit he hired on dozens of extra workers at Immergrun to keep Loretto's residents employed. Schwab also had twenty-seven friends and relatives on a monthly allowance and had co-signed for over $1 million in personal loans.

But commitments like that left Schwab in a bad position when the Depression severely dropped the value of his Bethlehem stock and other holdings. In 1936 he tried unsuccessfully to sell Riverside to the city of New York for $4 million. He said he was making the offer out of civic pride, but in fact he hadn't been able to afford the property taxes since 1933.

After his wife died in January 1939, Schwab announced he was closing Riverside and Immergrun permanently because he needed to "start life anew." In fact, Schwab was nearly bankrupt. Chase National Bank held on to the title to Riverside to cover some of Schwab's debts.

Still, Schwab was not penniless, and that summer he made his usual trip to Europe. In London on August 9 he suffered a heart attack. He returned home to his small apartment on Park Avenue and died there of a second attack on the evening of September 18. Schwab had done more than spend it all. He left an estate with assets of under $1.4 million and debts of over $1.7 million.

U.S. MAJOR GENERAL
JOHN SEDGWICK
September 13, 1813–May 9, 1864

GENERAL SEDGWICK—graduate of West Point and veteran of the Mexican War and several Indian campaigns—was commanding the Sixth Army Corps against Confederate forces at Spottsylvania, Virginia, in the spring of 1864. On May 9, while the robust, confident general was sitting under a tree talking with his aide about the upcoming battle, he noticed some of his troops were incorrectly positioned along the lines where the next fight would commence. Sedgwick got up and strode out to the front to adjust the lines when a Confederate sharpshooter started firing from somewhere out of sight. Sedgwick's troops began ducking, but the general just laughed and said, "What, what men! This will never do; dodging for single bullets! I tell you they could not hit an elephant at this distance."

One of his aides wrote the rest of the story after the war. "Before the smile which accompanied these words had departed from his lips, and as he was in the act of resuming conversation with the staff officer by his side, there was a sharp whistle of a bullet, terminating in a dull, soft sound; and he fell slowly and heavily to the earth."

Sedgwick was struck under his left cheekbone near his nose. He died instantly. More than a decade later his surviving troops erected a stone monument on the spot where he fell. It was twice as tall as a human being and larger than many elephants.

PERCY BYSSHE SHELLEY
August 4, 1792–July 8, 1822

PERCY BYSSHE SHELLEY, who has since been considered one of England's greatest poets, was little read during his scandalous, short life. "Mad Shelley," as the British called this son of a member of Parliament, shocked his fellow countrymen early on, having preached atheism at Eton and getting himself expelled from Oxford. His notions of free love, his early marriage to a 16-year-old girl who committed suicide after they broke up, and his several other real or alleged affairs finally amounted to such trouble that he settled in Italy in 1818, where he prolifically wrote most of his vast collection of poems that later won him acclaim.

In 1822 the boyish-looking poet was living with his wife, Mary Godwin, author of *Frankenstein*, in the Mediterranean coastal town of Leghorn, 45 miles north of Pisa. He was surrounded by many friends, including his most famous one, Lord Byron, and a mistress. He had bought a sailboat, which he adored even though he couldn't swim, and spent many days and moonlit nights floating in the Gulf of Spezia, reading Faust and working on his next long poem, *The Triumph of Life*. The sailboat was basically a large rowboat with sails and was hardly seaworthy. It rode dangerously high in the water and its hollow shell was equipped only with a writing table and bookshelves.

In early July, Shelley, tan and looking healthier than he had for some time, sailed to Pisa to visit some friends. He returned to Leghorn on July 7, and the next day set sail with two friends to go north along the coast to Lerici, his summer home, where his wife and mistress were. It was midafternoon, late to be starting the 20-mile journey, but Shelley was anxious to get back to his ladies. About 6 P.M. a sudden, violent squall burst over the sea. There were many boats on the water, and when the storm ended twenty minutes later only Shelley's was missing.

The three bodies, including Shelley's, washed ashore ten days later several miles apart. Shelley, a month shy of 30, was identified by the volume of Keats found doubled back in his coat pocket. The poet was buried in the sand until his cremation could be arranged on August 15. A friend, Edward Trelawny, wrote that after Shelley's body had burned slowly for hours, his heart remained unsinged. Trelawny snatched the organ from the fire and, in a gesture that perhaps only she could appreciate, sent it to Shelley's widow, Mary. The rest of his remains were interred in Rome.

Shelley's death brought no great mourning in England. One newspaper reported, "Shelley, the writer of some infidel poetry, has been drowned; now he knows whether there is a God or no."

BUGSY SIEGEL
February 28, 1906–June 20, 1947

THOUGH HE actually was the most powerful mobster on the West Coast in the 1930s and 1940s, Bugsy Siegel lived like a movie star. His friends included George Raft, Clark Gable, and Abbott and Costello; he carried on with starlets, and tourists often drove past his big house near Beverly Hills. It was all very glamorous and seemed to gloss over the fact that Siegel was suspected of committing several brutal murders and that he controlled most of the major rackets in California and ran a heroin-smuggling operation from Mexico. That he was considered one of the "Big Six" of New York's organized crime, a partner of Meyer Lansky, and a member of "Murder Inc." when he went west in 1933 did not prevent him from being welcomed into Hollywood parties.

Siegel, who was called "Bugsy" only by the police and the press—he was "Ben" to his friends—thrived for years in his double life. But as competition from other mobsters grew in the 1940s, Siegel began getting pressure from his New York bosses to increase profits. He blundered big in 1946 when his glitzy Flamingo Club opened in Las Vegas and promptly lost $6 million. And, some speculate, he blundered even worse when he took up with Virginia Hill, who was called an heiress but whose money actually came from her three ex-husbands and her mob-boss boyfriend back in Brooklyn.

On the early evening of June 20, 1947, Siegel returned to Hill's Moorish mansion in Beverly Hills with his longtime pal Al Smiley. At the time Hill was in Paris. She said later she had gone abroad after she and Siegel got into an argument because his shirt was dirty. That evening Siegel and Smiley were sitting on a sofa in the living room next to two tall French windows. Siegel was scanning a newspaper when four bullets quickly shot through the glass, hitting the 42-year-old mobster twice in his head and twice in his body and killing him instantly. The gunman apparently had crept up the driveway of the house next door, hidden by shrubbery, and then had fired a machine gun through a rose trellis a few feet from the windows and Siegel. Neighbors said they heard a car speed away soon after they heard the shots.

There was plenty of speculation as to who wanted Siegel dead. The list was not a short one and included the profit-hungry New York bosses, the growing West Coast competitors, and Hill's jealous Brooklyn boyfriend. Contacted in Paris, Hill said, "It looks so bad to have a thing like that happen in your house." Siegel's killer never was found, but that didn't make much difference in Hollywood or the press. As *Time* wrote, "Where the truth was, no one seemed to know—or care—but a wonderful time was had by all."

SITTING BULL
1831–December 15, 1890

In an earlier time Sitting Bull might have been a great and prosperous Indian chief. But in the second half of the 19th century he was the last ruler of a dying breed. His victory over General Custer at Little Big Horn in 1876 was but a glitch in the United States drive to corral the Sioux Indians onto reservations. A medicine man and never actually a chief, Sitting Bull led a dwindling number of Sioux away from federal troops for five more years, until finally, in 1881, he and fewer than 200 remaining followers surrendered. They were held in custody for almost two years before they were placed on the Standing Rock Reservation in South Dakota, near where Sitting Bull was born.

Sitting Bull, a tall, solid Indian with long, black, braided hair, was put on parade in several cities and in 1885 he toured with Buffalo Bill's Wild West Show along the East Coast. But when he was on the reservation Sitting Bull stubbornly continued to stir up unrest. Even after federal authorities prohibited the ceremony, Sitting Bull encouraged Indians to perform the new Ghost Dance, which the Indians had come to believe would lead to a rebellion and would bring a savior to defeat the White Man.

At dawn on December 15, 1890, about forty members of an Indian police force commissioned by federal authorities descended on Sitting Bull's cabin to arrest him. They pulled the 59-year-old naked man from his bed and ordered him to get dressed and go with them. Sitting Bull gathered his things, but he took a long time to do it, which allowed time for a restless crowd of Indians to gather outside. By the time Sitting Bull was roughly pushed out of his cabin into the freezing weather, the crowd was angry.

Sitting Bull stood waiting for his horse to be brought up. But then suddenly he yelled in the Sioux language—which the Indian officers, too, understood—"I am not going. Do with me what you like. I am not going. Come on! Come on! Take action! Let's go!" Another leader of unrest on the reservation, Catch the Bear, pulled out a gun and fired at the top Indian officer. Lieutenant Bullhead was hit in the leg and as he fell he fired at Sitting Bull, shooting him in his left side. Another officer also shot the Indian leader, killing him instantly.

The gun battle escalated, and when it was over fourteen men were dead, all Sioux, including six Indian police officers. Hundreds of others fled the reservation. Most were soon caught and sent to Wounded Knee, where, on December 29, an anonymous gunshot touched off the massacre of 300 Sioux.

BESSIE SMITH
April 15, 1894–September 26, 1937

BESSIE SMITH was called "Queen of the Blues," and Lord knows she had enough troubles to sing about. She had drinking problems, lover problems, and a violent temper, and she sang about them all and her popularity only grew. After a decade of traveling shows, she recorded "Down Hearted Blues" in 1923 and instantly became one of Columbia Records' hottest artists. That year she commanded $1,500 for a week's shows in Detroit—but the only accommodations available to her were still in black boardinghouses. By 1925 she was called "the Greatest and Highest Salaried Race Star in the World."

The Depression killed her recording contract and sent her back on the road. She was touring the South in 1937 in *The Broadway Rastus Show*, riding in her old Packard, driven by her longtime boyfriend Richard Morgan. They left Memphis on September 25 after the last Saturday-night performance and headed for Mississippi. About 75 miles south, a truck driver had stopped on the highway to check his tires. The road had a very narrow shoulder, so most of the truck was parked on the darkened highway. Morgan didn't see the truck in time. It had just started to move forward when Morgan skidded and swerved, turning the Packard sideways and slamming the passenger's side almost directly into the back of the truck. The car ended up lying on its left side diagonally on the highway. The truck didn't stop.

Smith, who was probably asleep, had had her right arm hanging out the window. Her arm was nearly severed, her ribs were crushed, and she was thrown from the car into the middle of the road. A white doctor, who happened to drive by moments after the crash, examined her and sent a friend to call an ambulance from a distant house. As they waited for the ambulance, a car carrying a young couple ran into the back of the doctor's car. The doctor said later that an ambulance took Smith directly to the black hospital in Clarksdale, Mississippi. She died there of her injuries at 11:30 A.M. Sunday.

But other accounts charged that the black singer died of neglect. The doctor could have driven Smith directly to a hospital without waiting for an ambulance. There was also a report that Smith was first taken to a white hospital, where she was denied admittance and lost precious hours of medical attention. That story, never substantiated, was the basis of Edward Albee's famous play *The Death of Bessie Smith*.

The truth was never resolved. Bessie Smith was buried in Philadelphia in a long silk dress in a gold-trimmed silver casket. Her grave had no headstone until 1970, when some fans began a drive to buy one. The $500 cost was split by a woman who had been Smith's maid and rock star Janis Joplin. The stone was installed August 7, 1970, 33 years after Smith was killed—and two months before Joplin died of a heroin overdose.

PYOTR ILYICH TCHAIKOVSKY
May 7, 1840–November 6, 1893

UNLIKE MANY in his field, Pyotr Ilyich Tchaikovsky didn't die poor. In fact, the most famous Russian composer—whose works, in addition to his famous symphonies, include *Swan Lake, Sleeping Beauty*, and *The Nutcracker* ballets as well as the *1812 Overture*—was at the height of his fame and fortune when his life ended at the age of 53. It was an amazing accomplishment, considering that the son of a mining engineer didn't begin his formal music training until his twenties and suffered long dry spells due to his lifelong torment with homosexuality, including a nervous breakdown caused by his disastrous three-month marriage in 1877.

By the late 1880s, Tchaikovsky was a celebrated man. He

lived comfortably in a large house, supported by a pension from the Czar. He was cheered on European tours and was treated like royalty when he made his one visit to America in 1891. In June 1893, Tchaikovsky was given an honorary degree from the University of Cambridge. That fall he went to St. Petersburg to conduct the premiere of his Sixth Symphony on October 28. The complicated work got a mixed reception, but Tchaikovsky seemed pleased with the performance.

Nine days later he was dead. The widely recounted cause of death was that the composer drank unboiled water and died of cholera. It was said he unwittingly drank the contaminated water on November 1 and soon began suffering painful stomach cramps, convulsions, and a high fever. He finally fell into a coma on November 5 and the next morning at 3 A.M. he died.

But in 1978 a new account of Tchaikovsky's final days was revealed by a Russian scholar who said she had heard a very different story in 1966 from an aged official of the Russian Museum in Leningrad, which was called St. Petersburg when Tchaikovsky died there. According to this account, Tchaikovsky was accused by a Russian aristocrat of having a sexual liaison with the man's nephew. To prevent the aristocrat from taking his claim to the Czar, Tchaikovsky was secretly tried by a panel of six high-ranking men. Their decision, on October 31, 1893, was that the composer must kill himself. It was the next day that he fell ill with stomach cramps. There is some speculation that Tchaikovsky intended to commit suicide by swallowing arsenic, and then may have drunk the contaminated water afterward to hide his motive.

DYLAN THOMAS
October 27, 1914–November 9, 1953

Do not go gentle into that good night,
Old age should burn and rave at close of day;
Rage, rage against the dying of the light.

Dylan Thomas wrote that poem in 1951, one of only nine poems he composed in the last seven years of his life. And although he wrote a scant ninety poems in his twenty-two-year career that began when he was 17, the stout Welsh writer was called the "modern Keats" long before he died. His poems were extremely popular, as was Thomas himself, a riveting storyteller and powerful reader of his work.

Thomas drew as much attention because of his life-style, which was the perfect prelude to the Beat Generation. The green-eyed, curly-haired poet was a self-promoting bohemian as early as 1935 in London, where he began drinking heavily and dangling a cigarette from his lips. When he crossed the ocean in 1950 to read his poems he said he had come to America "to continue my search for naked women in wet mackintoshes."

He arrived in New York for his fourth American tour on October 19, 1953, and, as usual, checked into the funky Chelsea Hotel. He stayed with his American girlfriend, since his wife of sixteen years had remained in England. On this trip he referred to his wife as his "widow." It was not out of dissatisfaction with her, but with his sickly physical self, which often was racked with the flu and bronchitis as a result of his excesses. "I've seen the gates of hell tonight," Thomas said after one night of heavy drinking. "Oh, but I do want to go on—for another ten years anyway. But not as a bloody invalid."

Thomas, who occasionally showed up drunk for his lectures,

conducted two seminars without incident on October 28 and 29, then had a week off until his next appearances. At 2 A.M. on Wednesday, November 4, Thomas left his girlfriend and went out for a drink. It is believed he went to the White Horse Tavern, his favorite neighborhood bar in the West Village, about a half mile from his hotel. When he returned more than an hour later he said, "I've had eighteen straight whiskeys. I think that's the record." He then told his girlfriend, "I love you, but I'm alone," and fell asleep.

He woke up midmorning. That he woke up at all probably means he had exaggerated the previous night's drinking binge. He said he needed air, and the two walked back to the White Horse, where Thomas had two beers but then had to return to the Chelsea because he didn't feel well. Back at the hotel, he began vomiting and suffered severe stomach spasms. His doctor arrived and is believed to have given him morphine to settle him. Thomas became delirious and by 2 A.M. the next morning he was unconscious.

He lingered in a coma for four and a half days at St. Vincent's Hospital, a few blocks from the White Horse. He finally died of pneumonia and a damaged liver. His wife, who had arrived from London and was with him when he died, lost control and smashed a crucifix and statue of the Virgin Mary in the Catholic hospital before she was straitjacketed and sent to a Long Island clinic to recover. Thomas had written, "Do not go gentle into that good night." He didn't.

JIM THOMPSON
March 21, 1906–March 26, 1967 (?)

WHEN WESTERN tourists arrived in Bangkok twenty-five years ago, often their first question was how to get to "Jim Thompson's place." What they meant was the Thai Silk Company, with which Thompson transformed a peasant art into a multimillion-dollar export business in the 1950s and 1960s. Thompson, a Princeton graduate and son of a prominent Delaware family, had been an American Army officer in Thailand at the end of World War II when he invested $700 to organize some home weavers. Within a few years thousands of weavers were spinning the beautiful, glistening fabrics that got shipped to the top clothing designers and were featured in *The King and I* and *Ben-Hur*.

Thompson, meanwhile, became perhaps the best-known foreigner in Southeast Asia. Divorced, the "silk king" lived alone with two servants and a pet cockatoo in a spectacular mansion that combined six transported Thai houses and was open for tours two days a week. His collection of Thai antiques and artifacts was envied, especially by the Thai government. And his famous, sparkling dinner parties usually featured a movie star like Katharine Hepburn or important politicians like Bobby Kennedy or dissident Vietnamese or Thai officials.

In the spring of 1967, Thompson, feeling overworked by plans to move the company into a larger store, traveled to Malaysia to spend Easter weekend with some close friends. He and a woman friend were staying with another couple at their summer cottage in the Cameron Highlands, a lush, mountainous resort area 7,000 feet above sea level, about 90 miles north of Kuala Lumpur. After going to church on Easter Sunday the four of them had a picnic lunch overlooking the dense jungle, then returned to the cottage for a rest. But Thompson apparently didn't take a nap like the others, and when they heard footsteps outside they assumed that he had gone for a walk.

Thompson never returned. The search began when he had not come back by nightfall. One hundred policemen and soldiers combed the surrounding thick jungles, assuming that the 61-year-old man had gotten lost or had fallen—possibly into one of many deep ravines—or had been attacked by a tiger or a snake. By the next day the search had expanded to 300 and included a Boy Scout troop, resort guests, and an aborigine tribe that served as guides. They found no trace of the famous foreigner, not even a piece of torn clothing or drops of blood. Officials were stymied by their lack of success. People had gotten lost in the jungle before, but they always had been fairly easy to find, dead or alive, when vultures circled.

Perhaps, some started to say, there was no body for the vultures to find. Perhaps Thompson had left the jungle, but not of his own accord. After all, Thompson was a chain-smoker, but his cigarettes and lighter were found in his room, indicating he hadn't planned to walk very far. Also, he left behind pills that he always carried with him for painful gallbladder attacks. And on top of those little things it was remembered that Thompson had first gone to Thailand as an officer in the Army's Office of Strategic Services, the forerunner of the CIA. The fact that he invited politically sensitive guests to his dinner parties led to suspicions that he had never ended his ties to the intelligence bureau.

The kidnapping theories were given great weight in Malaysia, especially after they were supported by the *bomohs*—highly respected Malaysian witch doctors—who all said Thompson was still alive. They were less certain as to why he had been abducted. Some said it was because he was rich, others said it was to stop the bombing in North Vietnam, and others insisted he was being held in Cambodia to stop recent incursions there. Some believed Thompson knew his captors and had met with them willingly, unaware that he was in danger. Any of those motives might have made sense, except that no one ever sought a ransom for the popular man. Further, why would kidnappers risk abducting him during an impromptu trip to Malaysia when Thompson followed a very routine and relaxed schedule in Bangkok?

After ten days the jungle search was halted. Five months later Thompson's eldest sister, a 74-year-old wealthy society matron, was found beaten to death in her isolated Delaware estate. Police found nothing missing and no motive. Finally, in 1974, Thompson was declared legally dead at his family's request. Jim Thompson's place in Bangkok remains a highlight for Western travelers, but the whereabouts of Jim Thompson is still a mystery.

JIM THORPE
May 28, 1888–March 28, 1953

THESE DAYS Olympic medalists can cash in big by hawking breakfast cereal and running shoes. Jim Thorpe, hailed as the greatest athlete of the 20th century decades after he won the gold in both the pentathlon and the decathlon in 1912, wasn't so lucky. The native Indian from Oklahoma already was a college track star and All-American football player under coach Pop Warner when he became the hero of the Stockholm Olympics. When Thorpe was presented his medals Sweden's King Gustav V told him, "Sir, you are the greatest athlete in the world." Thorpe replied, "Thanks, King."

Three months later the glory vanished. Olympics officials took back Thorpe's two gold medals after they learned that he had been paid for playing minor-league baseball one summer, thus disqualifying him as an amateur. Thorpe went on to have long though unspectacular careers playing baseball and football. He never made much money and wasn't too careful with what he did make. After Thorpe retired from football in 1929 at the age of 41, he tried Hollywood. He got a few bit parts playing Indian chiefs, but within a year he took a job with an oil company, painting gas stations and trucks. Several years later, whenever he needed the money to support one of his three wives and several children, the former star athlete toured the country in Indian costume, lecturing on sports, Indian culture, and his life. Through it all Thorpe never lost his good nature and his enthusiasm. Near the end of World War II the 57-year-old enlisted in the Merchant Marines.

Thorpe may not have been able to capitalize on his athletic triumphs, but he still had plenty of fans. In November 1951, after word got out that Thorpe couldn't afford to pay for his lip cancer surgery, a nationwide "Fair Play for Thorpe Committee" raised $4,500. The next fall Thorpe had a heart attack, his second in nine years. A few months later, on March 28, 1953, Thorpe and his wife were eating dinner in their trailer home in the suburban Los Angeles city of Lomita when the 64-year-old athlete suffered his third heart attack. A neighbor gave him artificial respiration for almost thirty minutes before a rescue squad arrived. They revived him well enough that he was able to talk to them. But a few minutes later Thorpe suffered a relapse and died.

Initially plans were for Thorpe to be buried in his native Oklahoma. But his wife wanted a bigger memorial than the state would provide. So instead Thorpe was put to rest in a town that used to be called Mauch Chunk, Pennsylvania, after the residents of this coal town in the eastern part of the state pleased Mrs. Thorpe by voting to change the town's name to Jim Thorpe, Pennsylvania.

LEO TOLSTOY

September 9, 1828–November 20, 1910

RUSSIAN NOVELIST Leo Tolstoy may be remembered for *War and Peace* and *Anna Karenina*, but his own life was just as rich and colorful. Called the "second czar of Russia" because his books were so popular, Tolstoy underwent a deep religious conversion in his fifties and spent the rest of his life trying to renounce his aristocratic upbringing. He wrote religious tracts promoting peace through nonresistance, prompting Gandhi later to call him "the highest moral authority." Devoted followers made pilgrimages to his huge country estate, of which the writer was so ashamed that he sought to give the land to local peasants.

That he did no such thing was the result of a deeper torment than his religion—his wife. Tolstoy married Sonya in 1862, when he was 34 and she was 18. They had nine children, but almost from the start their relationship was unpleasant. Sonya resented her husband's intense devotion to his work (he had just started *War and Peace* when they got married) and was angered far more when he began talking about giving up their earthly wealth and living like peasants. Sonya loved the Moscow parties and made herself Tolstoy's publisher so she could control profits from his writings, which Tolstoy himself renounced.

Tolstoy and Sonya bickered constantly. But whenever he suggested that he leave she would threaten to kill herself. He stayed, even after he discovered she had taken to following him and spying on him with opera glasses. In his last years, when he suffered from malaria, typhoid fever, and fainting spells, Tolstoy said, "My illness is Sonya."

On November 10, 1910, Tolstoy awoke to find his wife rifling through his papers looking for his latest diary. She had demanded it from him so she could publish it, but he had refused

to give it to her. Tolstoy pretended to remain asleep. After she
left without the diary he quietly got up and woke his daughter
and his doctor and told them to help him pack. Tolstoy was so
anxious to sneak away that he crept out into the dark, freezing
night and fell over a tree trunk on his way to the carriage stable.

Behind he had left a letter to Sonya thanking her for 48 years
of marriage and begging her not to follow him. The 82-year-old
man wrote, "I am doing what people of my age very often do:
giving up the world, in order to spend my last days alone and
in silence."

By the time Tolstoy and his daughter and doctor rode to a
train station, the writer's thick white beard was heavy with ice.
They traveled in second- and third-class sections to avoid being
recognized, but that did little good since newspapers the next
day reported his flight. When Sonya found her husband had
left she said to one of their children, "Wire your father that
I drowned myself." Tolstoy stopped at a monastery to rest, but
after a couple of days he abruptly left at 4 A.M. for fear that
Sonya was on his trail.

Tolstoy and his companions boarded a train for a 600-mile
journey to Novocherkassk, a trip that would take about thirty
hours. But early the first afternoon Tolstoy fell ill with fever
and chills. He was taken off the train that evening at a small
station at Astapovo and was put to bed in the stationmaster's
house. As Tolstoy grew worse the little town was besieged by
journalists from all over the world, who sent out hourly bulle-
tins on the famous writer's condition.

Sonya, of course, soon ordered a special train and arrived
with the rest of Tolstoy's children, many of whom sided with
Sonya and had wanted their father committed. But Tolstoy's
doctor refused to let Sonya see her husband, fearing that her
visit would upset the frail man. The blinds in his room were
drawn so that there would be no chance that Tolstoy would
awaken from his delirium and see his wife's face.

Sonya finally was let in to Tolstoy's room at 2 A.M. on November 20, when doctors decided he was so near death he wouldn't

know she was there. Less than four hours later, with no last words for his wife, Tolstoy died. Sonya immediately took sick, then lived another ten years.

LEON TROTSKY
November 7, 1879–August 21, 1940

ONE CAN ONLY speculate how things might have turned out if Leon Trotsky instead of Joseph Stalin had won the power struggle to rule the Soviet Union after Lenin died in 1924. Trotsky had been Lenin's right-hand man and was largely responsible for ensuring the early stability of the socialist regime. But Stalin's ruthless lust for power forced Trotsky into exile by 1929. It was nothing new for Trotsky, whose radical activities had caused him to spend many years in exile—including a few months as editor of a Russian radical newspaper in the Bronx—before the Russian Revolution in 1917.

But this time most nations refused to accept the deposed Russian leader. He lived in Turkey, then France, and then Norway, but his outspoken attacks against Stalin's regime soon made those countries nervous as well. Trotsky finally moved with his wife and son to Mexico in 1937, where he lived with Mexican painter Diego Rivera outside of Mexico City. Meanwhile, Stalin's purge against his enemies reached outside the Soviet Union. Trotsky was twice convicted in absentia for treason and some of his supporters were hunted down all over the world by Stalin's secret police.

Trotsky realized that he, too, probably was in danger, and he and his family moved into a house built like a fortress in a Mexico City suburb. On May 24, 1940, after machine-gun bullets shattered Trotsky's bedroom, guards were placed in concrete pillboxes atop a 15-foot brick wall that surrounded the house.

Sometime that summer Trotsky met a man who called himself Frank Jackson. He was the boyfriend of Sylvia Ageloff, a Brooklyn social worker whose sister used to work for Trotsky. Jackson had introduced himself to Ageloff in Paris some months before under the name Jacques Monard van den Dreischd. It turned out neither name was correct. He was Ramón Mercader, the son of a famous Spanish Communist, who had been sent by Stalin's police to assassinate Trotsky. The handsome Mercader, 36, wooed the homely Ageloff, 31, and professed no interest in politics. When they went to Mexico he told her he was using the name Frank Jackson to avoid passport problems.

Mercader met Trotsky a few times, and the 60-year-old exiled leader seemed barely to tolerate the visitor. Mercader visited on the afternoon of August 20, ostensibly to have Trotsky look over an article he had written. Mercader was wearing a raincoat, in which he had concealed a dagger, an automatic pistol, and a mountaineer's ice ax. While Trotsky sat at his desk in his study reading the article, Mercader pulled out the ax and struck Trotsky from behind in the back of his head. The sharply pointed pickax gouged two and three-quarter inches deep into Trotsky's skull.

But instead of collapsing Trotsky rose up and pushed Mercader away, then ran from his study screaming and dripping with blood. Guards rushed in and subdued Mercader as Trotsky finally fell in the dining room, saying, "I feel this time they have succeeded." Trotsky was rushed to the hospital, but doctors held little hope. As nurses cut away his clothes to prepare him for surgery, Trotsky looked at his wife and said, "I do not want them to undress me. I want you to undress me." Soon after, at 7:30 P.M., Trotsky fell into a coma. He never regained consciousness and died twenty-four hours later. After the United States refused to admit his body for burial, Trotsky was cremated and buried outside of Mexico City.

Mercader claimed he had killed Trotsky over a personal matter. He said the exiled leader had tried to convince him to go to the Soviet Union and commit sabotage and that Trotsky also had tried to prevent Mercader from marrying Ageloff. Mercader was convicted of the murder in 1943. When he was released in 1960 he first went to Cuba, then to Czechoslovakia.

WILLIAM MARCY "BOSS" TWEED
April 3, 1823–April 12, 1878

THIS IS NOT just another one of those corrupt-guy-gets-his stories. Boss Tweed's grip was too tight for his demise to be quite complete. In the 1860s, at his height as the Grand Sachem of Tammany Hall—the most powerful political machine in 19th-century New York—Tweed controlled everyone from the governor on down. He collected huge legal fees, though he had little knowledge of the law. His printing company did all the city's printing, as well as that of companies that wanted to do business with the city. He bought a quarry which then supplied all the marble for the new county courthouse. By his own later testimony, Tweed spent $600,000 bribing the state legislature to adopt a new city charter that gave him even more complete control. Estimates of the total amount milked by the heavyset five-foot-eleven-inch son of a chairmaker and his ring range from $30 million to $200 million.

The press finally started exposing the corruption in 1870. Tweed offered *The New York Times* $5 million not to publish evidence of his illegalities. He also offered *Harper's Weekly* cartoonist Thomas Nast $500,000 to stop drawing derogatory sketches. "Let's stop the damned pictures," Tweed raged. "I don't care much what the papers write about me—my constituents can't read. But, damn it, they can see pictures!"

Tweed was convicted in 1873 and sentenced to twelve years in prison and a $12,750 fine. A friendly appeals court reduced that to one year and a $250 fine. After his year in jail, Tweed was arrested again to recover the lost millions. He stayed in jail because he couldn't—or wouldn't—pay up, but it was an easy term. He took a carriage ride through the city every afternoon, and was allowed to visit his home under the escort of two prison guards. On December 4, 1875, Tweed slipped out the back door of his home while the guards relaxed in the parlor. A few months later he was captured in Spain, where he was identified by one of Nast's cartoons.

Tweed was sent back to jail, this time to a more secure facility on Ludlow Street. But even there, he orchestrated less-than-brutal conditions. He lived in two rooms, paying the warden $75 a month for such a suite. He had a black servant to tend him during the day. There were flower-filled pots on the window sill, a piano in the corner, several comfortable chairs, and walls covered with etchings and lithographs. The window, which overlooked a small courtyard where Tweed took his daily walks, had curtains to hide the steel bars outside.

But for all of his surrounding comfort, Tweed suffered from diabetes and a worsening heart condition. He volunteered to testify in the fall of 1877 in exchange for an early release, but by then most of the corruption had been cleaned out and no one was much interested. Tweed suffered a series of heart attacks that winter, but still the authorities would not release him.

On April 12, 1878, one of Tweed's daughters arrived in the morning for her regular visit. In the dim light, she didn't notice how pale and drawn the former power broker had become. As usual, she left to bring him some ice cream. She returned at the stroke of noon, just in time to watch her 55-year-old father give his last breaths. She dropped the ice cream to reach for him as he died.

There were only eight carriages in the funeral procession.

The family requested that as they passed City Hall, the flag be lowered to half-mast. The city said no.

RUDOLPH VALENTINO
May 6, 1895–August 23, 1926

FROM POOR Italian immigrant in 1913 to the silent screen's greatest lover in 1921, the story of Rudolph Valentino is classic Hollywood. His first leading roles in *The Four Horsemen of the Apocalypse* and *The Sheik* made him the biggest film phenomenon of the early era. Perhaps the clearest evidence of his hold on the passions of filmgoers came after his sudden, early death at the age of 31.

Valentino had just completed *The Son of the Sheik* in 1926 and was planning to go to Europe to drum up some publicity.

A few weeks before he was to leave he met with Adolph Zukor
to apologize to the powerful head of Paramount for his previous,
well-publicized star tantrums. "It's water over the dam," replied Zukor. "You're young. Many good years are ahead of
you."

But ten days later, on Monday, August 16, Valentino suddenly clutched his stomach and collapsed in his suite at the
Ambassador Hotel in New York. He had suffered stomach pains
for a few weeks, but even intense pain the night before hadn't
kept him from attending an all-night party. The star was rushed
to Polyclinic Hospital, where doctors performed surgery to repair a perforated ulcer and remove his ruptured appendix. By
then, however, infection was spreading throughout his abdomen.
At first news of his admittance the hospital was jammed with
fans and reporters. Valentino received thousands of telegrams
and hundreds of Bibles, flowers, and rosaries.

After the surgery Valentino asked for a mirror. "I just want
to see what I look like when I'm sick," he said, "so that if I ever
have to play the part in pictures, I'll know how to put on the
right makeup." By Saturday, Valentino seemed much better
and he was anxious to get out of bed. But suddenly that afternoon his temperature jumped to 104 degrees as the infection
couldn't be stopped. That night Major Bowes asked his radio
audience to pray for the screen star. Monday morning, drugged
to dull the pain, Valentino fell into a coma and four hours later,
at noon, he died.

It had been said that when Valentino appeared on the street,
he stopped traffic. So, too, in death. More than 20,000 people
jammed the streets around the Funeral Church at Sixty-seventh
and Broadway waiting to view the body. The frenzied throng
finally crashed through the front window, clawing at each
other and tracking mud into the Gold Room to get a glimpse
of the dead Sheik. More than 100 were injured in the near-riot,
but eventually 90,000 people filed through to see Valentino, laid
out in a silver-bronze coffin with a glass plate covering his body.
His head was turned to give a profile view.

A few days after Valentino died a woman named Peggy Scott committed suicide in London by drinking poison. She was found surrounded by photographs and autographed letters of the screen star. She left a note that said, "No one will ever know, but with his death the last bit of courage has flown." Later that fall Mrs. Angeline Celestina, a 20-year-old mother of two, drank iodine and fired two shots at herself. She didn't die, but was found lying on the floor of her home surrounded by photographs and news stories about the late legend.

Also that fall Natacha Rambova, Valentino's second divorced wife, arrived on an ocean liner from England to report that she had received "spirit messages" from Valentino through a medium. The late star had sent word that he was "in the astral plane and longed to be a legitimate actor," according to *The New York Times* account. Rambova said her former husband also had met Caruso, the Italian tenor who had died five years before, in that astral plane. Strangely, Valentino's messages did not mention his fiancée, Pola Negri, according to Rambova. Three days after this report Valentino's first wife issued a statement saying that she doubted any such spirit messages had been received, as her former husband didn't believe in them.

Meanwhile, as studio executives rushed to get his latest films into theaters—where they set box-office records—Valentino was taken by train from New York to Los Angeles, with a stop in Chicago for another viewing. Once he was installed in a Hollywood mausoleum, attendants for years afterward took to carrying smelling salts to revive women whom they found prostrated on the marble floor. And for decades a mysterious woman in black—who may or may not have been just one person—drew much attention by laying flowers under the screen lover's vault on the anniversary of his death.

VINCENT VAN GOGH
March 30, 1853–July 29, 1890

IT TOOK Vincent Van Gogh just ten years to leave his masterful impression on the art world. From 1880 to 1890 the Dutch painter created more than 1,600 paintings and drawings, driving himself along his prolific pace despite his mental torments and declining health. He explained himself in a letter to his close brother, Theo. "Not only did I begin painting late in life," wrote the artist who was an art dealer and lay preacher before he began painting at the age of 27, "but it may also be that I shall not live for so very many years. . . . So I go on like an ignoramus who knows only this one thing: in a few years I must finish a certain work."

The artist was most productive, in fact, when his life was in greatest turmoil. Living in Arles in 1888, Van Gogh painted 200 canvases in fifteen months amid severe depressions and hallucinations. After a quarrel with artist Paul Gauguin drove him to cut off his right ear, Van Gogh committed himself to an asylum at St. Rémy, where he painted "Starry Night" and others of his most important works. Doctors now speculate that Van Gogh exhibited signs of epilepsy and schizophrenia, but at the time little treatment was available.

In May 1890, Van Gogh moved to Auvers, just outside Paris, to be near Theo, who recently had gotten married. He continued to suffer mental problems and so was lodging with Dr. Paul Gachet, who also took a strong interest in Von Gogh's art. Van Gogh created seventy paintings in the last seventy days of his life, often standing all day in the hot sun to paint the fields around Auvers.

In late July, while Gachet was away for a few days, Van Gogh decided he could stand his hallucinations no longer. On

July 27 he took a revolver with him to the fields. Behind a manure pile in a farmyard near where he painted, the 37-year-old artist shot himself in the chest. He managed to stagger back to Gachet's home and up to his room before Gachet returned, and Van Gogh, clutching his chest, murmured, "I missed myself." Van Gogh smoked his pipe through the night. The next day he developed a high fever and became delirious. Finally, at 1 A.M. on July 29, the artist died. His last words: "There is no end to sorrow."

SID VICIOUS
1957–February 2, 1979

MANY PEOPLE die in ironic contrast to how they lived. For Sid Vicious the only irony would have been for him to go on living. As a member of the wildly popular British punk rock group the Sex Pistols, Mr. Vicious, according to one music reviewer, "played electric guitar and vomited." Vicious, born John Simon Ritchie in London's tough East End, said he did the latter "to show my disgust at everyone." He also tended to slash himself onstage and drip blood, inflicting cuts that occasionally required stitches. Those stunts helped make the Sex Pistols and their raw, monotonous music the darlings of England's alienated youth in 1976 and 1977. Other stunts, such as trashing the office of A&M Records and yelling obscenities during a live BBC interview, got the safety-pin-pierced band dumped by two record companies and banned from most British cities.

The Sex Pistols had released only one album, including the hits "Anarchy in the U.K." and "God Save the Queen," when they broke up in January 1978. That same month Vicious overdosed during a flight from Los Angeles to New York and had to be carried off the plane on a stretcher. After he recovered Vicious moved into the Chelsea Hotel in New York with his 20-year-old girlfriend, Nancy Spungen, a Philadelphia go-go dancer who became his manager. They were registered at the hotel as "Mr. and Mrs. John Ritchie."

On October 12, Vicious called police and told them he had awakened up and found his girlfriend dead. Police found her slumped over the bathroom sink, stabbed once in the stomach. Vicious was charged with murder but was released a few days later on $50,000 bail even though he was in the middle of a methadone treatment program. A few days after his release he was placed in the city's psychiatric ward after he tried to slash his wrists with a broken light bulb. Released again, Vicious was arrested in December for assaulting the brother of rock singer Patti Smith with a beer bottle at a New York disco.

This time Vicious was charged with assault and put in jail for two months. He completed a drug detoxification program and was released on February 1, 1979. That night he attended a party in honor of his release, given by a 22-year-old actress in Greenwich Village. Guests later said Vicious seemed in good spirits and not at all suicidal. He drank beer and took a shot of heroin, but seemed fine when everyone left him alone in the apartment at about 2 A.M. At 12:30 the next afternoon Vicious was found lying nude, faceup on the floor of the apartment, dead of a heroin overdose. Officials believed the 21-year-old probably had injected his usual dosage of heroin, unaware that because of his detoxification, his body no longer could withstand the amount. They ruled his death was accidental. But not surprising.

RAOUL WALLENBERG
August 4, 1912–July 16, 1947 (?)

RAOUL WALLENBERG, who is credited with saving 30,000 Hungarian Jews from the Holocaust, didn't seem cut out to be a hero. The scion of a prominent Swedish family, Wallenberg resisted a position in the family bank and spent much of World War II living the life of a handsome bachelor before he finally secured a job in an import-export firm. Then in 1944, Germany occupied Hungary and began sending thousands of the country's Jews to death camps. The Swedish government, working with Allied forces, wanted to send someone to Budapest to rescue as many people as possible. They needed a prominent business person who would be respected, but not a career diplomat who would be suspected. Wallenberg, who spoke German and had traveled in Nazi territory because of his job in the import-export business, was chosen and he eagerly accepted.

Backed by American money, Wallenberg arrived in Budapest on July 9, 1944. Within a month he had generated thousands of Swedish passports and protective passes which, at least temporarily, the Nazis honored. Wallenberg risked his life repeatedly, bribing Nazis and defying in person the Nazi mastermind of Jewish extermination, Adolf Eichmann. It was through Wallenberg's efforts that thousands survived until Soviet troops forced out the Nazis in January 1945.

That was also the month in which Wallenberg disappeared. He was seen last on January 17 when he left Budapest to meet with Soviet officials some miles away and inform them of the plight of the city's Jews. Allied government officials, beset by other problems at the end of the war, did little at first to try to locate Wallenberg. When inquiries finally were made the Soviets ignored the matter. Meanwhile, the new Soviet-backed Hungarian government said Wallenberg had been murdered by Gestapo agents as the Soviets advanced on Budapest in January. Hungarian officials even held a memorial concert and renamed a street in his honor.

But pressed further the Soviets finally in 1947 denied that Wallenberg was in their custody. Then ten years later, in 1957, Soviet officials released a statement saying that they had conducted a new investigation and determined that Wallenberg had died "suddenly in his cell" of a heart attack on July 16, 1947—a month after they had denied he was in custody. The Soviets acknowledged that Wallenberg had been arrested under false pretenses and offered their regrets.

That explanation, as well, was probably a lie. What really became of the young Swede? Much of the information about Wallenberg's fate is based on reports from others who were held in Soviet prisons and were later released. According to their accounts, Wallenberg met with Soviet officials outside Budapest on January 17, 1945, but then was ordered to go to Moscow. There he was imprisoned for two years in a small cell, surviving on bread and porridge. As to why the Soviets might have arrested the 32-year-old champion of the Allied cause, the best guess seems to be that Wallenberg's activities, which had involved extensive contact with the Nazis, might have seemed suspicious to the advancing Soviet troops. Why he remained in prison, however, has never been clear.

In 1947—the year the Soviets say Wallenberg died—other prisoners reported he was sent to Vorkula, a labor camp 70 miles north of the Arctic Circle. Wallenberg was seen at other prisons and labor camps as late as the mid-1960s. Generally he seemed healthy and in good spirits, though he occasionally conducted hunger strikes to no avail. Some who followed his case believe he died in a Soviet prison in 1964 or 1965, twenty years after he was arrested. There have been few reports of his being alive after that.

But interest in Wallenberg's fate has not died. In 1979 the Swedish government said there was evidence that Wallenberg was alive as late as 1975 and asked the Soviets to investigate. President Carter also pressed the case, as have British and Israeli officials. The Soviets have not released any new information. In 1987 a statue honoring Wallenberg appeared without fanfare in Budapest. A statue previously had been mounted in 1948, but the night before it was to be dedicated Soviet soldiers dragged it away with horses. The new statue, donated by a former American ambassador, includes a Latin inscription. It says, "When the weather is fine, you have many friends. When the skies are cloudy, you will be alone."

KARL WALLENDA
1905–March 22, 1978

EVEN AFTER the Great Wallendas' famous seven-person "Human Pyramid" collapsed on a high wire in Detroit in 1962, plunging two members of the family to their deaths and paralyzing his adopted son, patriarch Karl Wallenda said the family was not ready to give up walking the tightrope. "We can't lose our nerve," said the 57-year-old Wallenda, who survived the tragedy by tangling his legs around the high wire, which also enabled him to grab his niece. After Wallenda watched a son-in-law electrocuted as he climbed up to join him on a high wire in West Virginia in 1972, the 67-year-old performed again the next day. "Our life is show business," explained the German-born founder of the family's high-wire act. "Without show business, we don't survive, and we have to exist."

The question, it seemed, was not how the aging high-wire walker would die, but when. Instead of slowing down as he got older, the veteran of circuses since the 1920s performed more and more spectacular stunts. Far from the familiar circus ring, Wallenda teetered across the Houston Astrodome, the 1,000-foot Tallulah Gorge in Georgia, and the Thames River in London, pausing midway to stand on his head. He refused to work with a net, believing that would only invite a fall.

On March 22, 1978, the 73-year-old man was walking across a 750-foot steel cable stretched ten stories high between two hotels in San Juan, Puerto Rico. It was a publicity stunt to promote the Pan-American Circus, in which Wallenda and his 17-year-old granddaughter, Rietta, were performing nightly. There were strong winds as he made his way between the beachfront hotels and the wire wobbled. "Hold tight!" he yelled to members of his high-wire troupe who were holding the guide wires. "Sit, Poppy, sit!" they yelled back. When he was about two-thirds of the way across, a gust of wind caused Wallenda to lose his balance. He appeared to try to squat down and grab the wire. But then he fell, clutching his balance pole as he plunged more than 100 feet and landed on his back on a taxi cab before bouncing onto the pavement. Wallenda was pronounced dead at the hospital.

He was buried in Sarasota, Florida, next to the three other Wallendas who had been killed on the high wire. His grand-daughter, meanwhile, continued performing in the circus, which certainly is what Wallenda would have wanted. "The dead are gone," he once said, "and the show must go on."

GEORGE WASHINGTON
February 22, 1732–December 14, 1799

NOBODY CALLED the Father of Our Country's death an assassination, but by modern medical standards it was. It was a sad and bizarre end to the life of a man who had longed to retire after the Revolution, still hoped to retire after his first term as the President, and finally did go home in 1797 to find his estate at Mount Vernon financially and physically dilapidated.

Washington spent his long-awaited, brief two years of retirement selling off outside land investments to save his estate and to afford hosting the many friends and officials who visited the former President. For pleasure, though he told Thomas Jefferson that he "really felt himself growing old, his bodily health less firm," Washington would ride on horseback almost daily for hours to survey his farms.

On December 12, 1799, Washington took his usual ride despite blowing snow and freezing rain. The hefty 67-year-old man, who stood over six feet and had weighed nearly 200 pounds when he was younger, left at 10 A.M. When he returned at three that afternoon he was soaked and snow was crusted in his hair. By the next day he had a sore throat and began getting hoarse. He refused to do anything to relieve it, deciding he would "let it go as it came." But that night he awoke coughing so violently that his doctor was called.

When the doctor arrived the next morning he applied the usual remedy. He wrapped Washington's throat with a blister of cantharides—a preparation of dried beetles. He also applied a steam vapor of water and vinegar and made the former President gargle with vinegar and tea, but Washington was so congested that he almost choked on the liquids. Washington also was given a mixture of tartar and calomel to induce diarrhea, which also was supposed to help.

Worst of all, Washington was bled. The idea was that whatever disease was dirtying the blood could be sapped away. Washington was bled twice the morning of the fourteenth and twice that afternoon, draining a total of 32 ounces—two pints—of blood. All that was sapped was his strength. Of the three doctors treating Washington, at least one opposed the bleeding. And another wrote later, "He [the other doctor] was averse to bleeding the General, and I have often thought that if we had acted according to his suggestion—'He needs all his strength. Bleeding will diminish it'—our good friend might be alive."

Washington seemed reconciled that he was dying, which he had called "the debt which we all must pay." That evening, as the doctors tried to sit him up in bed, Washington waved them away. "I feel myself going," he said feebly. "You had better not take any more trouble about me, but let me go off quietly. I cannot last long."

At 10 P.M. the former President struggled with much effort to whisper what were his final words. "I am just going. Have me decently buried, and do not let my body be put into the Vault in less than two days after I am dead." He looked at the doctor. "Do you understand me?" "Yes, sir," the doctor replied. " 'Tis well," Washington said. He pulled his hand away from the doctor and felt his own pulse. A few minutes later, the day after he caught a cold, he was dead.

HORACE WELLS
January 21, 1815–January 24, 1848

THE NEXT TIME you lie back in a dentist's chair, thank Horace
Wells, one of the discoverers of anesthesia. Himself a successful
young dentist in Hartford, Connecticut, Wells saw a demonstra-
tion of nitrous oxide in 1844 and got the idea to apply it to surgery. The very next day he had himself put under the laughing
gas and became the first patient to have an aching molar pulled
painlessly. Wells went on to perform many successful extrac-
tions on his patients. But he also spent much of his time trying,
somewhat frantically, to prove that he deserved the credit for
introducing anesthesia, since other doctors were experimenting
with similar gases at about the same time.

The eager dentist firmly believed that laughing gas was the
best anesthetic, but to counter his competitors he also experimented with ether and chloroform. The problem was that, as
with his initial discovery, Wells experimented on himself. Soon
he became addicted to the intoxicating gas, and on January 21,
1848, his thirty-third birthday, he was arrested outside his new
New York office for causing a public disturbance while he was
high on chloroform.

Wells, a deeply honorable man, wrote a letter in jail that later
was published in the *Journal of Commerce*. He explained that
earlier in the week a friend had persuaded him to supply a vial
of sulfuric acid which the friend then threw on a local prostitute
for revenge. Wells became so distraught over providing the acid
that he gave himself a big dose of chloroform. He awoke "ex-
hilarated beyond measure," and in that state he grabbed the
partially used vial, ran into the street, and threw it on two passing women. "I cannot proceed," he wrote. "My hand is too un-

steady and my whole frame is convulsed in agony. My brain is on fire."

On his second day in jail Wells had been allowed to return to his office to get some personal items. Among them he picked up his razor and a bottle of chloroform. The next morning, on Sunday the twenty-third, he attended the prison church service, then returned to his cell to write the letter to the *Journal of Commerce* and also a note to his wife. "I feel that I am fast becoming a deranged man, or I would desist from this act," he wrote her. "I can not live and keep my reason, and on this account God will forgive the deed. I can say no more."

Wells was found dead in his cell the next morning. The dentist had slashed his left thigh to the bone with his razor. The empty bottle of his anesthetic, chloroform, lay nearby.

STANFORD WHITE
November 9, 1853–June 25, 1906

EVERY GENERATION has its pacesetters, and in turn-of-the-century New York City the pace was set by Stanford White. He was the most famous architect of the day, a founding partner of McKim, Mead and White, and the designer of the original Madison Square Garden, the exclusive Metropolitan Club, the arch in Washington Square Park, and many private mansions. But more than that, society watched White for what he wore, where he went, and who he paid attention to.

In 1901 he was paying lots of attention to Evelyn Nesbit, a 16-year-old girl whose mother had brought her from Pittsburgh to become a star. She was posing as an artist's model and had made her way into the chorus of the Broadway hit *Floradora* when she met White. The young girl began attending the architect's semisecret and highly sought-after stag parties in his private suites at Madison Square Garden, where she met many famous artists, actors, and politicians. She became his mistress and also the star of her own Broadway show in 1902.

Along the way Nesbit also met Harry Kendall Thaw, the neurotic heir of a Pittsburgh industrialist whose public temper tantrums were tolerated only because he was set to inherit $40 million. Thaw lavished his attentions on Nesbit even more than White did and got her to marry him in 1905. White tried to prevail on Nesbit not to marry Thaw, but once it happened he seemed content to turn his attention elsewhere. Thaw, on the other hand, was obsessed with his wife's former lover. He referred to White as "the beast" and hired detectives to follow his wife to find out if she still was seeing White.

White and Thaw were not still involved and didn't see each other—except once by chance in a dentist's office, which threw Thaw into a rage—until the day of White's death. Thaw told his wife they were going to see the opening of *Mamzelle Champagne*, the new revue at Madison Square Garden on June 25, 1906. Nesbit thought it odd that her husband would set foot in White's prized building and also wondered why he was wearing an overcoat on the muggy summer night. The couple dined that evening at Café Martin, near the Garden. In another room of the restaurant White and his son were also having dinner, though Thaw didn't see them.

Thaw and his wife proceeded to the rooftop restaurant of the Garden for the show, but Thaw soon left their table and mingled around the audience. Shortly after 11 P.M., as a singer crooned "I Could Love a Thousand Girls," White entered and took his seat near the stage. A few minutes later, as the chorus girls were doing a fencing routine, Thaw walked directly up to White, pulled a pistol from his coat, and fired three shots. One bullet entered White's left eye; the other two grazed his shoulders. The 52-year-old architect lunged forward, overturning his table as he collapsed dead on the floor of his most famous building.

Some members of the audience apparently at first thought that the shooting was part of the performance. But soon ladies started screaming as Thaw held up the gun and walked briskly toward the exit. The stage manager yelled to the performers, "Go on playing! Bring on that chorus!" but to no avail. Thaw, who was arrested as he tried to get on the elevator, was heard saying, "He deserved it. I can prove it. He ruined my life and then deserted the girl." Some thought they heard Thaw say "wife" not "life." Thaw was walked several blocks to the police station, where he gave his name as "John Smith, student." Asked why he shot White, Thaw said, "I can't say."

The most sensational trial of the decade lasted three months in 1907 and ended with a hung jury, seven voting to convict Thaw of first-degree murder, five voting for not guilty by reason of insanity. Afterward, Evelyn issued a statement saying, "My husband was justified in killing Stanford White. He will be tried again and triumphantly acquitted." A second trial in 1908 found Thaw to be insane. He was moved from jail to an asylum. He was released in 1915, only to be recommitted in 1917 for kidnapping a young boy. After another seven years in the asylum, Thaw spent the rest of his life in only minor trouble until he died of a heart attack in Miami in 1947.

Nesbit, meanwhile, divorced Thaw while he was committed, thus losing the second man who had kept her. Her stage career revived briefly because of White's murder, but she later became a heroin addict and a failed nightclub owner. A movie of her life, *The Girl in the Red Velvet Swing*, was made in 1955 starring Joan Collins. Nesbit lived on until 1966, when, at the age of 81, she died of a heart attack in a nursing home.

OSCAR WILDE
October 16, 1854–November 30, 1900

"To THE WORLD I seem, by intention on my part, a dilettante and dandy merely—it is not wise to show one's heart to the world—and as seriousness of manner is the disguise of the fool, folly in its exquisite modes of triviality and indifference and lack of care is the robe of the wise man. In so vulgar an age as this we all need masks." So wrote Oscar Wilde in 1894, the year before his crowning achievement, *The Importance of Being Earnest*, opened in London. And for most of his life the Irish-born playwright's cheerful, witty facade held up quite well. It has held up even better since he died, which probably is why Wilde still regularly shows up on lists of favorite historical dinner guests.

But in his last years Wilde was welcome at no tables in England. Though married and the father of two children, Wilde was for years involved with a younger man, Lord Alfred Douglas, called "Bosie," and he engaged in many anonymous scenes with male prostitutes and pickups. His double life proceeded without incident until soon after *Earnest* opened, when he received a calling card from Bosie's eccentric father, the Marquess of Queensbury. It read, "To Oscar Wilde, posing as somdomite [*sic*]."

To maintain his mask Wilde felt he had to charge the Marquess with libel. And when the trial began in April 1895, Wilde charmed the jury with his punchy testimony. But the Marquess had hired private detectives, and when that evidence began to be presented Wilde abruptly dropped his suit. Later the same day he and Bosie were arrested for immorality. Wilde's new play continued its successful run, but his name was removed from the programs. At his own trial Wilde again maintained his witty upper lip. The first jury could not reach a verdict. But the second jury convicted him, and Wilde was sentenced to two years' hard labor. He spent the time in solitary confinement, where he was poorly fed and slept on a wooden plank bed. He was put to work sewing mailbags.

When he was released in May 1897, Wilde was bankrupt, his manuscripts had either been auctioned or stolen. Friends paid his way to France, where he finally settled in Paris. He wrote a little about prison life, including his famous *Ballad of Reading Gaol*, and continued to whisk his way through dinner engagements. But he confessed, "I don't think I shall ever really write again. Something is killed in me." He picked up boys more frequently than before and began drinking large amounts of absinthe, though doctors had told him it would kill him. Wilde laughed off the warnings, as he did his constant worry about money, quipping, "I am dying beyond my means."

In October 1900, Wilde developed a painful ear infection from an injury he had suffered in prison when he fainted one morning in chapel and perforated an eardrum. Doctors performed surgery, but the infection spread and caused him to develop encephalitis, swelling of the brain. He was taken back to his hotel room, the last in a series of cheaper and cheaper rooms that he could barely afford.

The legend is that his last words were "It's the wallpaper or me—one of us has to go." But Wilde did not depart with a clever remark. He grew delirious through the month of November. On the thirtieth two close friends near his bed could hear only a painful grinding sound from his throat. A nurse regularly had to dab blood that was drooling from his mouth. Slowly his breathing and his pulse weakened until he died at about 2 P.M. that afternoon.

VIRGINIA WOOLF
January 25, 1882–March 28, 1941

IF EVER SOMEONE led a literary life, it was Virginia Woolf. The British novelist and essayist, granddaughter of William Makepeace Thackeray, was educated in the tremendous library of her father, a literary critic, in a home often visited by Robert Louis Stevenson, Thomas Hardy, and other prominent writers of the day. Later her own home became the center of the "Bloomsbury group," a self-select gathering of intellectuals that included economist John Maynard Keynes, philosopher Bertrand Russell, and novelist E. M. Forster.

It was in such an environment that Woolf wrote her difficult, subtle novels, including *A Room of One's Own, Jacob's Room*, and *The Waves*. It was also in that rich environment that the writer suffered a series of nervous breakdowns. The first came in 1904, after her father died, and most seemed to occur near the completion of one of her novels. Some were brief, while others lasted more than a year and led to at least one suicide attempt in 1913.

In 1940, Woolf, a fine-featured woman with a long face, saw her world shattered by World War II. After the Germans invaded Paris in June, Woolf and her husband, who was Jewish and a socialist, discussed committing suicide. They stored extra gasoline in the garage in the event that they decided to kill themselves by inhaling fumes from the car. Later they acquired lethal doses of morphine. Woolf described one air raid spent huddled with her husband when the Battle of Britain began that fall. "Bombs shook the windows of my lodge," she wrote. "Will it drop I asked? If so, we shall be broken together. I thought, I think, of nothingness—flatness, my mood being flat. Some fear

I suppose." Later she wrote, "I can't conceive that there will be a 27th June 1941."

Woolf and her husband were bombed out of their London home. After the house they moved to was also destroyed, they fled to their weekend home outside the city. "They are destroying all the beautiful things!" Woolf cried. In the midst of the bombings Woolf finished her latest novel, *Between the Acts*, a story about the struggle of civilization against brutality. As had happened so often before, Woolf was depressed after she completed the initial draft in November 1940. "I didn't realize how bad it was till I read it over," she said.

But this time, as her depression deepened through the winter, there was nothing to pull her out of it. On March 28, a clear, cold day, Woolf went to her studio in the garden and wrote letters to her husband and her sister. At about 11:30 A.M. she took her walking stick and walked down to the Ouse River. She put down the stick, forced a large stone into her coat pocket, and then entered the water for "the one experience, I shall never describe," as she had termed death to her longtime female lover, writer Vita Sackville-West. Woolf's body was not recovered until April 18, three weeks later.

Woolf had left the letter to her husband, Leonard, on the mantel of the sitting room. Their marriage had been passionless but devoted. "I have a feeling I shall go mad," Woolf wrote to him. "I cannot go on any longer in these terrible times. I hear voices and cannot concentrate on my work. I have fought against it but cannot fight any longer. I owe all my happiness to you but cannot go on and spoil your life."

INDEX

Fitzgerald, F. Scott, and Zelda, September 24, 1896–December 21, 1940; July 24, 1900–March 11, 1948, *99*
The '20s' most famous flappers flamed out.

Fixx, Jim, April 23, 1932–July 20, 1984, *101*
He died with his running shoes on.

Flagler, Henry, January 2, 1830–May 20, 1913, *102*
Robber baron was killed by his opulent mansion.

Forrestal, James, February 15, 1892–May 22, 1949, *104*
The Secretary of Defense jumped out the window.

Foster, Stephen, July 4, 1826–January 13, 1864, *106*
Sentimental composer died unrecognized in a city hospital.

Franklin, Benjamin, January 17, 1706–April 17, 1790, *107*
Just wore out.

Freud, Sigmund, May 6, 1856–September 23, 1939, *109*
Preferred to think clearly rather than to dull the pain of his cancer death.

Gable, Clark, February 1, 1901–November 16, 1960, *111*
"[Marilyn Monroe] damn near gave me a heart attack," he said a few days before he had one.

Gagarin, Yuri, March 9, 1934–March 27, 1968, *113*
Soviet astronaut died in a plane crash.

Garfield, James, November 19, 1831–September 19, 1881, *114*
"I am a Stalwart," the assassin said.

Garland, Judy, June 10, 1922–June 22, 1969, *116*
"She was just tired," Liza said of her mother's overdose.

Gary, Elbert, October 8, 1846–August 15, 1927, *118*
U.S. Steel founder fell out of his chair.

George V, June 3, 1865–January 20, 1936, *119*
"Goddamn you," said the king to his doctor before he was given a fatal injection.

Gershwin, George, September 26, 1898–July 11, 1937, *121*
The brain of a music-making genius stilled.

Gibbons, Euell, 1912–December 29, 1975, *122*
Health food expert died of a stomach ailment.

Goering, Hermann, January 12, 1893–October 15, 1946, *123*
Nazi leader just beat the hangman by a few hours.

Gordon, Charles "Chinese," January 28, 1833–January 26, 1885, *126*
British general orchestrated his own martyrdom.

Gorky, Arshile, April 15, 1904–July 21, 1948, *128*
Committed suicide after his painting arm was paralyzed.

Grant, Ulysses S., April 27, 1822–July 23, 1885, *129*
Died poor, but his family reaped the memoirs.

Griffith, D. W., January 22, 1875–July 23, 1948, *131*
The "Father of Film" died alone in Hollywood.

Guggenheim, M. Robert, May 17, 1885–November 16, 1959, *133*
He died leaving the house of his mistress.

Hamilton, Alexander, January 11, 1757–July 12, 1804, *134*
Burr didn't refuse to pull the trigger.

Hammarskjöld, Dag, July 29, 1905–September 18, 1961, *136*
UN leader's thankless job ended in a plane crash.

Harding, Warren, November 2, 1865–August 2, 1923, *139*
When the scandals broke, they wondered how he died.

Hari, Mata, August 7, 1876–October 15, 1917, *141*
Flirtatious dancer smiled at her firing squad.

Harlow, Jean, March 3, 1911–June 7, 1937, *143*
Her mother wouldn't let her go to the hospital.

Harrison, William Henry, February 9, 1773–April 4, 1841, *144*
Pneumonia made him President-of-the-Month.

Hay, Josslyn, 1901–January 24, 1941, *146*
The Earl was brutally murdered in "Happy Valley."

Hemingway, Ernest, July 21, 1899–July 2, 1961, *149*
"We have an obligation to kill cleanly," said the writer who committed suicide.

Hendrix, Jimi, November 27, 1942–September 18, 1970, *150*
Rock star died a nauseous death.

Hickok, Wild Bill, May 27, 1837–August 2, 1876, *152*
Lawman shot in the head holding aces and eights.

Hoffa, Jimmy, February 14, 1913–July 30, 1975(?), *154*
Like magic, his enemies made him disappear.

Holiday, Billie, April 17, 1915–July 17, 1959, *156*
Blues singer wore out at 44.

Holly, Buddy, September 7, 1936–February 3, 1959, *158*
Died in a plane hired to give the singer time to rest.

Houdini, Harry, April 6(?), 1874–October 31, 1926, *159*
Felled by a blow he hadn't prepared for.

Howard, Leslie, April 3, 1893–June 1, 1943, *161*
Screen's Civil War survivor killed in World War II.

Hudson, Henry, d. 1611, *162*
Explorer was cast adrift by his crew.

Ivan the Terrible, August 25, 1530–March 18, 1584, *164*
The czar of torture died a monk.

James, Jesse, September 5, 1847–April 3, 1882, *166*
Shot by one of his own men, he thought.

Jefferson, Thomas, born April 13, 1743; John Adams, born October 19, 1735. Both died July 4, 1826, *168*
Founding Fathers died on their creation's Golden Anniversary.